NOTES ON GALATIANS

Machen's
Notes on Galatians

NOTES ON BIBLICAL EXPOSITION
AND OTHER AIDS TO THE INTERPRETATION
OF THE EPISTLE TO THE GALATIANS

J. Gresham Machen

EDITED BY

John H. Skilton

Solid Ground Christian Books
Birmingham, Alabama USA

Solid Ground Christian Books
2090 Columbiana Rd, Suite 2000
Birmingham, AL 35216
205-443-0311
sgcb@charter.net
http://solid-ground-books.com

NOTES ON GALATIANS

John Gresham Machen (1881-1938)
Edited by John H. Skilton

Solid Ground Classic Reprints

First printing of new edition January 2006

Copyright belongs to P & R Publishing Company 1972
All rights reserved.

Cover work by Borgo Design, Tuscaloosa, AL
Contact them at nelbrown@comcast.net

*Cover image of J. Gresham Machen furnished by Wayne Sparkman
of the PCA Historical Center, 12330 Conway Rd .St. Louis, MO 63141.
Call them at 314-469-9077.*

ISBN: 1-59925-037-3

TABLE OF CONTENTS

PART I

NOTES ON BIBLICAL EXPOSITION

I.	A Man Who Could Say "No" (Galatians 1:1-2)	1
II.	The Witness Of Paul (Galatians 1:1-2)	9
III.	Plain Speaking In A Time Of Peril (Galatians 1:1-2)	17
IV.	The Freedom Of The Christian Man (Galatians 1:3-7)	26
V.	The Gospel Of Christ (Galatians 1:6-7)	35
VI.	The Message And The Messenger (Galatians 1:8-11)	46
VII.	How Paul Received The Gospel (Galatians 1:11-17)	56
VIII.	The Call Of God (Galatians 1:13-17)	61
IX.	After The Conversion (Galatians 1:15-19)	68
X.	Paul And The Jerusalem Church (Galatians 1:18-24)	76
XI.	Harmony Of Acts And Galatians (Galatians 2:1-2)	86
XII.	Paul At Jerusalem (Galatians 2:1-2)	94
XIII.	False Brethren And A True Gospel (Galatians 2:1-5)	99
XIV.	Paul's Commission And Its Importance To Us (Galatians 2:6-10)	108
XV.	"The Apostolic Decree" (Galatians 2:6-10)	118
XVI.	The Right Hand Of Fellowship (Galatians 2:6-10)	127

XVII.	Consequences Versus Truth (Galatians 2:11-14a)...................	133
XVIII.	The Power Of Example (Galatians 2:14).......	140
XIX.	Justification By Faith (Galatians 2:15-16)......	144
XX.	The Peril Of Inconsistency (Galatians 2:17-19a)..	148
XXI.	The New Life (Galatians 2:19-21).............	155
XXII.	The Cross Of Christ (Galatians 3:1)...........	162
XXIII.	The Spirit Of God (Galatians 3:2-5)...........	166
XXIV.	The Authority Of The Bible (Galatians 3:6-7).....................	172
XXV.	The Atonement (Galatians 3:10-14)...........	176

PART II

ADDITIONAL AIDS TO THE INTERPRETATION OF GALATIANS FROM VARIOUS WRITINGS OF J. GRESHAM MACHEN

I.	EPISTLE TO THE GALATIANS [Questions on the Exegesis of Galatians 1:1—4:4 prepared by Dr. Machen for his students]...............................	182
II.	SURVEYS OF GALATIANS [From *The Literature and History of New Testament Times*, Teacher's Manual and the corresponding Student's Text Book]	200
III.	THE COUNCIL AT JERUSALEM [From *The Literature and History of New Testament Times*, Teacher's Manual]	214
IV.	FAITH AND WORKS [Excerpt from Student's Text Book issued with *The Literature and History of New Testament Times*].............................	219
V.	REVIEW of E. D. Burton *Commentary on Galatians* [From *The Princeton Theological Review*]......	222
VI.	INDEX OF REFERENCES TO GALATIANS IN VARIOUS OTHER WORKS OF MACHEN	231

INTRODUCTION

The chief feature of this volume is that it makes available in convenient form the "Notes on Biblical Exposition" which Dr. J. Gresham Machen published in the earlier *Christianity Today* from January 1931 to February 1933. Students at Westminster Seminary have made profitable use of these Notes on Galatians 1:1—3:14 by following them, with minor inconvenience, through bound periodical volumes; but for many others who might greatly benefit from them, they have long been virtually inaccessible.

In the four decades which have passed since these Notes began to appear, they have not lost their instructive value and their power to arouse and move the Christian soul. By design they were more popular and less technical than Dr. Machen's brilliant classroom instruction in Galatians and, unlike his classroom presentation, they did not refrain from making specific applications to the ecclesiastical controversies of their time; but they are not in the slightest degree superficial; they present the teaching of Galatians with an exemplary penetration and clarity; and their contemporary references and applications still have a lively relevance. Machen's Notes should encourage a Pauline and Reformation testimony today.

It is of course to be regretted that the "Notes on Biblical Exposition" carry us only to Galatians 3:14. We might sincerely wish that their author had found occasion or opportunity in the crowded and demanding years between 1933 and his death in 1937 to give the rest of the epistle similar coverage. However, compensation for our loss is not completely lacking. The enlightened grammatico-historical method of interpretation employed by Machen did not sanction the viewing of a portion of Scripture in a kind of atomistic isolation. He was aware of the grand particularities of a given text or passage, but he did not lose contact with the nearer and the more distant context. For him the part contributed to the whole and the whole contributed to the part. Accordingly, his treatment of the earlier text of Galatians was written without neglect of the epistle as a whole. It drew upon the whole and it also laid a substantial foundation for the interpretation of the remaining portion of the epistle. But in addition to this, there are in Machen's other writings many references to Galatians, some very extensive and some to verses or passages not directly covered in the Notes, and these provide a most welcome supplement. Part II of this volume draws upon these references by reproducing a number of them and by providing an index of others. Included in Part II, along with other materials, are the syllabus of questions dealing with the exegesis of Galatians 1:1—4:4 which Dr. Machen prepared for the use of students in his introductory course in New Testament Exegesis and surveys of Galatians as a whole from *The Literature and History of New Testament Times* (from both the Teacher's Manual and the corresponding Student's Text Book).

The text of the Notes and of Machen's other writings included in this book has been left almost untouched. A few minor changes have been made to remove typographical or other minor imperfections in the available printed form. The Rev. George R. Demass has helped greatly by making copies of the "Notes on Biblical Exposition" in the form in which they were originally published. Gratitude is also expressed to Mrs. Robert H. Skilton, III, and to Miss Margaret Anne Skilton for assistance in proofreading.

Under the caption "Teaching Galatians" in his biographical Memoir of Machen, Dr. Ned B. Stonehouse, Machen's successor as Professor of New Testament at Westminster Seminary and himself one of Machen's students at Princeton, paid his professor the following tribute:

"The Epistle to the Galatians was traditionally chosen as the portion of the New Testament with which the seminary students [at Princeton] grappled in the required course in Exegesis. Though Machen had heard Armstrong, Jülicher and Bousset lecture on the Epistle, he never seemed to be passing on a rehash of the opinions of others. He engaged indeed in a thorough study of the literature, and his analysis of exegetical problems and questions, which he came to prepare for the students, exhibits his insistence upon the most painstaking evaluation of the text in its minutest details. Nevertheless, Machen possessed an unusual gift of bringing into bold relief the larger questions, and thus giving a vision of the forest as well as the trees.

"The Epistle to the Galatians, moreover, was admirably suited to the purpose of exegetical study as well as to bring to expression Machen's special gifts as a teacher. Historical questions currently in hot dispute and doctrinal issues bearing upon the very nature of the gospel confronted the student in forceful and fascinating fashion and stimulated him to engage his best powers of analysis and decision. The message of Galatians may take on an extraordinary freshness and contemporaneity, especially in an age when the gospel of the grace of God in Christ is undergoing eclipse, as Luther had discovered. And in the hands of Machen it became alive and relevant to the present situation, though his devotion to his task of expounding the text was such that he did not yield to the temptation of making direct applications to the ecclesiastical scene of his own day. At least when the present writer was in his classroom, it was not felt merely that Luther had been reborn, but that Paul himself had become alive, and was teaching and proclaiming as a fresh message the evangel that stands in irreconcilable opposition to 'another gospel which is not another.' " [1]

It is hoped that through the writings included and referred to in this volume Machen's special gifts as a teacher will long continue to be exercised for edification and reformation.

John H. Skilton

---

[1] *J. Gresham Machen: A Biographical Memoir* (Grand Rapids: Wm. B. Eerdmans Publishing Company, 1954), pp. 170f.

PREFACE TO THE SECOND EDITION

The chief distinctive feature of this edition is the inclusion in Part II of Dr. Machen's review of Ernest DeWitt Burton's *Commentary on Galatians*. This review originally appeared in *The Princeton Theological Review,* Volume 20 (1922), pp. 142ff. Thanks is expressed to Professor Leslie W. Sloat of Westminster Theological Seminary for recommending the inclusion of this important review.

John H. Skilton

PART I

NOTES ON BIBLICAL EXPOSITION

I. A MAN WHO COULD SAY "NO"

"Paul an Apostle, not from men nor through a man, but through Jesus Christ and God the Father who raised Him from the dead, and all the brethren who are with me, to the churches of Galatia..." (Gal 1:1, 2, in a literal translation).

Letters, Ancient and Modern

The words just quoted, with the three verses that follow, constitute the opening, or the "address," of the Epistle to the Galatians. We know more about the openings of ancient letters than we did thirty years ago; for within the last thirty years there have been turning up in Egypt, where the dry air has happened to preserve the perishable papyrus on which they were written, great numbers of private letters written on all sorts of occasions and by all sorts of people during the very age and in the very language in which this Epistle was written.

These papyrus letters differ widely among themselves. Some of them are written by educated people; some, by uneducated: some concern business affairs; some, the most intimate matters of family life. But widely though they differ in many particulars, they all *begin*, at least, in practically the same way. We discover when we examine them that there was a fixed epistolary form for the opening of Greek letters in that age.

We too, in our day, have an epistolary form for the opening of letters. We begin our letters with "Dear Sir," even when we are tempted to think that some other adjective would be far more in place than that adjective "dear." It is a mere form, and we follow it with great uniformity, no matter what the particular occasion of our letters may be.

So in Paul's day there was a regular form for the opening of letters. The Greek papyrus letters that have been discovered in Egypt begin, with only slight variations, according to the form: "So-and-so to so-and-so, greeting."

The Originality of Paul

How interesting that is—so we may be tempted to exclaim—for our understanding of the Epistles of Paul! How interesting it is to discover that these Epistles, which we have been accustomed to regard as so stiff and sacred, are just "letters" after all, and that Paul begins them in the way in which ordinary letters were begun at that time! How near that brings them to us, how very "human" it shows these Biblical Epistles to be!

Well, it is all very interesting, no doubt. The only trouble with it is that it is not true. As a matter of fact, no matter what we may think about it, Paul does *not* begin his letters according to the customary epistolary form.

Even the grammatical skeleton of Paul's openings is different from that which appears in the papyrus letters that have been discovered in Egypt. Those letters begin with one sentence: "So-and-so to so-and-so (says) greeting." Paul's letters, on the other hand, begin with the form: "So-and-so to so-and-so," then a pause, then: "Grace be with you and peace." But what is far more important is that Paul, in the openings of his Epistles, is not a slave to *any* form, not even his own form. He follows this latter form for the most part, but into it he sometimes pours the most distinctive things that in each Epistle he has to say.

So the opening of this Epistle to the Galatians, far from being merely formal or stereotyped, as one might expect the opening of a letter to be, is one of the most characteristic passages in all the Epistles of Paul; it contains in summary all that the writer has to say in the glorious Epistle that follows.

In general, an examination of the papyrus letters of which we have just spoken, instead of impressing us with the similarity between Paul's letters and other letters of that day, impresses us rather with the profound difference. As has well been observed, we have still to find, among these Egyptian letters, anything that compares even for a moment with the Epistle to Philemon, the briefest and most informal of the Epistles of Paul.

The Meaning of the Word "Apostle"

This distinctive quality of Paul's letters is connected, no doubt, with the second word that appears in this Epistle to the Galatians, the word "apostle." It is not merely "Paul," who is designated as the writer, but "Paul *an apostle.*" "Apostle," as we all learned in Sunday School, means "one who is sent," and not merely "one who is sent," but "one who is sent with a commission." So the word could be used in the ordinary affairs of life to designate a "delegate" or a "commissioner." It is used in this way in II Cor. 8:23 to designate "delegates of the churches"—men, that is, who were commissioned by the Gentile churches to carry the proceeds of the collection to the Jerusalem Church. But where, in the New Testament, the word is used without anything corresponding to the phrase "of the churches," where, in other words, it is not expressly said from whom the commission comes, the understanding is that it comes from Christ, and that it is a commission of a very special and very lofty kind.

So when Paul calls himself at the beginning of this Epistle an "apostle," he plainly is using the word in its highly specialized, extremely lofty and sacred, meaning. He means that the Lord Jesus has given to him, as to the original Twelve, a very special authority to speak, in Christ's name, for the guidance of the Church.

"Letters" or "Epistles"?

Professor Deissmann has asked, indeed, whether these Pauline Epistles are really "epistles" and are not rather "letters," and he has decided in favor of the latter alternative. An "epistle," he says, is intended for the general public; a "letter" is addressed to local and temporary needs. According to this distinction, he says, the Pauline Epistles are "letters" and not "epistles"; they were not intended for publication, but dealt with special needs as those needs arose among persons whom Paul knew.

This observation has an element of truth in it, and also has an element of error; but the error far overbalances the truth.

It is true that the Epistles of Paul are addressed to special needs and show intimate knowledge of local and temporary conditions. They are not treatises merely put by a literary fiction into an epistolary form, but were intended to answer the questions and deal with the difficulties that had actually arisen in the churches of Paul's day. In so far, they can be called "letters" in Deissmann's sense of the word.

Paul's Epistles Not Ordinary Letters

On the other hand, however, although they are letters, they are certainly not ordinary letters; they are not letters that were intended, like the letters that have recently turned up on the rubbish-heaps and in the mummy-cases of Egypt, to be read once and then thrown away. Despite their individual occasions, they are not private letters, but were intended from the beginning to be read in the meetings of the Church. Even the Epistle to Philemon, which is the most informal of them all, is addressed not only to Philemon but to the "church" that was in his house; and the Epistles to Timothy and Titus, though they are addressed to individuals, are addressed to them not merely as individuals but as leaders of the Church, and were plainly intended from the first to be read in the congregations over which Timothy and Titus had charge. If, therefore, the Epistles of Paul are "letters," they are not private letters but at least pastoral letters—letters written by a leader of the Church for the edification of those over whom God had made him an overseer. Hence they partake, to some extent at least, of the nature of what Deissmann calls "epistles"; they are letters intended, to say the very least, to be read publicly—and, we may add, certainly not just once but again and again—in the churches to which they are addressed.

The Authority With Which Paul Writes

But there is something else that differentiates them even more sharply from the private "letters" with which Deissmann is inclined to bring them into connection. It is found in the peculiar character of the commission which gave Paul his right to speak to the Church. Paul did not think of himself merely as an ordinary "bishop" or "overseer," but he thought of himself as an apostle of Jesus Christ, a man who, however unworthy in himself, had been invested by the Lord Jesus with supernatural authority and supernatural power.

We may approve of Paul's thinking of himself thus, or we may not approve of it; but at least we cannot deny that he did so think. A consciousness of divine authority runs all through the Epistles of Paul.

The Epistles deal sometimes, it is true, with very intimate and individual matters. We can rejoice in that fact. It gives to these writings much of their power to move the heart. They are not cold, theoretical treatises, but are written by a man whose heart was stirred by the actual needs of his spiritual children, and who, because his own heart was thus stirred, can stir the hearts of others from that day to this. But despite this individual and intimate character of parts of the Epistles, Paul never forgets that he is an apostle of Jesus Christ. There is a loftiness of tone in these letters, a dignity, a profound consciousness of authority, that differentiates them sharply from merely private or casual or temporary communications. Despite their special occasions, and the intimate details into which they sometimes enter, they are written throughout by an apostle of Jesus Christ, in the conscious plenitude of apostolic authority, for the upbuilding of the Church of God.

If we forget that fact, as so many readers do today, we may understand some details in these Epistles; we may learn how to construe the sentences grammatically; we may obtain a superficial and piecemeal knowledge of what is said: but the real heart of the writer will remain forever hidden from us. Unless we recognize the consciousness of authority which runs through these Epistles from beginning to end, all the detailed learning in the world will give us nothing but a superficial knowledge of Paul.

The Duty of Saying "No"

So far we have dealt with only two words of this Epistle to the Galatians, the word "Paul" and the word "apostle." What is the next word after these?

It is a word that is now regarded as highly objectionable, a word that Paul, if he had been what modern men would have desired him to be, never would have used. It is the small but weighty word "not." "Paul an apostle," he says, "*not* from men nor through a man, but . . . ."

That word "not," we are today constantly being told, ought to be put out of the Christian's vocabulary. Our preaching, we are told, ought to be positive and not negative; we ought to present the truth, but ought not to attack error; we ought to avoid controversy and always seek peace.

With regard to such a program, it may be said at least that if we hold to it we might just as well close up our New Testaments; for the New Testament is a controversial book almost from beginning to end. That is of course true with regard to the Epistles of Paul. They, at least, are full of argument and controversy—no question, certainly, can be raised about that. Even the hymn to Christian love in the thirteenth chapter of I Corinthians is an integral part of a great controversial passage with regard to a false use of the spiritual gifts. That glorious hymn never would have been written if Paul had been averse to controversy and had sought peace at any price. But the same thing is true also of the words of Jesus. They too—I think we can say it reverently—are full of controversy. He presented His righteousness sharply over against the other righteousness of the scribes and Pharisees.

That is simply in accordance with a fundamental law of the human mind. All definition is by way of exclusion. You cannot possibly say clearly what a thing is without contrasting it with what it is not.

When that fundamental law is violated, we find nothing but a fog. Have you ever listened to this boasted non-controversial preaching, this preaching that is positive and not negative, this teaching that tries to present truth without attacking error? What impression does it make upon your mind? We will tell you what impression it makes upon ours. It makes the impression of utter inanity. We are simply unable to make head or tail of it. It consists for the most part of words and nothing more. Certainly it is as far as possible removed from the sharp, clear warnings, and the clear and glorious promises, of Holy Writ.

No, there is one word which every true Christian must learn to use. It is the word "not" or the word "No." A Christian must certainly learn to say "No" in the field of conduct; there are some things that the world does, which he cannot do. But he must also learn to say "No" in the field of conviction. The world regards as foolishness the gospel upon which the Christian life is based, and the Christian who does not speak out against the denial of the gospel is certainly not faithful to his Lord. That is true with respect to the denials in the world at large, but it is even more obviously true of the denials within the visible Church. There the obligation of bearing testimony, negatively as well as positively, is particularly strong. A Christian testimony that makes common cause with men in the same church who, like the thirteen hundred "Auburn Affirmationists" in the Presbyterian Church in the U.S.A.,[1] cast despite upon the holiest things of

---

[1] (Editor's Note) The "Auburn Affirmation" was issued in January, 1924, in Auburn, N. Y., as "An Affirmation designed to safeguard the unity and liberty of the Presbyterian Church in the United States of America." It was signed by 150 ministers of that denomination. In May of 1924 it was published again, this time with the signatures of almost 1300 — or more than a tenth — of the ministers of that church. It attacked the doctrine of the inerrancy of the Bible and maintained that certain teachings of the Scriptures such as the Virgin Birth and the Bodily Resurrection of Christ were theories which ministers were not obliged to accept. Later in these *Notes*, more than once, Dr. Machen will comment further on the "Auburn Affirmation." For the text of the Affirmation and comments about it, the reader is referred to *The Auburn Betrayal* by Murray Forst Thompson (Philadelphia: The Committee on Christian Education of the Orthodox Presbyterian Church).

The Presbyterian Church in the United States of America, the largest of the Presbyterian churches in the United States, subsequently joined with the United Presbyterian Church of North America to form the present United Presbyterian Church in the United States of America.

the Faith, is hardly worthy of being called Christian testimony at all. The Church of our day needs above all else men who can say "No"; for it is only men who can say "No," men who are brave enough to take a stand against the sin and error in the Church—it is only such men who can really say "Yea and amen" to the gospel of the Lord Jesus Christ.

We know not in detail what will take place when the great revival comes, the great revival for which we long, when the Spirit of God will sweep over the Church like a mighty flood. But one thing we do know—when that great day comes, the present feeble aversion to "controversy," the present cowardly unwillingness to take sides in the age-long issue between faith and unbelief in the Church—will at once be swept aside. There is not a trace of such an attitude in God's holy Word. That attitude is just Satan's way of trying to deceive the people of God; peace and indifferentist church-unionism and aversion to controversy, as they are found in the modern Church, are just the fine garments that cover the ancient enemy, unbelief.

May God send us men who are not deceived, men who will respond to the forces of unbelief and compromise now so largely dominant in the visible Church with a brave and unqualified "No"! Paul was such a man in his day. He said "No" in the very first word of this Epistle, after the bare name and title of the author; and that word gives the key to the whole Epistle that follows. The Epistle to the Galatians is a polemic, a fighting Epistle from beginning to end. What a fire it kindled at the time of the Reformation! May it kindle another fire in our day—not a fire that will destroy any fine or noble or Christian thing, but a fire of Christian love in hearts grown cold!

Next Month

We have covered just three words of the Bible, and yet here we are at the end of two pages of *Christianity Today*. It may seem like slow progress, but we make no apologies for it. It is worth while, we think, to linger over these words of Paul. Next month, however, we hope to cover more ground than that, if our readers have patience to follow us as we examine further this wonderful Epistle to see what word of God it contains for the Church of our day and for our own minds and hearts.

II. THE WITNESS OF PAUL

"Paul an Apostle, not from men nor through a man, but through Jesus Christ and God the Father who raised Him from the dead, and all the brethren who are with me, to the churches of Galatia . . ." (Gal. 1:1, 2, in a literal translation).

Human Merit vs. the Grace of God

Last month we called attention to the fact that the very first word of the Epistle to the Galatians, after the bare name and title of the author, is the unpopular word "not." Unlike many men in the modern Church, Paul was not afraid to say "Not" or to say "No"; he had no sympathy with the feeble notion that a man can speak the truth without opposing error: and so this Epistle is a fighting epistle from beginning to end.

The enemy against which Paul is fighting in the Epistle can be reconstructed fairly well from the Epistle itself. Paul was fighting against the doctrine that a man can earn a part, at least, of his salvation by his own obedience to God's law; he was fighting against the doctrine that a man is justified not by faith alone, but by faith *and* works.

That doctrine was being propagated by certain teachers who had come into the Galatian churches from the outside. These teachers were men of Jewish race; and since they sought to induce Gentile people to "Judaize"—that is, to adopt the Jewish manner of life—they are commonly called "Judaizers."

The Judaizers agreed with Paul about many things: they agreed in holding that Jesus was the Messiah; they seemed to have no quarrel whatever with Paul's lofty doctrine of the deity of Christ; they believed in the resurrection of our Lord from the dead. Moreover, they even held, no doubt, that a man must believe in the Lord Jesus Christ if he is to be saved.

But their error lay in holding not only that a man must believe in the Lord Jesus Christ if he is to be saved, but that he must also do something else—namely, keep at least a part of the law of God. Salvation according to those Judaizers, in other words, is attained partly by the grace of God and partly by the merit of man.

The Modern Judaizers

The particular form of merit which they induced men to seek was the merit of keeping the law of Moses, particularly the ceremonial law. At first sight, that fact might seem to destroy the usefulness of the Epistle for the present day; for we of today are in no danger of desiring to keep Jewish fasts and feasts. But a little consideration will show that that is not at all the case. The really essential thing about the Judaizers' contention was not found in those particular "works of the law" that they urged upon the Galatians as being one of the grounds of salvation, but in the fact that they urged any works in this sense at all. The really serious error into which they fell was not that they carried the ceremonial law over into the new dispensation whither God did not intend it to be carried, but that they preached a religion of human merit as over against a religion of divine grace.

So the error of the Judaizers is a very modern error indeed, as well as a very ancient error. It is found in the modern Church wherever men seek salvation by "surrender" instead of by faith, or by their own character instead of by the imputed righteousness of Christ, or by "making Christ master in the life" instead of by trusting in His redeeming blood. In particular, it is found wherever men say that "the real essentials" of Christianity are love, justice, mercy and other virtues, as contrasted with the great doctrines of God's Word. These are all just different ways of exalting the merit of man over against the Cross of Christ; they are all of them attacks upon the very heart and core of the Christian religion. And against all of them the mighty polemic of this Epistle to the Galatians is turned.

The Authority of Paul

But it is time to return to our word "not" in the first verse of the Epistle. We have seen that that word is typical of the whole Epistle, since this letter is a polemic from beginning to end. But the particular reference of the word in this verse is not directly to the false gospel of the Judaizers, but to their personal attack upon Paul. The Judaizers had not been able to gain an entrance for their false teaching so long as the authority of the great Apostle remained beyond dispute. So they had proceeded to undermine that authority as best they could; they had said that Paul was at best an apostle of the second rank—that he had not been with Jesus in Galilee as had Peter and the others of the original Twelve, and that consequently whatever authority he possessed had come to him only through them.

It is against this attack that Paul utters the "not" in this first verse; in this verse he defends his apostolic authority, not his gospel. But of course the defence of his apostolic authority was altogether for the sake of his gospel; he is not interested in his apostolic prerogatives for their own sake, but only for the sake of the message which those prerogatives had been given him to proclaim. Hence the "not" of this verse is a very weighty word indeed; it involves, indirectly at least, the whole mighty conflict between pride in human goodness and the all-sufficiency of the Cross of Christ.

With this understanding, let us see how Paul defends his authority as an apostle of Jesus Christ. He is "an apostle," he says, "not from men nor through a man."

When he says that he is not an apostle *from* men, he denies that the *source* of his apostleship was found in men. So far, perhaps, even the Judaizers may have agreed with him; they may perhaps have admitted that ultimately his authority to preach came from Christ.

But the real point of his defence comes in the following words. "My apostleship not only did not come *from* men," he says—so much perhaps even his opponents admitted—"but it did not come even *through* a man." There is where the dispute arose. The Judaizers said that if Paul had any authority at all it came *through* those who had been apostles before him, but Paul says that it came to him directly from Christ without any human intermediary at all: not only was the source of his apostleship divine, but also the channel through which it came to him; the Lord Jesus did not use any intermediary to give him his commission as an apostle, but appeared to him directly on the road to Damascus.

Paul's Commission and Ours

Thus in the words, "nor through a man," Paul refers to a prerogative that differentiates him sharply from ordinary Christians.

Every humble Christian can in a certain sense go with Paul in the former of the two phrases that we have just discussed. Every humble Christian can say: "My commission comes to me not from men but from Christ." Of course, the ordinary Christian cannot say, as Paul could say, that his commission is an apostolic commission; for by the term "apostle" is designated a high function that has not been continued in the Church. Nevertheless, even the very humblest Christian can say that he has a commission which has come to him not from men but from God. That is true of a preacher, and it is just as true of the sexton who sweeps out the church and of the treasurer who takes care of the funds.

But we ordinary Christians, whether preachers or sextons or treasurers, cannot go with Paul in the second of the two phrases; we cannot say that our commission did not come to us *through* a man; for as a matter of fact it did come to us through some true evangelist who preached the gospel to us, or through some faithful pastor or teacher, or through some godly parent. Christ gave us our commission, but He used human emissaries in doing so; we are not eyewitnesses of the risen Christ. But in the case of Paul there was no such human emissary; to him Christ appeared on the road to Damascus and gave him directly his high commission.

The reference to Paul's conversion is plain in the words that immediately follow those with which we have just dealt. "I am an apostle," says Paul, "not from men nor through a man, but through Jesus Christ and God the Father *who raised Him from the dead.*" The reference to the resurrection of

Christ is not, at this point, a mere general reference to something that was fundamental in the Christian faith, but Paul is thinking specifically of the fact that his apostleship came to him from the *risen* Christ. "I am an apostle," he says, "through Jesus Christ—yes, and through God the Father, since God the Father raised Christ from the dead and is concerned in all that the risen Christ does, including that call to me that came on the Damascus road."

The Contrast Between Christ and Man

So far we have explained the words that Paul uses in this verse. But it is to be wondered whether all readers are aware of the stupendous implications of those words. When Paul says, *"Not* through a man *but* through Jesus Christ," has it struck the reader that that is a very strange contrast; does it seem at all strange that the Apostle should set Jesus Christ sharply over against humanity in this way, as though He belonged in an entirely different category, as though "a man" and "Jesus Christ" were two entirely distinct things?

If it does not seem strange to us, that is simply because our Christian conviction about Jesus Christ has become so ingrained in us that the wonder of it has been lost from view. Thank God that it does not seem strange to us! But to most modern historians, both within and without the Church, it seems very strange indeed.

A Contemporary Witness

Who was this "Jesus Christ" who is separated thus by Paul so sharply from ordinary humanity and is placed on the side of God? Who was this person who is treated thus as a stupendous heavenly being to whom divine honors were to be paid, along with the honors paid to the eternal God, the Maker of heaven and earth? Was He a mythical personage of remote antiquity, around whom the legends of the ages would have been free to grow?

Not at all. He was a Jewish teacher, a contemporary of Paul, who had lived in Palestine and had died a shameful death only a few years before this Epistle was written. He was a person one of whose brothers Paul had actually met

(Gal. 1:19). The genuineness of the Epistle to the Galatians is admitted by all serious historians, whether friends or foes of Christianity. The Epistle was admittedly written, then, by Paul; and the date of it can be fixed within rather narrow limits. It was written not later than about A. D. 55, only some twenty-five years after the death of this Jesus of whom Paul speaks. When, therefore, Paul speaks of Jesus Christ as in such contrast with humanity and as standing so clearly on the side of God, he is not speaking about a personage of the dim and distant past, but about one of his own contemporaries. How shall so strange a phenomenon be explained?

The real Christian will have no difficulty in explaining it. "Paul speaks of Jesus as God," he will say, "because as a matter of fact Jesus *was* God, because He was the eternal Son of God who came voluntarily to this earth for our salvation, worked redemption for mankind, rose from the dead, and is now seated on the throne of all being to be worshipped and glorified by all who are His."

But to most modern historians, who regard Jesus as a mere man, the first verse of Galatians, together with all the rest that Paul says, presents a very strange problem indeed. How did a mere man, a Jewish teacher, come to be regarded thus as God, not by later generations but by one of His own contemporaries?

One God, Yet Christ Is God

The thing would not be quite so strange if Paul, who attests this strange view of Jesus, had been a man of polytheistic training and belief. Had he believed in many gods, the adding of one more would not be quite so difficult to understand. But as a matter of fact Paul was a monotheist of the monotheists. Pharisaic Judaism of the first century was nothing if not monotheistic; it held with heart and soul to the doctrine that there is but one God. Paul shared that doctrine, both before and after his conversion, to the full. How could such a monotheist, such a believer in the awful separateness between the one God and the world that He had made, possibly come to exalt a mere man, Jesus, to the godhead and pay to him the reverence which belongs only to God?

That Paul does just that is attested not only by our verse but by his Epistles from beginning to end. He does, indeed, in certain passages, speak of Jesus as a man. In Rom. 5:15, for example, he contrasts the one man, Adam, with "the one man, Jesus Christ"; and a similar contrast between "the first man" and "the second man" occurs in the fifteenth chapter of I Corinthians. So also in I Tim. 1:5, Paul speaks of the "one Mediator between God and men, the man Christ Jesus." But in these passages the careful reader receives somewhat the impression that the Apostle regards it as a strange thing, worthy of special note, that Jesus Christ should be a man as well as something other than man. At any rate, these passages do not in the slightest invalidate the fact that in the Epistles as a whole, as in our verse in Galatians, Jesus Christ is separated sharply from ordinary humanity and placed clearly on the side of God. Everywhere Paul stands in a truly religious relationship to Christ. Christ is for him not primarily an example for faith but the object of faith; his religion does not consist merely in having faith in God like the faith which Jesus had in God, but in having faith in Jesus.

That fact is enough to give the thoughtful historian pause. Who was this Jesus who could be exalted to the throne of God not by later generations but by a man of His own generation, only a few years after His shameful death?

But we have not yet mentioned what is perhaps the most surprising thing of all. The surprising thing is not merely that Paul holds this stupendous view of Jesus, but that he does not argue about it, that he seems to be under no necessity whatever of defending it against attack within the Church. Even the Judaizers, so far as we can see, had no quarrel with Paul's lofty view of Christ. Paul said: "I am an apostle not through a man but through Jesus Christ"; the Judaizers said: "No, you are an apostle not through Jesus Christ but through a man"; but it never seems to have occurred to anyone in the Church to say: " You are an apostle through Jesus Christ and therefore you are an apostle through a man, since Jesus Christ was a mere man."

Certainly, at any rate, whatever may have been the attitude of the Judaizers, it is perfectly clear that even if they did differ from Paul about the person of Christ, the original apostles—Peter and others of the Twelve—gave them no slightest color of support on this point. The Judaizers may possibly have appealed to those original apostles on another point—namely, the attitude that was to be assumed in the Church toward the Mosaic law. Even that appeal—supposing they did make it, which is by no means perfectly certain—was, as we shall see, an utterly unjustified appeal. But with regard to the person of Christ, at any rate, they did not venture to make any appeal to the original apostles at all.

Here, then, we have the truly amazing thing. Not only does Paul hold to his stupendous view of the person of Christ, but he assumes that everyone agrees with him about it; in particular, he assumes that Peter agrees with him, and others of the intimate friends of Jesus. Those men had seen Jesus subjected to all the petty limitations of human life, as He had walked with them on the Galilean hills; and yet they agreed perfectly with the lofty view, which Paul presents in his Epistles, of Jesus as the Son of the living God.

That fact presents to the modern naturalistic historians, who reject the picture of Jesus which the New Testament contains, a serious problem. According to those historians, Jesus was a mere man, and His first disciples regarded Him at first as such. That, then, according to these historians, was the original, the "primitive," view of Jesus; Jesus presented Himself and was first regarded, as a mere prophet of righteousness, or at most as a purely human Messiah. Yet the plain fact is—a fact which no historian can deny—that if that was the original view of Jesus it gave place to a totally different view not in some later generation but, as attested by the Epistles of Paul, in the very first Christian generation, when the intimate friends of Jesus were leaders in the Church.

The rapidity of the transition is very strange. But still more strange is the utter absence of any conflict at the time when the change was produced. The absence of conflict, the absence of any throes of transition, is eloquently attested by the Epistles of Paul. What we are asked by naturalistic historians to believe is that the true, the original, the "primitive," view of Jesus as just a great religious teacher, proclaiming the fatherhood of God and the brotherhood of man, suddenly gave place, just after His shameful death, to a totally different, a totally incongruous, view, and that that mighty transition was effected without the slightest trace of any conflict in the Church!

That is really too much to believe. No, the matter-of-course way in which Jesus, as the Epistles of Paul attest, was regarded as a supernatural person in the earliest apostolic Church shows that there was something in His person from the very beginning that justified such a view.

Such is the witness of Paul to Christ. It is not dependent upon details in the Epistles, but is involved, rather, in the total phenomenon which the Epistles present. It has not been invalidated in the slightest by modern research.

III. PLAIN SPEAKING IN A TIME OF PERIL

"Paul an Apostle, not from men nor through a man, but through Jesus Christ and God the Father who raised Him from the dead, and all the brethren who are with me, to the churches of Galatia . . . " (Gal. 1:1, 2, in a literal translation).

"All the Brethren Who Are With Me"

In the two previous numbers of *Christianity Today* we have considered the significant addition which Paul makes in the opening of this Epistle to the bare name and title of the writer. He is an apostle, he insists, not through any merely human intermediation, as the Judaizing opponents contended, but by a direct commission from the Lord Jesus Christ.

But with himself Paul associates certain other persons. The letter comes, he says, not only from him, but from "all the brethren" who are with him when he writes. Such association of other persons with Paul occurs in the openings of a number of the Epistles. Thus I and II Thessalonians are sent in the name of Paul and Silvanus and Timotheus; I Corinthians, in the name of Paul and Sosthenes; II Corinthians, Philippians and Colossians, in the name of Paul and Timothy.

What is the meaning of this association of other persons with Paul in the openings of these letters? What part did these persons have in the letters that follow?

The true answer to that question is readily determined when we find a mean between two extremes.

Paul Alone the Author

It is perfectly clear, on the one hand, that these persons did not have any actual share in the composition of the Epistles. That view is excluded by the whole character of the Epistles. It would be difficult to imagine any writings that present more clearly than these the marks of one very distinctive mind. Whatever else may be thought of them, it is perfectly clear that they are not composite productions. Moreover, the first person singular is used in the Epistles in the freest possible way. Thus in Galatians, immediately after the opening, Paul says, "*I* marvel that ye are so soon removing . . ."; and he proceeds to write throughout the Epistle in the same thoroughly individual and personal manner. It is evident, therefore, that whatever this association of other persons with Paul in the openings of the Epistles may mean, it does not mean that these persons shared in the actual composition; these persons clearly were not joint authors with Paul.

On the other hand, an opposite extreme should also be avoided. It will hardly do to say that this association of other persons with Paul in the openings is only a polite way of indicating that these persons send greetings to the churches that are addressed; for the Pauline way of sending such greetings is to put them at the end. At the end of I Corinthians, for example, it is said: "Aquila and Priscilla, with the church that is in their house, salute you much in the Lord" (I Cor. 16:19); yet I Corinthians is one of the Epistles where another person—in this case, Sosthenes—is associated with Paul in the opening. Evidently the two things, the sending of greetings at the end and the association with Paul in the opening, cannot be exactly the same in meaning.

Others Agree with Paul

If, then, the association of these persons with Paul in the openings does not mean so much as that they have shared in the actual composition of the Epistles, and on the other hand means more than that they merely send greeting, what does it mean? Evidently it means something in between these two extremes. No doubt it means that these persons are acquainted, in at least a general way, with the contents of the Epistles, and unite with Paul in hoping for a favorable and obedient reception of them on the part of the churches to which they are addressed.

So here Paul no doubt means to say to the Galatians: "All the brethren who are with me join in what I am saying to you; will you, then, agree with me any less than they?"

By the words, "all the brethren who are with me," Paul hardly means to designate the whole church in whatever city he may have been residing in when he wrote the Epistle; for, as has well been observed, in Phil. 4:21 "the brethren who are with me" are distinguished from "all the saints" (verse 22), by which latter phrase Paul means to designate all the Christians in the city, Rome, in which the Epistle was written. Evidently the phrase, "the brethren who are with me," designated some smaller group, more intimately associated with Paul than were the members generally of that church at Rome. So here in Galatians Paul associates with himself in the Epistle not all the Christians in the city where he was residing, but some smaller and more intimate group of persons who could really be cognizant of what the Epistle contains.

No Time for Pleasant Words

So far we have dealt with only one of the three parts into which the opening of the Epistle is divided. We have dealt only with the part that is in the nominative case, the part that designates the writer of the letter and his associates. The next part is the part in the dative case, the part which designates the persons to whom the letter is addressed. This part is very brief; it consists simply of the words, "to the churches of Galatia."

We have already seen that the nominative part of this opening is very peculiar as compared with the other Epistles of Paul; it contains a long addition directed against the attack which the Judaizers had made against the independent apostolic authority of the writer. But the dative part of the opening is no less peculiar than is the nominative part.

At first sight, that may seem to be rather a surprising assertion. "To the churches of Galatia," Paul says. What could be simpler than that? What is there so peculiar about it? We answer that there is nothing peculiar about it, and that that is just exactly what is so peculiar about it! In almost every one of the other Epistles of Paul, there *is* something peculiar about the way in which those to whom the Epistle is addressed are designated in the opening; Paul uses words which designate in some way the high Christian state in which the readers find themselves. So in Rom. 1:7 the readers are called "beloved of God, called to be saints"; in I Corinthians the church is called "the church *of God* which is at Corinth," and the members of the church are called "saints"; and similar words of recognition of the Christian state of the addressees are found in other Epistles of Paul. But here the Epistle is addressed, in the briefest and most formal kind of way, simply "to the churches of Galatia."

This brevity and formality in the designation of the recipients of the Epistle, this complete absence of words recognizing their Christian state or their progress in the Christian life, is without doubt significant. These Galatians were on the point of turning away from the gospel of Christ, and Paul has no intention whatever of commending them. It is true, he does address them, later in the Epistle, as "brethren"; and "brethren," in Paul's writings, means, "fellow-Christians." He does not, therefore, give them up. Though they are in danger of falling away, there is yet a possibility —if we may speak after the manner of men—of saving them. But certainly it was no time for pleasant words. He calls them, therefore, simply "the churches of Galatia"; he does not call them "saints"; he does not go out of his way to call them a part of the Church of God. Whether they were truly to be designated by these high terms remained to be seen;

they could not rightly be so designated unless they should reject the error of the Judaizers and should stand fast in the freedom with which Christ had set them free.

What Would Paul Say Now?

How would Paul designate our churches of the present day? Would he fall in with the customary practice of saying that all is well? Would he sign the reports of the various Moderatorial commissions in the Presbyterian Church in the U. S. A., which have as their function the crying of "Peace, peace, when there is no peace"? Would he go out of his way to commend as a true church of Jesus Christ an ecclesiastical body that includes among its ministers the thirteen hundred "Auburn Affirmationists" who have signed a formal document derogatory to the very vitals of the Christian faith? Would he commend an organization that has placed those men in positions of the highest ecclesiastical authority and is plainly dominated by the point of view that they represent, an organization that has recently removed from office the old Board of Directors of Princeton Seminary for no other cause but that with too great honesty and fearlessness it maintained the Confession of Faith of the Church? Would he speak with any essentially greater commendation of many other Reformed or Presbyterian Churches in this country? Would he commend the Presbyterian Church in the U.S.,[1] which is drifting away from the Bible and from the historic Faith almost without knowing it? Would he commend the United Presbyterian Church,[2] with its recent adoption of a feeble, compromising "Confessional Statement," to supplement, and really to supplant, its great historic Westminster Confession which was founded squarely upon the word of God? Would he commend any of these churches that are toying with a plan of union which would substitute the power of committees and boards for a true, free unity of the Spirit in the bond of peace, and which, in its tentative form already announced, would do

---
[1] The so-called "Southern Presbyterian Church." (Editor's Note)
[2] The United Presbyterian Church of North America, which later joined with the Presbyterian Church in the U.S.A. to form the present United Presbyterian Church in the United States of America. (Editor's Note)

away with any effective creed-subscription on the part of the ministry and would give free course to indifferentism and unbelief? Would he commend churches so complacent toward those advocates of indifferentist church-union who, ever since the proposal of the "Plan of Organic Union" of 1920, have been engaged in undermining, undermining, undermining, where their office would have required them to be engaged in edification on the basis of God's holy Word?

We are convinced that he would utter no such commendation at all, but that he would speak the same earnest word of warning that he spoke in the presence of the Judaizers of old. And in these sad days, when Christian language so often conceals a profoundly unchristian mind and heart, would to God that we had, in all our churches, less of empty pious words, less of a foolish optimism, and more of the fearless honesty of Paul.

The Churches of Galatia

Where were these "churches of Galatia," to which this Epistle was addressed? There are two views about this question. According to one view, called "the North Galatian theory," the churches were in the north central part of Asia Minor, in Galatia proper, the country of the "Celts"—the word "Galatians" is the Greek word for "Celts"—which was occupied by people of Celtic race after a back-migration into Asia Minor in the third century before Christ. According to the other view, "the South Galatian theory," the churches addressed in the Epistle were not in Galatia proper, but were the well-known churches in Pisidian Antioch, Iconium, Lystra and Derbe, which were in those parts of Phrygia and Lycaonia that had been united, or been left united, with Galatia proper in 25 B. C. to form the large Roman province of "Galatia."

Upon this "Galatian question," the question as to which of these two views regarding the destination of the Epistle is correct, depends to some extent the question of the date of the Epistle. Apparently Paul had visited "the churches of Galatia" twice before he wrote the letter; for he says in Gal. 4:13, according to the most natural interpretation of his words: "Ye know that on account of a weakness of the flesh I preached the gospel to you *the former time.*"

If the North Galatian theory is correct, the former of these two visits to the churches is to be put at Acts 16:16 (near the beginning of the second missionary journey) and the second of the visits to be put at Acts 18:23 (near the beginning of the third missionary journey), in both of which passages the phrase, "the Galatian country," is used. On the North Galatian theory, therefore, the Epistle could not have been written prior to the time of Acts 18:23, and in all probability it was written during the long stay of Paul at Ephesus which came just after that time.

If, on the other hand, the South Galatian theory is correct, the former of the two visits to the churches addressed in the Epistle took place on the first missionary journey, when Paul founded the churches in Pisidian Antioch, Iconium, Lystra and Derbe; and the second visit—at least so our first impulse would be to say—took place at the beginning of the second missionary journey, when the Book of Acts distinctly says that Derbe and Lystra were visited and when it apparently intends us to understand that Paul went on also to Iconium and Pisidian Antioch. On the South Galatian theory, therefore, the Epistle may have been written at any time after Paul's passage through South Galatia at the beginning of the second missionary journey.

Indeed, it is possible, on the South Galatian theory, to place the Epistle even earlier than that. On the first missionary journey, it will be remembered, Paul went first through Pisidian Antioch, Iconium, Lystra and Derbe; and then he went back again over the same route. May not that return journey be regarded as the second of the two visits of Paul to the Galatian churches? If so, both of the visits may be placed in the first missionary journey, and the Epistle may have been written at any time after that journey was over.

In particular, the Epistle, on this view, may have been written *immediately* after that journey, or at Syrian Antioch during the period mentioned in Acts 14:26—15:2, a period prior to the "Apostolic Council" at which Paul met the Jerusalem Church in the manner described in Acts 15:3-29.

The Importance of "the Galatian Question"

This early dating of Galatians would have rather important consequences for our understanding of the history of the apostolic age. If the Epistle to the Galatians was actually written before the Apostolic Council, then of course it cannot contain an account of the Apostolic Council; and the meeting described in Gal. 2:1-10 between Paul and the pillars of the Jerusalem Church cannot be identical with the Apostolic Council of Acts 15:3-29, but must be identical with a previous visit of Paul to Jerusalem, the "famine visit" of Acts 11:30; 12:25, when Paul and Barnabas took up to Jerusalem the gifts of the Antioch Church.

Now a large part of modern negative criticism of the New Testament has been based upon the assumption that Acts 15:3-29 and Gal. 2:1-10 are two accounts of the same event. Since they are two accounts of the same event, it has been said, they can be checked up by comparison with each other; and if they are found to be contradictory, one account or the other is untrue. But in any case it is clear that the account given by Paul in Galatians is essentially true, since Paul was actually an eyewitness of the events and since the genuineness of the Epistle is not denied today by any serious critics, whatever their general attitude toward the New Testament may be. If, therefore, it is said, there is contradiction between Gal. 2:1-10 and Acts 15:3-29, the fault must lie on the side of Acts; and if Acts is thus discredited at this point, where we can check it up by comparison with a recognized authority, it is discredited elsewhere as well; and since the Third Gospel was written by the same man, that is discredited also, and the whole account which Luke-Acts gives of the life of Christ and the beginnings of the Christian Church is shown to be untrustworthy.

This method of attack falls to the ground if Galatians was actually written before the Apostolic Council of Acts 15:3-29 took place; for in that case Gal. 2:1-10 is an account of an entirely different event from that which is narrated in

Acts 15:3-29, and differences between the two accounts cannot possibly be regarded as contradictions. Thus the dating of Galatians before the Apostolic Council, which becomes possible on the South Galatian theory, constitutes one way, and a very effective way, of refuting what is perhaps the most serious modern attack upon the trustworthiness of the New Testament. This early dating of Galatians can no longer be regarded as a mere curiosity or baseless vagary of criticism; for it has received the support of several able modern scholars of widely differing views.

We do not, indeed, desire to create the impression that we adopt the early dating of Galatians. In particular, we do not desire to create the impression that we think it provides the only way of defending the trustworthiness of Luke-Acts. Even if Galatians was written after the Apostolic Council, and even if Gal. 2:1-10 and Acts 15:3-29 do constitute, as the vast majority of scholars think they do, two accounts of the same event, still we hold most emphatically that there is no contradiction between them but that they present only those differences which are natural in two independent, but equally trustworthy, witnesses.

However, the early dating of Galatians, with identification of the event of Gal. 2:1-10 with the famine visit of Acts 11:30; 12:25, constitutes one possible, even though perhaps not probable, way of exhibiting the harmony between Acts and Galatians. It must be treated, therefore, at least with respect, and unquestionably it would serve to solve some of the problems. If there were no other way of defending the trustworthiness of Luke-Acts, then, because of the great weight of independent evidence to the effect that Luke-Acts *is* trustworthy, and that it was really written by a companion of Paul, we should regard as thoroughly scientific the adoption of this view.

The possibility of this early dating of Galatians is open only on the basis of the South Galatian theory. That constitutes, we think, the chief interest of the much debated "Galatian question" as to the destination of the Epistle.

We shall not endeavor to decide that question here, and indeed the decision is exceedingly difficult. Plausible arguments may be adduced on either side. The North Galatian theory has the advantage of placing the Epistle chronologically together with the Epistles of the third missionary journey—I and II Corinthians and Romans—with which it is very closely connected in thought and in style. Perhaps that theory may provisionally be adopted, though the South Galatian theory, with or without the dating before the Apostolic Council, must be kept in mind as a possibility which ultimately we might be led to adopt.

Fortunately the essential teaching of the Epistle is quite independent of the question where the churches to which it is addressed are to be found. Whether those churches were in North Galatia or in South Galatia, they were falling into a very modern, as well as a very ancient, error, and the Epistle which Paul wrote to them in the first century is eminently a tract for our twentieth-century times.

IV. THE FREEDOM OF THE CHRISTIAN MAN

"Grace be to you and peace from God our Father and the Lord Jesus Christ, who gave Himself for our sins, in order that He might deliver us from the present evil age, according to the will of Him who is God and our Father, to whom be the glory for ever and ever, Amen.

"I marvel that you are so soon turning, from Him who called you in the grace of Christ, to another gospel, which is not another—only, there are some who are disturbing you and wishing to subvert the gospel of Christ" (Gal. 1:3-7, in a literal translation).

Grace and Peace

In the last three numbers of *Christianity Today*, we have discussed two of the three parts into which the opening of this Epistle is divided: we have discussed the nominative part, which indicates the person or persons from whom the Epistle comes; and we have discussed the dative part, which indicates the persons to whom the Epistle is addressed.

The remaining part is the greeting. It begins with the words: "Grace be to you and peace from God our Father and the Lord Jesus Christ." So far there is nothing peculiar about it at all. Exactly these same words occur in the greetings in Romans, I and II Corinthians, Ephesians, Philippians, II Thessalonians; and very similar words occur in all the other Epistles of Paul.

In this Pauline greeting, "grace" designates the undeserved favor of God, and "peace" the profound well-being of the soul which is the result of it.

"God Our Father and the Lord Jesus Christ"

This grace and this peace come not only from "God our Father" but also from "the Lord Jesus Christ"; these two divine Persons are placed in the closest possible conjunction. Thus the greeting involves the most stupendous ascription of deity to our Lord. Yet that ascription of deity appears not at all as something new, but altogether as a matter of course. So deeply rooted in the life of the apostolic Church is the belief in the deity of Christ that it has determined the very form with which practically every one of the Pauline Epistles begins. Neither Paul nor his readers detected anything strange in this amazing separation of Jesus Christ from all created beings and this amazing inclusion of Him with God the Father as the source of all grace and all peace.*

So much appears in almost every one of the Epistles of Paul. The greeting is the most constant part among the three parts into which the openings of the Epistles are divided. But here in Galatians this constant formula of greeting has joined with it an addition which is entirely unique. "Grace be to you and peace," says Paul to the Galatians, "from God our Father and the Lord Jesus Christ"—so much appears in the other Epistles—but then he adds here alone, "who gave Himself for our sins in order that He might deliver us from the present evil age according to the will of Him who is God and our Father, to whom be the glory for ever and ever, Amen."

What is the reason for this addition just here, this addition which is entirely without parallel in the other Epistles?

---

* See the fine article by B. B. Warfield, "God Our Father and the Lord Jesus Christ," now published in the second volume, *Biblical Doctrines*, in his selected works, pp. 213-231.

The answer is perfectly clear. Paul is adding these words in reply to the propaganda of the Judaizing teachers who were making the cross of Christ of none effect. "Christ died to set you free," says Paul in substance; "yet now you are returning into bondage; by your effort to earn a part of your salvation by your own good works you are returning into that very bondage from which you were released at such enormous cost; you are trying to undo the effects of Christ's unspeakable gift." That is the central thought of the Epistle to the Galatians. It is set forth in epitome in this remarkable addition which the Apostle makes to the regular form of greeting that appears in the other Epistles.

"Who Gave Himself for Our Sins"

"The Lord Jesus Christ," says Paul, "who gave Himself for our sins." When Paul says "gave Himself," he is referring very specifically not to the incarnation, but to the cross; not to the life of Christ, but to His death. Certainly the incarnation and the life of Christ on earth were necessary to the saving work of Christ; without them the redemption which He accomplished on Calvary would have been impossible. But here it is unquestionably the death that Paul has in mind. There might conceivably be a doubt about that if this language appeared in some other writer, but in Pauline usage the matter is not open to doubt.

The word "for" in the English translation of the phrase "for our sins" represents either of two Greek prepositions, of which some manuscripts have one and some the other.

One of these two prepositions, *peri*, means simply "concerning" or "in the matter of." If that preposition was what Paul wrote, then the phrase simply indicates that Christ's death was connected in some way with our sins, without any indication of what the connection was. Of course, the connection is made perfectly plain by other passages in Paul; the Apostle clearly believed that when Christ died on the cross He died in our stead, bearing the just punishment of our sins. That wonderful thought was always in the background of his mind when he spoke of the connection between our sins and Christ's death. But it is not designated specifically by the preposition *peri*.

The other preposition, *hyper*, means "in behalf of," "for the benefit of"; it has the idea not merely of a connection between what precedes it and what follows after it, but of an active interest of the former in the latter. But how can Paul possibly have said that Christ died "for the benefit of" *sins?* The thought seems at first sight to be blasphemous.

In reply, it may be said, in the first place, that Paul does say just that in I Cor. 15:3. Whichever reading is correct at Gal. 1:4, the preposition *hyper* is certainly used in the clause, "Christ died for *(hyper)* our sins," in the precious summary that Paul gives in I Cor. 15:3 ff. of the tradition of the early Jerusalem Church. It is important, therefore, to determine what the preposition means in this connection. What does Paul mean when he says that Christ died "in behalf of our sins"?

The answer can be made clear by the example of a modern English colloquial usage. We sometimes say to a sick person, "How is your cold this morning?"; and he sometimes replies: "It is very much better; I took some medicine for it last night, and the medicine helped it very much." Now that sick person does not mean, strictly speaking, that he took the medicine *for* ("for the benefit of") the cold, or that the medicine *helped* the cold, or that the cold is now *better.* On the contrary, he means that he took the medicine *against* the cold and that the cold was *hindered* by the medicine and that the cold is *less flourishing* than it was before. Yet the colloquial usage in question is very common and very natural. When we say that a cold is better, we really mean that the person is better because the cold is not so flourishing as it was before; and when we say that we give a sick person some medicine for his cold, we really mean that we give the medicine for him and against his cold.

So here, when it is said that Christ died for the benefit of our sins—supposing that to be the correct reading—that really means that Christ died for the benefit of us, laden with our sins as we were; or, in other words, that He died for the benefit of us and for the destruction, or counteraction in some way, of our sins.

The manuscript evidence is rather evenly divided in Gal. 1:4 between *peri,* "concerning" or "in the matter of," and *hyper,* "for the sake of" or "for the benefit of." But fortunately it does not make very much difference which of these two readings is correct: for if *peri* (the more general word) is the correct reading here, we have the more precise word used in exactly the same connection in I Cor. 15:3; and in any case the phrase is of course to be understood in the light of the full, rich teaching of Paul in other passages as to the meaning of Christ's death.

The Two Ages

Christ "gave Himself for our sins," Paul says, "in order that He might deliver us from the present evil age." "The present age" is clearly to be regarded as contrasted with a future age. In Eph. 1:21, in the phrase "not only in this age but also in that which is to come," the contrast becomes explicit; and it is implied in all the passages in Paul's Epistles where "the present age," or "this age," is mentioned. By "the present age" Paul means the whole period from the fall of man to the second coming of Christ; by "the age which is to come" he means the glorious time which is to be ushered in by this latter event.

This doctrine of the two ages was not originated by the Apostle Paul, but had a considerable history before his time. It appears with the utmost clearness, for example, in the teaching of Jesus, as when He speaks of the sin that shall be forgiven "neither in this age nor in that which is to come" (Matt. 12:32). But Jesus does not speak of it as though it were a new thing. On the contrary, He seems to assume that it is already well known to his hearers.

It is not surprising, therefore, to discover that the doctrine of the two ages was a well-known Jewish doctrine at the time of our Lord and of His apostles. Ultimately the doctrine had an Old Testament basis in such passages as the prophecy in Isaiah 65: 17-25 regarding the new heavens and the new earth. The later Jews were quite in accordance with Old Testament teaching when they looked forward to a new and glorious age which was to take the place of the present age of misery and sin.

Thus far we have found nothing peculiar in the teaching of the New Testament and of the Apostle Paul upon this subject. In holding that the age in which we are living is to be followed by a glorious age which is to be ushered in by an act of God, Paul is teaching what his Jewish contemporaries already taught.

Already Free

But at this point an important difference enters in. The difference is that according to the Jews a man must be either in one age or in the other, whereas according to Paul (and really also according to Jesus) a man, through Christ, can already, here and now, be free from the present age and a citizen of the future kingdom. In one sense we look to the future for our salvation, but in another sense we have it here and now. Outwardly we are still in the present evil age, but inwardly we are already free from its bondage.

This double aspect of salvation—in one sense, future; in another sense, present—runs all through apostolic teaching, and is quite basic in true Christian life of all ages. Here in Galatians it is especially the present aspect of salvation that is in view. "You have already been made free from the present evil age," Paul says to the Galatians; "what folly then it is to return into bondage! Christ died to set you free; will you then do despite to His love by becoming again slaves?"

Bondage Versus Freedom

Certainly a man is a slave if, as the Judaizers desired, he seeks to earn even a part of his salvation by his obedience to God's law, if he seeks to enter into an account with God. We are already hopelessly in debt; we are under the awful curse which the law pronounces against sin. If we try to pay the debt by our own miserable works, the debt is not really paid but is heaped up yet more and more. There is one way of escape and one way only. It is open because Christ has paid the debt and set us free.

Have the men of our time really known that freedom? Will they ever really be able to atone for sin by "making Christ Master" in their lives, by trying, unredeemed and unregenerate, to live as Christ once lived? The whole Word of God answers, "No." Freedom is found only when a man, like Christian in Bunyan's allegory, comes to a place somewhat ascending where he sees a cross and the figure of Him that did hang thereon, and where, at that sight, the burden of sin, which none in the village of Morality could remove, falls of itself from the back. That is a freedom that is freedom indeed. Right with God, fear removed, the slate wiped clean, all lightness and joy!

It is a freedom, first of all, from sin—freedom from its guilt and freedom from its power. But the freedom from sin brings also a freedom from this whole evil world. What cares the true Christian what the world may do; what cares he what ill fortune, as the world looks upon it, may bring? These things hold the unredeemed in bondage, but over the redeemed man they have no power.

The Meaning of Freedom

The Christian does indeed live still in this world. It is a travesty on this Pauline doctrine when it is held to mean that when he escapes, inwardly, from the present evil world by the redeeming work of Christ the Christian can calmly leave the world to its fate. On the contrary, Christian men, even after they have been redeemed, are left in this world, and in this world they have an important duty to perform.

In the first place, they do not stand alone, but are united in the great brotherhood of the Christian Church. Into that brotherhood it is their duty to invite other men by the preaching of the gospel; and they should pray that that preaching, through the supernatural operation of the Holy Spirit in the new birth, may be efficacious, and that the great brotherhood may expand yet more and more.

In the second place, Christians should by no means adopt a negative attitude toward art, government, science, literature, and the other achievements of mankind, but should consecrate these things to the service of God. The separateness of the Christian from the world is not to be manifested, as so many seem to think that it should be manifested, by the presentation to God of only an impoverished man; but it is to be manifested by the presentation to God of all man's God-given powers developed to the full. That is the higher Christian humanism, a humanism based not upon human pride but upon the solid foundation of the grace of God.

But these considerations do not make any less radical the step of which Paul speaks. It remains true that the Christian has escaped from this present age—from this present world with all its sin and all its pride. The Christian continues to live in the world, but he lives in it as its master and not as its slave. He can move the world because at last he has a place to stand.

The Author of Freedom

This freedom which Paul attributes to the Christian is not a freedom that the Christian has arrogated to himself; it is not a freedom that has been attained by rebellion against God's holy law. So the Judaizers represented it, but in representing it so they were wrong. "No," says Paul; "we are not free by rebellion against God, but by His own gracious will. Christ gave Himself for our sins that He might deliver us from the present evil age *according to the will of Him who is God and our Father*; and to Him, our supreme Liberator, we can ascribe all the glory and all the praise." So the address of this Epistle ends with a triumphant doxology: "To whom be the glory for ever and ever, Amen."

It is a wonderful passage—this "address" or opening of the Epistle to the Galatians. In it is contained a summary of the whole rich content of the glorious Epistle that follows. In the unique addition to the nominative part ("not from men nor through a man, but through Jesus Christ and God the Father who raised Him from the dead"), we have a summary of the first main division of the Epistle (Gal. 1:10-2:21) in which Paul defends his independent apostolic authority against the Judaizers' contention that he was an apostle only in a secondary sense; in the unique curtness and brevity of the dative part ("to the churches of Galatia"), we have an indication of the deadly seriousness of the crisis in which the Epistle was written; in the unique addition to the greeting part ("who gave Himself for our sins, in order that He might deliver us from the present evil age according to the will of Him who is God and our Father, to whom be the glory for ever and ever, Amen"), we have a summary of Paul's defence of his gospel in the great central part of the Epistle. Paul was not like some modern preachers, who are inclined to mention the blessed doctrine of the cross only when they are taken to task for neglecting it. Paul regarded it as the very foundation of Christian life; and when it was belittled, as in Galatia, he put his whole heart into its defence.

Thanksgiving True and False

Immediately after the address we find in nearly all of the other Epistles of Paul an expression of thanksgiving for the Christian state of the readers. That appears in Romans, I Corinthians, Philippians, Colossians, I and II Thessalonians, II Timothy, Philemon; and II Corinthians and Ephesians are only apparent, rather than real, exceptions. But in Galatians there is nothing whatever of the kind. The first word of the Epistle, after the address is over, is not "I give thanks" but "I am surprised"; Paul plunges at once into the matter that caused the Epistle to be written. "You are turning away from the gospel," he says in effect, "and I am writing this Epistle to stop you."

What is the reason for this absence, in the Epistle to the Galatians, of the usual thanksgiving? The answer is really very simple. Paul omitted giving thanks, for the simple reason that there was nothing to be thankful for.

No doubt he did give thanks to God on the very same day when he wrote this Epistle. He gave thanks for the gospel of Christ; he gave thanks for news that he had received from other churches. But the news that he had received from Galatia was bad and only bad, and Paul had not the slightest intention of telling God that it was good.

Many persons seem to think that it is eminently pious to give thanks to God whether or not there is anything to be thankful for. They seem to think that loyalty to the Church means blind loyalty to a human organization or to agencies and boards; they seem to think that sin in individual or ecclesiastical life can be removed by saying that it is not there; they cover up the serious issues of the day, in the councils of the Church, by a sad misuse of the sacred exercise of prayer.

Paul's way was very different. A sterling honesty ran all through his devotional life. He thanked God for what was good; he prayed to God, sometimes with tears, for the removal of what was bad. But always he was honest with God. When he got down upon his knees he did not try to conceal the real facts either from God or from himself. He made God a sharer in his joys, but also he made Him a sharer in his sorrows. Like Hezekiah, he spread the threatening letters of the adversaries unreservedly before the throne of grace. So here, with regard to the Galatian churches, he faced the facts. The Galatians were turning away from the faith. There was no honorable possibility of concealment or palliation. The facts were too plain. Paul had not the slightest intention of concealing them. Thanksgiving at such a moment would have been blasphemy; praise of the Galatians would have been cruelty. Paul engaged neither in thanksgiving nor in praise. Instead, he wrote this mighty Epistle, with its solemn warning, with its flaming appeal.

There is one advantage about a man like that. He may not always give you praise when you desire praise; but when he does give you praise you know that it comes from the heart.

V. THE GOSPEL OF CHRIST

"I marvel that you are so quickly turning from Him who called you in the grace of Christ, unto a different gospel, which is not another—only, there are some who are disturbing you and are wishing to subvert the gospel of Christ" (Gal. 1:6, 7, in a literal translation).

Another Gospel Which Is Not Another

In the last number of *Christianity Today,* we pointed out the strange absence, in the Epistle to the Galatians, of the usual thanksgiving for the Christian state of the readers.

There was nothing to be thankful for in the news which Paul had received from the Galatian churches, and Paul had not the slightest intention of expressing a thankfulness which was not justified by the facts.

The news which had come from the churches was bad and only bad, and the Apostle plunges at once into his treatment of it. "I marvel," he says, "that ye are so quickly turning away, from Him who called you in the grace of Christ, to another gospel, which is not another—only, there are certain men who are troubling you and are wishing to subvert the gospel of Christ."

The Person whom Paul means when he speaks of Him from whom the Galatians are turning away is of course God the Father. God had called them by that majestic call at the beginning of their Christian life which had been made possible only by the gracious gift which Christ had made for them on the cross; yet now they are turning away from such a call and despising such grace. No wonder that the Apostle marvels at a perversity so great!

The thing to which they are turning away so quickly is designated as "another gospel, which is not another." But in the Greek two different words are used here for "another." The word which is used in the former place is *heteros;* the word which is used in the latter place is *allos.* The former word, *heteros,* often, though not always, has in it the notion of difference in kind between one thing and another. Thus it is said in the Gospel according to Luke, in connection with the transfiguration, that "the fashion of His countenance became other." Here the word *heteros* is used for "other," and the plain implication is that the fashion of His countenance was *different* from what it had been before.

The other word, *allos,* on the other hand, designates merely numerical distinctness of one thing from another. If I give a man an apple, and he asks me whether I have "another," the word that he will naturally use is not *heteros* but *allos.*

In view of this distinction, the scoffing observation that "orthodoxy is my doxy, and heterodoxy is the other man's doxy," is seen to illustrate rather clearly the principle that a little learning is a dangerous thing. As a matter of fact, *orthos* means "straight" and "orthodoxy" means "straight doxy"; whereas *heterodoxy* means a doxy that is *different* from straight doxy—in other words, it means "crooked doxy"!

We trust that the readers will pardon this slight digression and will now return with us to the matter in hand. Paul says that the Galatians are turning unto a different gospel, but that that different gospel is not really a second gospel to be put alongside of the gospel already preached, as though it could be a companion with it in a series. "No," says Paul, "it is not really a gospel at all; there is only one gospel, and that is the gospel already preached to you. This other teaching, though it purports to be a gospel, is not really a gospel at all. It is not really another gospel, but only a perversion of the one true gospel."

Christ's Gospel Or the Gospel About Christ?

The one true gospel is "the gospel of Christ." What does Paul mean when he designates it so? In what sense is it to be called a gospel "of Christ"?

That question is closely connected with another question, the question what *we* mean today when we speak of the gospel of Christ. Upon this latter question there depends the whole vast question as to the truth or falsehood of the Christian religion.

The English phrase, "the gospel of Christ," with the corresponding phrase in Greek, may mean at least two things. In the first place it may mean "the gospel which Christ preached," and in the second place it may mean "the gospel which sets Christ forth," "the gospel about Christ." In the English language, each of these two uses of the word "of" is perfectly well established, and so is each of these two uses of the genitive case in Greek.

Thus when we speak in English of "the gospel of Paul," we are using the word "of" plainly in the former of the two senses; we mean not at all a gospel about Paul or a gospel which proclaims Paul, but a gospel which Paul proclaimed. On the other hand, when we speak, for example, of "the gospel of the cross," we are using the word "of" just as plainly in the latter sense; we mean not a gospel which the cross proclaims, but a gospel which proclaims the cross.

But how is it when we speak of "the gospel of Christ"? Do we mean "the gospel which Christ proclaimed" or "the gospel which proclaims Christ"; do we mean "Christ's gospel" or "the gospel about Christ"?

According to the Modernist tendency now so largely dominant in the Church, we mean, or at least ought to mean, the former and not the latter. We ought, it is said, to think of the gospel as being the gospel which Christ preached, not the gospel which sets Christ forth; a message of which Christ was the great exponent, not a doctrine of His person or of His work. We ought, in other words, it is said, to return from this gospel *about* Christ and have recourse to Christ's own gospel; we ought to abandon the theological subtleties of atonement, redemption and the like, and have recourse to the simple message that was proclaimed by Jesus of Nazareth on the shores of the sea of Galilee nineteen hundred years ago.

That formulation of the great issue in the Church is by no means altogether new. It has been known for a hundred years or so, if not even far longer than that. It raises rather clearly the very greatest of all questions, and it ought to be dealt with in the most careful possible way.

Ought we to yield to the demand of modern "Liberal" preachers that we should abandon the gospel about Christ and have recourse, in distinction from that, to the gospel which Christ preached?

Which Gospel Exalts Christ More?

Before we answer that question, we ought at any rate to clear up one strange misconception—the strange misconception, namely, that represents "Christ's gospel," in this modern sense, as bringing us nearer to Christ or as giving Christ a greater place in our lives than "the gospel about Christ" which is being abandoned. As a matter of fact, "Christ's gospel," so understood, puts Christ in a very small place in our lives and makes him very remote from us. If the gospel to which we hold is merely the gospel which Christ preached nineteen hundred years ago, then our relation to

Christ is not different in kind from our relation to many other great teachers. We can speak in that sense of "a gospel of Paul" or "a gospel of Spurgeon" or "a gospel of D. L. Moody." But it would be blasphemous to hold to a gospel *about* Paul or a gospel *about* Spurgeon or a gospel *about* D. L. Moody. That would put mere human teachers in a position that belongs only to Christ. Others may proclaim a gospel, but Christ alone is the substance or content of the gospel.

How remote, too, Christ is made from us by this modern rejection of the gospel about Christ in the supposed interests of a gospel which Christ preached! It is amazing that men can be so blind as not to see that the blessed "doctrine" of the eighth chapter of Romans, far from putting a barrier between us and Jesus, really is the only thing that can unite us to Jesus. He died nineteen hundred years ago. How may we hold fellowship with him today? It is this much despised "theology" which alone can tell us how—this theology that sets forth the meaning of His death and the fact of His glorious resurrection.

The Gospel That Christ Preached

In holding to this gospel about Christ, are we rejecting the gospel which He preached when He was on earth? Far from it. For the gospel which He preached was also a gospel about Him; He put His own person and work into the center of the gospel that He proclaimed.

He could not, indeed, proclaim that gospel fully when he was on earth. He had come into this world to redeem men by His death and resurrection, and the recounting of that great event was to constitute the gospel by which He was to be presented as the Saviour of men. The meaning of the great event could not be set forth in all its fulness until the event had taken place. Much, therefore, was left to the teaching of the Holy Spirit through the Apostles. A gospel that neglects the Epistles of Paul and holds only to the teaching of our Lord on earth is not really loyal to Christ; nay, it is profoundly disloyal to Him, and it impoverishes woefully and sinfully our knowledge of His teaching and His person and His work.

Nevertheless, our Lord did proclaim the gospel about Himself even when He was on earth. He did put His own person into His gospel.

That fact has often been denied in modern times. The denial of it lies at the root of the reconstruction called "the Liberal Jesus" in its typical forms. The real Jesus, according to that reconstruction, did not present a doctrine of His own person; neither did He have the slightest notion of a redeeming significance of His approaching death; but He proclaimed with wonderful simplicity the fatherhood of God and the brotherhood of man, and we are His true disciples when we cease disputing about His place in the scale of being and hearken to His simple message.

The Jesus of the Gospels

To reconstruct Jesus in this way, it is of course necessary to reject much that the Gospels contain. The gospel of John has to be eliminated at the start, since throughout that Gospel Jesus is represented as making His own person and the nature of His redeeming work the express subject of His teaching. If the Gospel of John is true, then Jesus most emphatically did put His own person into His gospel, and the "Liberal" reconstruction is wrong.

But even after the Fourth Gospel has been eliminated, much still remains to be done. In the Synoptic Gospels also, Jesus is represented as putting His own person into His gospel; and hence by a mere appeal from John to the Synoptic Gospels the simple teacher of the fatherhood of God and the brotherhood of man is not yet found. He can be found, therefore, if at all, not by taking as they stand the utterances attributed to Jesus even in the Synoptic Gospels, but by regarding some of those utterances as authentic and by rejecting the rest.

The Jesus of the Supposed "Sources"

How can the choice be made? Conceivably it might be made by the discovery of earlier sources underlying our Synoptic Gospels. Possibly, it might be said, the unauthentic elements in the teaching attributed to Jesus have been introduced by the authors of our Gospels, whereas if we could only reconstruct the sources that they used we should find that Jesus was really such a one as we modern men desire.

As a matter of fact, however, this method of reconstruction has been found to fail. The two chief sources supposed, rightly or wrongly, to underlie our Gospels of Matthew and Luke are (1) Mark and (2) a source commonly called Q, which is supposed to contain chiefly sayings, as distinguished from deeds, of Jesus. And in both of these supposed sources the undesired element appears in the teaching which Jesus is represented as carrying on; in both of these sources Jesus is represented as holding a lofty view of His own person. The well-known utterance of Jesus in Matt. 11:27, beginning, "All things have been delivered unto me of My Father," appears in practically the same form in Luke 10:22, and so must be thought to have stood in the supposed source, Q. Yet this utterance presents the same lofty view of our Lord's person as that which is presented in the Gospel according to John.

Even more impressive than such individual utterances is the entire tenor of the two supposed sources. Neither Mark nor the supposed Q really presents a Jesus who was a mere preacher of the fatherhood of God and the brotherhood of man; both of them present a Jesus who offered Himself not merely as teacher but as Saviour. As James Denney (in a book sadly mistaken and unduly concessive in some ways)[1] correctly insisted, Jesus is represented, even in the earliest sources which have been reconstructed, rightly or wrongly, by modern criticism, as offering Himself not merely as an example for faith but as the object of faith. He did, in other words, even according to the earliest sources or supposed sources, put His own person into His gospel; His gospel, even according to the earliest sources, was a gospel *about* Him.

Thus if we are to discover a gospel *of* Jesus which was not also a gospel *about* Jesus, we must certainly go back of the earliest written sources of information which, rightly or wrongly, have been discovered by modern criticism; we must suppose that, in a period of oral tradition prior to those

---

[1] Denney, *Jesus and the Gospel*, 1909.

earliest written sources, the information about Jesus became contaminated and thus the Jesus who really lived in Palestine, a pure and simple teacher of the fatherhood of God and the brotherhood of man, came falsely to be presented as one who attributed to Himself superhuman functions as the Redeemer of mankind.

"The Liberal Jesus"

But how are we to separate what is true from what is false in an oral tradition now preserved for us only in written sources already vitiated by a false view of Jesus' person? Surely the process of separation must be very difficult. And when it has been completed, what sort of Jesus remains? Is the Jesus who remains even then exactly the sort of Jesus that the "Liberal" historians desire?

At one point even the Liberal historians (or most of them) admitted that He is not. Even their reconstructed Jesus, they had to admit, thought that He was the Messiah; and His Messianic consciousness introduced a totally discordant element into their picture of Him. Their simple preacher of the fatherhood of God did after all claim a stupendous dignity for Himself. What becomes then of their fundamental thesis? Even their reconstructed Jesus was not exactly the kind of person whom they desired to find.

They did, indeed, try to minimize the importance of Jesus' claims; they represented the claim of Messiahship by Jesus as a mere means to an end, a mere means that He adopted almost against His will. But such palliative treatment evidently did not go to the root of the matter. It remained true that the claim of Messiahship was totally out of character if Jesus was the kind of teacher that the Liberal historians represented Him as being. Yet that claim was rooted too deep in the sources for it to be removed save by a few extremists.

Thus it is not surprising to find in our day evidences that the whole imposing reconstruction of "the Liberal Jesus" is destined soon to fall to the ground. If Jesus was not the divine Redeemer whom the Gospels represent Him as being —and of course according to the current naturalism He could not have been that—then it is increasingly being admitted that we can never determine just exactly what He was.

Sixty or seventy years ago, when "the Liberal Jesus" was first constructed on the basis of the Gospel of Mark (or a supposed earlier form of Mark) and of the supposed source later called Q, there was vast enthusiasm. Scientific history, it was supposed, had had a beneficent result. At first, indeed, it was admitted, it had given many persons pain; it had removed from the pages of history many things about Jesus that the Church had held dear. But in removing things that were false or uncertain, it had, men were told, established with all the greater firmness the things that remained. For the first time, it was thought, "the life of Christ" was put upon a firm scientific basis; the assured results of modern criticism of the gospels could at last, it was supposed, be summed up, and on the basis of these assured results the real Jesus could be presented to the Church.

That real Jesus lacked, indeed, many things that had hitherto been found in the Jesus of Christian faith. Gone were His stupendous "metaphysical" attributes—His preëxistence, His omnipotence, His omniscience, His Trinitarian oneness with God. Gone were His miracles, His redeeming death, His resurrection from the tomb, His final judgment of the world. But to balance these losses, it was thought, how much had been gained! The true humanity of Jesus at last had been rediscovered. Jesus at last had been brought near to us: He was no longer a pale metaphysical abstraction, but had become a living person of flesh and blood; He had become a true example and teacher and guide, a true leader into a larger and more glorious life. Let the Church forget its dry theology, it was urged; let it take Jesus as its leader and go forth to more glorious conquests than it had ever seen before!

Such, in essentials, was the program of the Liberal historians. That program had a great vogue in the modern Church. The reconstruction of the Liberal Jesus appeared in all essentials in H. J. Holtzmann's book on the Synoptic Gospels in 1863; it was repeated in many learned and many popular treatises; it was raised to the highest pitch of popular enthusiasm by Harnack's *What Is Christianity?* in 1900.

The Fall of "The Liberal Jesus"

But today the vogue of "the Liberal Jesus" has entered upon a sad decline. Scholars who, like the older Liberal historians, reject the supernatural in the Gospels are no longer at all clear about the "assured results" of modern criticism on the positive side. All our sources of information, it is seen with increasing clearness, are imbued with a supernaturalistic view of Jesus' person; all of them represent Him as offering Himself to men not as a mere prophet or teacher, but as a Saviour. How, then, can the historian ever hope to discover the real Jesus beneath these gaudy colors of the supernatural that have so hopelessly defaced His portrait? In the attempt to answer that question, modern scholars are falling more and more into despair. Gone is the almost lyrical enthusiasm with which Holtzmann in 1863 set forth the purely human Jesus whom he supposed to have been rediscovered by modern historical research. More and more the sobering conviction is gaining ground that the naturalistic criticism of the Gospels, rejecting the miracles, has been able only to destroy and not to build. It has shown, in the opinion of the naturalistic historians, that the Jesus of the Gospels was not the real Jesus—but what sort of person the real Jesus was—that question, it is increasingly admitted, must forever remain unanswered. We can show what sort of person the primitive Church held Him to be, but what sort of person He really was —this remains hidden from our eyes.

The Real Jesus

Against such skepticism must be placed at least one solid fact. It is the stupendous picture of Jesus which the Gospels contain. That picture presents unmistakable marks of truth. It is totally unlike all that we know of the fancies of the early Christian Church; it is irreducibly original; it is amazingly vivid and concrete.

Yet about one thing modern skepticism is unquestionably correct. The Gospel picture of Jesus is suffused with the supernatural throughout. It is not the picture of a mere prophet and teacher simply overlaid with a few supernatural elements. Rather does the supernatural, both in the presentation of fact and in the presentation of Jesus' claims, enter into the very warp and woof. If the supernatural be rejected, then there is really nothing that certainly remains. No wonder that an increasing skepticism has taken the place of enthusiasm for "the Liberal Jesus"! Increasingly it has become evident that unless Jesus was essentially what He is represented in the Gospels as being, His true person and character can never be rediscovered by any historical research.

Such skepticism will always be condemned by a sound common sense. The picture of Jesus in the Gospels is too self-evidently true ever to be removed thus radically from the pages of history. If, then, we cannot reject the supernatural element and retain the rest, what remains for us to do? One thing and one thing only remains—that we should accept the whole, that we should accept the miracles and accept Jesus' stupendous claims.

When we take that step, everything in early Christian history falls into its proper place. The beginnings of the Christian Church, which before seemed to be a mass of contradictions, a jumble of kaleidoscopic changes, become the inevitable result of one stupendous fact; and the historian wonders at the blindness with which he formerly groped for the solution of a problem to which the key lay so ready to hand. There is really no other solution. A great building was never founded upon a pin point. At the foundation of the Christian Church there stands the supernatural Christ.

The One True Gospel

If that be so, the whole distinction between the gospel of Christ and the gospel about Christ falls to the ground. The gospel of Christ, the gospel which He proclaimed, is seen also to be a gospel about Him. He came into this world to make that gospel possible by His redeeming death and glorious resurrection. While He was on earth He proclaimed that gospel afore, and He left the fuller presentation of it to the apostles whom he chose. But always He is both the author and the substance of His gospel; the gospel that He proclaimed was also the gospel in which He was proclaimed.

Hence it makes comparatively little difference whether in any particular case Paul means by "the gospel of Christ" the gospel that Christ proclaimed or the gospel that proclaims Him. Usually when he speaks of the gospel he is thinking certainly of the latter rather than of the former; he is thinking of the gospel as that which sets forth Christ's redeeming work rather than as that which Christ proclaimed when He was on earth.

What does he mean in our verse in Gal. 1:7, when he speaks of the "gospel of Christ"? Does he mean the gospel which Christ proclaimed or the gospel which proclaims Christ? If he means the former, he is no doubt thinking not so much of Christ's proclamation of the gospel when He was on earth, as of His proclamation of it to him, Paul, after He had risen from the dead, when He appeared to him on the road to Damascus. Possibly he might mean that. More probably, perhaps, he might mean the gospel about Christ, the gospel which sets Christ forth.

But in this particular place we are inclined to think that he means neither. Rather is he designating the gospel here simply as the gospel that *belongs to* Christ. It is Christ's property; yet these Judaizers are seeking to lay violent hands upon it. They are seeking to deal as they will with what is not really theirs but Christ's.

Would God that every modern preacher might avoid the Judaizers' sin! The gospel is not ours to change as we will; in proclaiming it we are but stewards. God grant that we may be faithful stewards; God grant that we may truly proclaim the gospel which is not ours but the gospel of the Lord Jesus Christ!

VI. THE MESSAGE AND THE MESSENGER

"But even if we or an angel from heaven should preach to you contrary to the gospel which we preached to you, let him be accursed. As we have said before, now also again I say: 'If anyone is preaching to you contrary to what ye received, let him be accursed.' Now am I persuading men—or God? Or am I seeking to please men? If I were still pleasing men, I should be no servant of Christ. For I make known to

you, brethren, as to the gospel which was preached by me, that it is not according to man" (Gal. 1:8-11, in a literal translation).

An Inviolable Gospel

In the verse which we dealt with last month, Paul has stated with the utmost clearness the occasion for the writing of the Epistle: the Galatians are turning away from the Gospel of Christ to another teaching. That other teaching purports to be a gospel, but in reality it is no gospel at all. It is a perversion of the one true gospel. The Judaizing teachers who are leading the Galatians astray are laying violent hands upon a gospel which does not belong to them but belongs only to Christ.

But in denying to the Judaizers the right to change the gospel, the Apostle is not denying to them anything that he is attempting to reserve for himself. "Even we who preached the gospel to you," he says, "have no right to change it; it is not our property any more than it is any other man's property; we were the instruments of preaching it to you, but it belongs exclusively to Christ." Indeed, Paul continues, even the angels in heaven have no power over this gospel; it is fixed and sure once for all. "But even if we," says the Apostle, "or an angel from heaven should preach to you contrary to what we preached to you, let him be accursed."

The Meaning of "Anathema"

The word *anathema,* here translated "accursed," is an interesting word. The derivation of it is very simple: *ana* means "up"; *the* is a root meaning "to place" or "to put"; *-ma* is a noun ending with a passive significance. Hence an *anathema* is "a thing that is placed up." The word came to refer especially to what is "placed up" in a temple as a votive offering to a god. So the word is used in Lk. 20:5: "And when certain men said concerning the Temple, that it was adorned with beautiful stones and *offerings.* . . ." The spelling is a little different in this passage, a long *e* standing for a short *e* in the *the* of *anathema;* but essentially it is the same word.

How then can a word that means "votive offering" possibly come to have the bad sense, "accursed"? The answer to that question seems fairly clear. The fundamental idea, when a thing is called an *anathema,* is that the thing has been taken from ordinary use and has been handed over to God. If it is a good thing, it has been handed over to Him for His use; if it is a bad thing, it has been handed over to Him for destruction: but in either case men have no more to say about it; it is taken out of ordinary relationships and is "devoted" to God.

So here Paul says—if the original sense of the word is to be regarded as still in view—that the punishment of the man who attempts to lay violent hands upon the gospel of Christ should be in God's hands: that man should be regarded as beyond men's power to help; he should be regarded as having fallen into that state about which the Epistle to the Hebrews says: "It is a fearful thing to fall into the hands of the living God."

The Intolerance of Paul

Upon what sort of error does the Apostle pronounce this tremendous condemnation? It was not an error which the modern Church, according to its present tendency, would be inclined to take very seriously. The Judaizers agreed with Paul about many things: they believed that Jesus was the Messiah; they seem to have had no quarrel with Paul's lofty view of Jesus' person; they believed in His resurrection from the dead. Moreover, they believed that a man must have faith in Christ if he is to be saved. They differed from the Apostle only in thinking that a man must also contribute something of his own if he is to be saved—namely the keeping of the law of God.

Paul also held that the Christian man must do what the law commands. The Apostle did differ from the Judaizers, it is true, with regard to the meaning of the law; he did hold that certain ceremonial requirements of the Old Testament, though entirely divine and authoritative, were intended by God only for the old dispensation and not for the new dispensation that had been ushered in by the redeeming work of

Christ. But that difference is not really the main point in the Epistle to the Galatians. The central point at issue between Paul and the Judaizers concerned merely the logical—not even the temporal—order of three steps. Paul said: (1) "Believe on the Lord Jesus Christ; (2) at that moment you are saved; and (3) immediately you proceed to keep the law of God." The Judaizers said: (1) "Believe on the Lord Jesus Christ, and (2) keep the law of God the best you can; and then (3) you are saved."

To the men that dominate the life of the modern Church it would seem to be a subtle, hair-splitting distinction at the most. Surely, they would say, Paul ought to have made common cause with those Judaizers who had such a zeal for righteousness and furthermore exalted the Lord Jesus Christ so high!

As a matter of fact the Apostle did nothing of the kind. What he actually said with respect to the Judaizers was: "Let them be anathema." He seemed to have none of the modern virtue of tolerance at this point.

Tolerance Right and Wrong

Yet on occasion the Apostle could display tolerance of the broadest possible kind. He displayed it, for example, when he was in prison in Rome, at the time when he wrote the Epistle to the Philippians. At that time, certain men had tried, apparently, to use the Apostle's imprisonment in order to seize the place of preëminence in the Church, which otherwise would have been his. They preached Christ, says Paul, "of contention, not sincerely, supposing to add affliction to my bonds." It seems to have been about as mean a piece of business as could possibly be imagined. But Paul was very tolerant about it. "What then?" he said, "Notwithstanding, every way, whether in pretence or in truth, Christ is preached; and I therein do rejoice, yea, and will rejoice."

What was the reason, on the one hand, for the broad tolerance in Rome and, on the other hand, for the vigorous anathemas in Galatia? Why was Paul tolerant in the one case and not in the other? The answer is perfectly plain. He was tolerant in Rome because the message that was being proclaimed by the rival preachers was true; their motives were wrong, but their message was right. And it was with the truth of the message that Paul was chiefly concerned. In Galatia, on the other hand, it was the message that was wrong. No doubt the motives of the Judaizers were by no means all that they should be; these men preached circumcision in order to avoid persecution for the cross of Christ and in order to obtain credit from their non-Christian Jewish countrymen (Gal. 6:12f.). But it was not such faults in their motives that afforded the primary ground for Paul's attack upon them. His opposition to them would have been exactly the same, as he says in our passage, if they had all been angels from heaven!

Tolerance and Intolerance in the Modern Church

The prime question for Paul in dealing with any message was not the personality of the messengers but the question whether the message was true. In the modern Church, on the other hand, it is exactly the other way around. Paul was intolerant about the content of the message but tolerant about the personality of the messengers; the modern Church is tolerant about the message but intolerant about the personality of the messengers and about the methods by which the message is proclaimed.

Thus Paul was just as tolerant as the modern Church; only his tolerance appeared at an entirely different place. It is a mistake to say that the modern Church is really practising tolerance. On the contrary, there is nothing more intolerant than the ecclesiastical machinery that governs, for example, our Presbyterian Church in the U. S. A. It seems at first sight to be tolerant in the doctrinal sphere, though even there its tolerance is apparent rather than real, being extended much more to Modernist opponents of the truth than to those who would proclaim in its fulness and in its solemn exclusiveness the gospel of the Lord Jesus Christ. But even if the ecclesiastical machinery were really tolerant in the doctrinal sphere, its intolerance in the sphere of administration would still be apparent.

A Recent Example

The difference between the two kinds of tolerance can be made clear if we take as an example the contrast between the methods of the two parties in the recent debate regarding the reorganization of Princeton Theological Seminary.

In that conflict, the gentlemen representing the ecclesiastical machinery, who finally succeeded in bringing about the reorganization of the seminary, certainly displayed intolerance enough, even though the president of the Seminary who agreed with them, advocated an "inclusive" seminary.[1] They carried on the conflict, moreover, by the introduction of all sorts of personalities. Such personalities appeared at the beginning, and they also appeared not only throughout the conflict but also at the very end. An official bulletin issued by Princeton Theological Seminary in November, 1929, soon after the reorganization, actually speaks (without any specific citations whatever) of "insinuations," "slanders," "false statements," "defamers," a "disingenuous" attitude on the part of the opponents.[2] It seems almost unbelievable that an official organ of an educational institution should use such language as that; yet such language certainly was used.

We, on the other hand, opposing the reorganization, and opposing the present government of Princeton Seminary, have avoided such personalities. We are strongly opposed to the policy of these gentlemen who brought about the destruction of the old Princeton; but we are not interested in carrying on a guerilla warfare against their character or in analyzing their motives. Their character and their motives are for God to judge; all that we feel obliged to say is that their policy is hostile to the spread of the gospel of the Lord Jesus Christ. Our objection to them, like Paul's attitude to his opponents in Galatia, would be exactly the same if they were angels from heaven. Not the character of the messen-

---

[1] See *Proceedings of the General Assembly's Special Committee on Princeton Theological Seminary* (on file in the office of the Stated Clerk of the General Assembly), p. 170.

[2] See *Princeton Seminary Bulletin*, xxiii, No. 3, November, 1929, pp. 5-8.

gers, but the truth and clearness of the message is our concern in this entire conflict. And in that attitude we have tried very humbly to follow the teaching and example of the Apostle Paul.

The Cost of Loyalty

There could scarcely be a better guide in controversy than the verse with which we have just dealt: "Even if we or an angel from heaven should preach to you contrary to the gospel which we have preached to you, let him be anathema." That text excludes unworthy personalities in debate; but it also demands the most unswerving loyalty to the gospel of Christ, no matter what personalities may be opposed, and no matter what sacrifices loyalty may involve.

The sacrifices involved in loyalty will, in our Presbyterian Church in the U.S.A., in all probability not be small. In the Permanent Judicial Commission just appointed by the General Assembly, four out of eight ministerial members are signers of the "Auburn Affirmation," which declares that a man may be a minister in the Presbyterian Church without believing in one single one of the following verities of the Faith: the full truthfulness of Scripture, the virgin birth, the substitutionary atonement, the bodily resurrection, the miracles of our Lord. A leader of the Affirmation movement, Dr. Robert Hastings Nichols of Auburn, is among the four. It seems altogether probable, therefore, that the highest judicial body in the Church, which is charged with the all-important duty of interpreting the creed, is dominated by this point of view so derogatory to the very vitals of the Christian religion.

A consistent Christian man will hold that in any doctrinal issue it will be a disgrace to be acquitted by such a court and an honor to be condemned. But the honor of being condemned will of course involve worldly sacrifices and the revilings of the visible Church, at the same time that it involves the favor of God. Unless all signs of the times fail, Christian men in the Presbyterian Church in the U. S. A. will soon be called upon to decide very definitely which they love more—the Lord Jesus Christ or the favor of men.

The Law or Grace

Certainly the point of difference between Paul and the Judaizers—to return to our passage in Galatians—was no trifling difference, no matter how trifling it may seem to the modern Church. It was the difference between a religion of merit and a religion of grace. The Judaizers' teaching required a man to earn at least part of his salvation by his own keeping of God's law. Paul saw clearly that to follow such teaching was to do despite to the cross of Christ. If we have to fill up even the slightest gap by our own works, then we are still lost in sin; for the awakened conscience sees clearly that our own works are insufficient to bridge even the smallest gap. We must trust Christ for nothing or for all; to trust Him only for part is the essence of unbelief. There are two ways of being saved, according to the Apostle Paul. One way is to keep the law of God perfectly. That way is closed because of sin. The other way is to accept the gift of salvation which Christ offers us freely by His cross. The two ways cannot both be followed—that is the burden of the Epistle to the Galatians. A man must choose as the way of salvation either the law or grace. In bidding men choose the latter way the Apostle was contending for the very heart of the Christian religion.

So important did the utterance which we have just discussed seem to the Apostle Paul that he repeats it, in slightly different form, in the next verse. "As we have said before," he says, "now also again I say: 'If anyone is preaching to you contrary to what ye received, let him be accursed.'" The reference here is no doubt to a warning which had been given on the last visit by the Apostle to the Galatian churches. "I gave you the warning at that earlier time," he says, "and I am giving you exactly the same warning now."

Was Paul Inconsistent?

Then he continues, with reference to the uncompromising language which he has just used: "Now am I persuading men—or God? Or am I seeking to please men? If I were still pleasing men, I should be no [true] servant of Christ." Apparently the Apostle had been accused of vacillation and timeserving. When he was among the Gentiles where circumcision was unpopular, it was said, he could preach freedom from the Mosaic law; but when he was among the Jews, where circumcision was popular, he could preach circumcision. Such a charge seems to be implied in Gal. 5:11, where Paul says: "And I, brethren, if I still preach circumcision, why am I still persecuted?"

At first sight, this charge might seem too preposterous ever to have been made even by the bitterest opponents. But closer examination reveals things in Paul's life which might conceivably have given color, though certainly not real justification, to the charge. One may think, for example, of the circumcision of Timothy, the half-Jew (Acts 16:3); or one may remember that Paul himself in his Epistles says that he "became all things to all men" (I Cor. 9:22), and particularly that he became to the Jews as a Jew, to those who were under the law as being himself under the law (I Cor. 9:20). Where no principle, but merely his own convenience, was involved, Paul could be the most concessive of men. Such concessiveness may well have been misunderstood, or wilfully misinterpreted, by the Judaizing opponents. So the Apostle has to defend himself against a charge from which he might at first sight have been thought to be immune.

"You say that I am a time-server," says the Apostle; "you say that I change my attitude toward circumcision to suit the likes or dislikes of my hearers. Well, the language that I am using now hardly seems to justify such a charge. If any man preaches a different gospel, let him be accursed. I said that some time ago on my last visit. I am saying exactly the same thing now. Does *that* look like persuading or cajoling men? Does that look like vacillation? Surely not. Surely that language is uncompromising enough."

"No," says the Apostle, "if I am 'persuading' anyone, it is God. It is his favor, not men's, that I am seeking to win. Indeed, if I were still seeking men's favor I should be no true servant of Christ; for the commission that Christ has given me excludes all man-pleasing. The gospel that Christ has entrusted to me is not according to man, and now that I have been entrusted with that gospel I must put all thought of men's favor aside. I must preach that gospel without fear or favor: it is not my gospel, but Christ's; and I have no power to change it to suit the fancies of men."

Various Interpretations

Such, we venture to think, is the most natural interpretation of a passage that has been much discussed. The commentators dispute, for example, over the meaning of the word "now" at the beginning of verse 10. Does it mean "now since I have become a Christian," or "now since the error has become so serious as to call forth an uncompromising stand"; or does it mean, as we have taken it, "now when I am using such uncompromising language as that which appears in the two preceding verses"?

So also there is dispute over the meaning of the Greek conjunction, usually translated "for," which appears at the beginning of that same verse 10. Does Paul mean (1): "I pronounce this severe judgment upon the Judaizers; for I am no man-pleaser"? Or does he mean (2): "This severe judgment of mine upon the Judaizers is correct; for I am speaking the truth as in the sight of God and am not swayed by my likes or dislikes"? Or, is the "for" best left untranslated in English, as we have left it untranslated, the meaning of it being, if it had to be analyzed, very similar to that which appears in (1).

Then what is the meaning of the word "still" in the clause, "If I were still pleasing men"? Does the word mean, "still after I have become a Christian," or "still after the error has attained such proportions as to call forth an uncompromising stand"; or does it mean, as we have taken it, "still after I have been entrusted with a gospel which by its very nature excludes man-pleasing in the messenger who proclaims it"? It must be said that this last interpretation seems to depend upon the correctness of those manuscripts that read "for" at the beginning of verse 11, as over against other manuscripts that read "but" or "and." We are inclined to hold rather strongly to our interpretation and to the reading that supports it.

Fortunately these questions about the meaning of the passage in detail do not seriously affect the general sense. Paul has been entrusted with a gospel that is not his own and that demands unswerving loyalty in the man who proclaims it. That gospel in its very nature is not "according to man"; it does not conform to any standard which man might set up.

VII. HOW PAUL RECEIVED THE GOSPEL

"For I make known to you, brethren, the gospel that was preached by me, that it is not according to man. For no more did I receive it from man, nor was I taught it, but I received it through revelation of Jesus Christ. For ye have heard of my manner of life formerly in Judaism, how that excessively I persecuted the Church of God and laid it waste and advanced in Judaism beyond many contemporaries in my race, being more exceedingly zealous for the traditions of my fathers. But when He who set me apart from my mother's womb and called me through His grace was pleased to reveal His Son in me that I might preach Him among the Gentiles, immediately I conferred not with flesh and blood, nor did I go up into Jerusalem to those who were apostles before me, but I went away into Arabia and again I returned into Damascus" (Gal. 1:11-17, in a literal translation).

Paul and Paul's Gospel

In the last number of *Christianity Today* we discussed the first verse of this passage in connection with what precedes. "You are turning away from the gospel," Paul says (if we may summarize and paraphrase his words), "to another teaching. That other teaching purports to be a gospel, but it is really only a perversion of the one true gospel. These Judaizers have laid violent hands on a gospel that belongs only to Christ. Even we who preached that gospel to you have no right to do that, and even the angels in heaven may not do it. If anyone is doing it, let him be anathema! I said that when I was with you, and I am saying exactly the same thing now. Surely *that* does not look like the vacillation and inconsistency with which I have been charged; surely it does not look as though I were seeking to please men. Nay, if I were still pleasing men, I should be no true servant of Christ at all; for the gospel with which I have been entrusted by Christ conforms to no human norm, and a man who has been entrusted with such a gospel must put all thought of human favor aside."

In verse 12, Paul passes from the gospel itself to his own connection with the gospel. "I make known to you, brethren, *the gospel* which was preached by me, that it is not according to man (verse 11); for no more did *I* receive it from man" (verse 12). The pronoun "I" in this last clause is emphatic; for if it were not emphatic, it would not be expressed separately in Greek at all, but would be regarded as expressed sufficiently by the ending of the verb form.

Emphasis is nearly always a matter of contrast, either expressed or implied. If I say, *"I* did not do it" (with the emphasis on the "I"), that implies that someone else did do it or may have done it. The contrast is here between *me* and someone else. If, on the other hand, I say, "I did not *do* it" (with the emphasis on the "do"), that implies that whereas I did not *do* it I may have *thought* it or *said* it. The contrast is here between *doing* and some other action of mine.

What, then, in our passage, is the contrast that is implied by the emphasis on the "I"? The commentators have held various views about this question. Does Paul mean: *"I* did not receive the gospel from men, though the Judaizers did so receive it"; or does he mean: *"I* did not receive it from men, though the ordinary Christian who is not an apostle does so receive it"; or does he mean; "I did not receive it from men any more than the original apostles did?" These various views—with the exception of the first—yield a good enough sense. But in point of fact we think that the emphasis on the "I" is to be explained in a very much simpler way. It is due, we think, to the simple contrast between the gospel that Paul preached and Paul himself in his connection with that gospel. "The gospel that I have preached," says Paul, "is not according to man; for, what is more, I, the preacher of that gospel, did not receive it from man. It might have been a divine gospel and yet have been handed over to me by a purely human agent. But as a matter of fact that was not the case. Not only was the gospel that I was to preach divine, but I received it in a divine manner—namely by direct revelation from Jesus Christ."

Revelation of Jesus Christ

Paul says that he received the gospel "by revelation of Jesus Christ." That might mean one of two things. It might mean (1) that he received the gospel by having Jesus Christ revealed to him, or it might mean (2) that he received the gospel by having Jesus Christ reveal the gospel to him. In the former case, the Greek genitive case of the noun "Jesus Christ" (translated into English by the preposition "of") would be an "objective genitive"; "Jesus Christ" would be the *object* of the verb, "reveal," underlying the verbal noun "revelation." In the latter case, the genitive would be a "subjective genitive"; "Jesus Christ" would be the *subject* of the verb underlying the verbal noun.

Both usages are perfectly grammatical in English just as they are in Greek. When we speak of the revelation "of holy mysteries" to us by God in His Word, the preposition "of" indicates that the mysteries are the things that *are revealed*. That corresponds to the Greek objective genitive. But when we say of some piece of knowledge that we possess that it was no product of our own research but came to us by revelation "of God," the preposition "of" indicates that God was the One who *revealed* the thing to us. That corresponds to the Greek subjective genitive.

In our passage, it is perfectly clear from the context that the genitive "of Jesus Christ" is subjective genitive and not objective genitive. Paul means that he received the gospel by a revelation which Jesus Christ gave him, not that he received it by the fact that God revealed Jesus Christ to him. The objective genitive would, indeed, in itself yield a perfectly good sense; it is perfectly true that Paul received the gospel through the fact that God revealed Jesus Christ to him, and indeed he says practically that just below, in verse 16, when he says that God revealed His Son in him. But here the point plainly is concerned not with the content of the revelation but with the source of it. "I received the gospel," Paul says, "not from man but from Jesus Christ." Plainly the same contrast between Jesus Christ and ordinary humanity is intended as that which appears in the first verse of the Epistle—"not through a man but through Jesus Christ." Lightfoot admirably paraphrases as follows: "I received it not by *instruction* from man but by *revelation* from Christ."

Paul's Apostolic Independence

In this verse Paul is enunciating the thesis which he proceeds to prove in the first great division of the Epistle, running through to the end of the second chapter. His proof of the thesis may be divided into three parts. "In the first place," he says, "before my conversion I certainly did not receive my gospel from the original apostles, because I was then an active persecutor of the Church; and even after I was converted (suddenly and without human intermediation, by a sovereign act of God) I had in the early period no extensive contact with the apostles and so could not have become their disciple (Gal. 1:13-24). In the second place, when I did finally hold a conference with the pillars of the Jerusalem Church, they themselves recognized that the gospel had already been given to me by God and that they had nothing to add (Gal. 2:1-10). In the third place, so independent was I of the original apostles that on one occasion I could even withstand the chief of them to his face, though my objection was altogether to his practice and not at all to his gospel, which was the same gospel of divine grace as that which I myself preached" (Gal. 2:11-21).

"Ye have heard of my manner of life formerly in Judaism," says Paul, as he begins his defence of his apostolic independence, "how that excessively I persecuted the Church of God and laid it waste, and advanced in Judaism beyond many contemporaries in my race, being more exceedingly zealous (than those contemporaries were) for the traditions of my fathers."

The Church of God

It is interesting to observe that Paul here calls the whole body of the disciples "the Church of God." The Greek word *ecclesia*, which is translated "church" in our English Bible, is derived from the Greek word for "call" and the preposition *ek* which means "out." An *ecclesia*, therefore, is a company of those who are called out from their homes to a common meeting place.

So the word designates, first of all, any ordinary assembly, or an assembly in civil or political life. It is used in this way, for example, in Acts 19:32, where, with reference to the mob in the theatre at Ephesus, it is said that the "assembly" (*ecclesia*) was confused. So also in verse 39 of the same chapter the town clerk is represented as saying: "And if ye seek anything further, it will be attended to in the lawful assembly (*ecclesia*)." In both of these passages the word appears in its ordinary secular use.

But in the Septuagint, the Greek translation of the Hebrew Old Testament, which was the Bible of the Greek-speaking Jews in the first century and was also the Greek Bible of the New Testament writers, the word *ecclesia* is used to translate a Hebrew word that designates the solemn assembly of God's covenant people. This solemn, religious sense of the word was taken over by the writers of the New Testament books.

In the New Testament, at least three special uses of the word may be distinguished. The word designates (1) the little company of disciples meeting in an individual house, as in I Cor. 16:19, where Paul speaks of Aquila and Priscilla and the "church" (*ecclesia*) which is in their house. It also designates (2) the whole company of Christians living in any city, as in I Cor. 1:2, where "the Church (*ecclesia*) of God which is at Corinth" includes, presumably, not only the "church" in Aquila and Priscilla's house but also other house-churches in Corinth. Finally, it designates (3) the whole body of Christians throughout the world, as in our passage.

We cannot say that this third usage came as any mere later development from the other two uses of the word. At any rate, it appears plainly in the apostolic age, in the universally accepted Epistles of Paul. With our passage is to be compared particularly I Cor. 15:9, where Paul says: "For I am the least of the apostles, that am not meet to be called an apostle, because I persecuted the Church of God." In both places, Paul is speaking of his guilt as a persecutor, and in both places, as though to enhance his guilt, he calls the Church that he persecuted by its full title. What a terrible thing it was to lay violent hands upon a company of disciples which, though despised by the world, was in reality nothing less than "the Church of God"!

Certainly it required faith to designate those little groups of humble people, insignificant in numbers, insignificant in the judgment of men, by any such title as that. But Paul was right in so designating them. The future really belonged to those little groups. God does not judge as man judges; He does not look upon the outward appearance but upon the heart, and in His sight those humble little companies were His Church, forever under His care and keeping, not to be separated from Him by principalities or powers or things present or things to come.

VIII. THE CALL OF GOD

"For ye have heard of my manner of life formerly in Judaism, that excessively I persecuted the Church of God and laid it waste, and advanced in Judaism beyond many contemporaries in my race, being more exceedingly zealous for the traditions of my fathers. But when He who set me apart from my mother's womb and called me through His grace was pleased to reveal His Son in me in order that I might preach Him among the Gentiles, immediately I conferred not with flesh and blood, nor did I go up to Jerusalem to those who were apostles before me, but I went away into Arabia and again I returned to Damascus" (Gal. 1:13-17, in a literal translation).

The Conversion

It has been shown in the last number of *Christianity Today* that Gal. 1:12 enunciates the thesis which is to be proved in the first main division of the Epistle. "I received the gospel," Paul says in effect, "not by instruction from men but by direct revelation from Jesus Christ."

The first proof of this assertion is found in Paul's life before his conversion: certainly he was not then coming under the influence of the original apostles, but was an active persecutor. "Ye have heard," Paul says, "of my manner of life formerly in Judaism, that excessively I persecuted the Church of God and laid it waste, and advanced in Judaism beyond many contemporaries in my race, being more exceedingly zealous (than those contemporaries were) for the traditions of my fathers."

We learn something more about those traditions from Phil. 3:5, where Paul himself, in one of the Epistles that are universally accepted as genuine by modern criticism, says that he was "as touching the law a Pharisee." Since he was a Pharisee, it is natural, when he speaks of the traditions of his fathers, for us to think especially, though perhaps not exclusively, of the Pharisaic additions to the written Law.

"Such," Paul says in effect, "was my life before my conversion. Far from coming nearer to Christ, I was if anything moving farther away. I was an active persecutor of the Church of God; I was as far as possible from becoming a disciple of those from whom the Judaizers say that I received my gospel."

Then came the conversion. It was not according to Paul what it is according to modern naturalistic historians, the result of a psychological process; but it was utterly sudden, and was brought about by a sovereign act of God. "When He who set me apart," says the Apostle, "from the very beginning of my life—from my mother's womb—and called me through His grace was pleased to reveal His Son in me that I might preach Him among the Gentiles. . . ." Three acts of God are here mentioned. In the first place, God set Paul apart from his mother's womb. Although Paul did not know it, God had really, from the very beginning of his life, designated him for the special work of preaching the gospel to the Gentiles. In the second place, God carried out that plan, which He had had for him from the beginning, by calling him through His grace. There is no doubt whatever but that this divine call is to be regarded as having taken place definitely and specifically at the conversion. The word "call" in such connections does not refer to the plan of God from all eternity; and it does not refer to the general divine ordering of a man's life in the execution of that plan: but it refers to the majestic divine act by which at a definite moment of time the divine purpose becomes effective in those who are saved. Such a "call" is more than a mere invitation; it is, rather, a call which brings its answer with it; it is what the Shorter Catechism calls "effectual calling." That sovereign call of God came to Saul of Tarsus when he saw the Lord Jesus on the road to Damascus and became instead of a persecutor a servant and an apostle.

The Revelation of God's Son

But if the call refers to the conversion, what is referred to by the revelation of God's Son which is mentioned next, as the third of the things which God did in the case of the Apostle? At first sight, it might seem to be something subsequent to the call and hence something subsequent to the conversion. Paul says: "When He who (1) set me apart and (2) called me (at the conversion) was pleased (3) to reveal His Son in me that I might preach Him among the Gentiles. . . ." At first sight, it might seem as though three successive acts were here mentioned: (1) the setting apart, (2) the call, (3) the revelation of God's Son. Thus the revelation of God's Son in Paul would not be identical with the conversion but would be some later event in the Apostle's life.

There are, however, other indications which tend to show that this view is incorrect and that it is really the event on the Damascus road which is referred to here as it is referred to by the "call" which has just been mentioned. The trouble with regarding the revelation of God's Son as an event distinct from the conversion is that it seems to be treated as the turning-point in Paul's life, the event with reference to which all subsequent events in the experience of the Apostle are to be dated. Paul tells what did *not* happen immediately after this event, then he tells us what happened three years after it, etc. But surely the event which is treated in this way as the turning-point in Paul's life can only be the conversion.

At any rate, it would seem clear that if the revelation of God's Son is not the conversion it must at least be placed very soon after the conversion and in close connection with it. We might think, for example, of possible revelations within the three days of blindness which the Book of Acts mentions as having followed immediately upon the event on the road to Damascus.

But is it really necessary, from the form of the sentence, to regard the revelation of God's Son as being subsequent to the "call"? That does not seem to be by any means perfectly clear. Paul first designates God by means of the two outstanding things which He had done for him in his life taken as a whole up to the time of the writing of the Epistle; he designates God as the One who had set him apart and had called him. Then he tells what the One so designated had done to fit him particularly to be a preacher to the Gentiles. It is perhaps not necessary to reflect upon the question what the temporal relation is between this third act of God and the other two acts. Paul may mean simply to say: "When the One who can be designated as the One who set me apart and called me was pleased (whether before or after or simultaneously with the calling) to reveal His Son in me that I might proclaim Him among the Gentiles. . . ." In that case, the revelation of God's Son in Paul might be regarded as having taken place on the road to Damascus and as being, like the call, identical with the conversion.

Paul's Meeting with Christ on the Damascus Road

It must be admitted, indeed, that another difficulty seems to arise against this identification. If the revelation of God's Son here spoken of was a revelation *in* Paul, it seems at first sight to be designated as an inner, rather than as an external, revelation. But if so, how can it be identified with that meeting of Paul with Christ which is described in the ninth and twenty-second and twenty-sixth chapters of the Book of Acts? In that meeting, not only the Book of Acts (which is under fire in modern criticism) but also Paul himself in one of his universally accepted Epistles says that he actually saw Christ, so that the revelation at that time was an outward and not merely an inward event. In I Cor. 9:1 Paul says, (plainly with reference to the conversion): "Have I not seen Jesus our Lord?"; and in I Cor. 15:8 he says that Christ "appeared" to him, the verb "appeared," which is here used, being the passive voice of the verb "to see," which is used in the other passage, so that "appeared" in Greek is the same as "was seen." Moreover, Paul evidently regarded his meeting with Jesus on the Damascus road as being entirely different from such an experience as that which he describes in II Cor. 12:1-4.

That does not mean that this latter experience did not possess high value; it does not mean that it was a mere illusion. But Paul speaks of it with the utmost reserve and with the utmost reluctance. He was caught up into the third heaven, he says, but whether in the body or out of the body he does not know, and the words that he heard were unspeakable. Indeed, he even hesitates to use the pronoun "I" in speaking about that experience; he ventures only to say, with regard to the recipient of it: "I knew a man in Christ above fourteen years ago. . . ." When he speaks about his meeting with Christ on the Damascus road, on the other hand, there is none of this reserve. Far from having to be forced to speak about that meeting, as about the strange experience described in II Cor. 12:1-4, he made it basic in all his preaching; he presented it publicly to his converts (or, as it is perhaps more accurate to say, to those who by the presentation of it became converts) "among the first things" (I Cor. 15:3). Evidently he regarded it as a plain matter of fact, attested by the senses like any other event. It was not merely an inner experience, according to Paul, but a happening in the external world.

If that be so about Paul's meeting with Christ on the Damascus road, how can it be that event that is referred to in our passage when Paul says that God revealed Christ *in* him? Paul plainly regarded the event on the Damascus road as an external event, whereas in our passage the revelation of God's Son is designated as a revelation *in* him and not as a revelation *to* him.

Revelation to Paul or to Others?

This difficulty, when taken with the difficulty already mentioned, that the revelation of God's Son seems, at first sight at least, to be presented as subsequent to the call and not identical with it, made it not altogether surprising that so able a scholar as Bishop Lightfoot adopted an interpretation totally distinct from those that we have so far considered. Lightfoot held that the revelation here referred to is not at all a revelation either to Paul or within Paul's soul, but a revelation through Paul to others. The wonderful change in Paul's life, since it was wrought by the grace of Christ, was a revelation of Christ to all who might behold it. On this interpretation, the use of the preposition "in" in the phrase "in me" would be similar to that in verse 21 when Paul says, "They glorified God *in me*." "When God was pleased," Paul would be made by this interpretation to say, "to reveal His Son in me by the revelation of His Son's power in my whole life. . . ." An objection to this view is usually found in the fact that the passage seems to put the revelation of God's Son in Paul as something prior to the proclamation of God's Son by Paul to the Gentiles—something which had that proclamation as its purpose—whereas if Lightfoot's interpretation is correct the revelation of God's Son in Paul would seem rather to be identical with that proclamation of God's Son or continuously contemporary with it. This objection is perhaps not quite decisive, and the interpretation against which it is raised is at least not beyond the bounds of possibility.

However, the commoner view, that the revelation of God's Son in Paul does refer to the Damascus event or to something immediately subsequent to that event and closely connected with it, and that it does refer to a revelation that had Paul as its recipient, is also not impossible. Why may not Paul be referring here to an inner aspect of what he designates elsewhere as an external event? If the conversion was wrought by a revelation of God's Son *to* Paul, does that exclude the fact that it was also a revelation of God's Son *in* Paul?

A special reason for the use of the preposition "in" here is perhaps to be found in the parallelism with the immediately following phrase, "among the Gentiles." In that latter phrase we have to use the preposition "among" in English. But in Greek it is exactly the same preposition as the preposition "in" which occurs in the phrase "in me." Quite possibly the parallelism is intentional. "God revealed His Son *in me,*" Paul says, "that I might preach Him *in the Gentiles;* God revealed Him in the little sphere of my life that I might proclaim Him in the large sphere of the Gentile world."

The Value and the Limitations of Exegesis

Thus three interpretations are possible in this difficult passage. By the revelation of God's Son in Paul, Paul may be referring (1) to his meeting with Christ at his conversion, (2) to a revelation closely following upon the conversion, or (3) to the revelation of Christ to the world which was found in the wonderful change which Christ wrought in Paul's life.

Which of these three interpretations is correct? We confess that we do not know, though we lean rather strongly to the first. That confession of our ignorance may be painful, but at least it is honest.

In making the confession, we are particularly desirous of not being misunderstood. We are not falling in the slightest into the current agnosticism about the interpretation of the Bible; we are not acquiescing at all in the current impression that the Bible can with equal propriety be made to support (1) Christianity and (2) a non-doctrinal religion which is almost the diametrical opposite of Christianity. We are by no means acquiescing in the notion that everything in the Bible may be "interpreted" to mean its exact opposite, and that there is no disputing about interpretations any more than there is disputing about tastes. On the contrary, we believe that in the great body of its teaching the Bible is as plain as day, and that no honest man who really attends to it can reasonably be in doubt as to what it means. It is perfectly clear, moreover, that the real issue in the Church of the present day concerns not the question what the Bible means but the question whether, meaning what it plainly does, the Bible is true or false.

But if there are many things in the Bible that are plain, there are some things that are obscure, and it is important not to be too cocksure in our views about those things. Sound and cautious exegesis will demolish many a sermon, but it is salutary in the end; and few things are more needed than sound and cautious exegesis is needed today. Contact with the really great exegetical tradition of the Christian Church will preserve us from many vagaries; it will keep us from many dangerous by-paths; it will save us from the sad waste of time into which some devout people fall.

Let us not be ashamed, therefore, to say sometimes with reference to the interpretation of the Bible: "We do not know." But on the other hand, let us never rest complacently in that ignorance, but let us strive rather by diligent study and by earnest and prayerful meditation to learn more and more of what God has said to us in His Word.

IX. AFTER THE CONVERSION

"But when He who set me apart from my mother's womb and called me through His grace was pleased to reveal His Son in me, that I might preach Him among the Gentiles, immediately I conferred not with flesh and blood, nor did I go up to Jerusalem to those who were apostles before me, but I went away into Arabia and again I returned to Damascus. Then after three years I went up to Jerusalem to make the acquaintance of Cephas, and I remained with him fifteen days; but another of the apostles I did not see—only I saw James the brother of the Lord" (Gal. 1:15-19, in a literal translation).

No Conference with Flesh and Blood

In the last number of *Christianity Today*, we discussed the revelation of God's Son in Paul, which is mentioned at the beginning of this important passage. That revelation, we observed, is to be regarded either (1) as the inner aspect—the effect within Paul's soul—of the outward appearance of

Christ at Paul's conversion or (2) a revelation soon after the conversion or (3) a revelation to others which was involved in the wonderful change which Christ wrought by the conversion in Paul's life. In accordance with the first and third of these interpretations, it is distinctly the conversion which is referred to here; and in accordance with the second interpretation it is an event immediately subsequent to the conversion and closely connected with it. We shall not go wrong, therefore—especially since the second interpretation is probably incorrect—if we say that it is the conversion of Paul on the road to Damascus that is here treated not only as the turning-point of Paul's life but as the event that gave him the gospel that he was to preach.

"Before the conversion," Paul's argument runs, "I certainly did not become a disciple of the original apostles; for I was then an active persecutor. I was then certainly not being brought to Christ gradually by any instructions or persuasions of men. My conversion was utterly sudden, and it was produced by an act of God; I received my gospel directly from Jesus Christ."

Up to this point, we have already discussed Paul's argument in the last number. "But then," Paul goes on, "even after my conversion, even after I had received the gospel from Christ, I did not become a disciple of the men upon whom the Judaizers say I am dependent. In the early period, I did not even have any contact with them at all. After my conversion I did not go up to Jerusalem to those who were apostles before me; but the journey that I made was to Arabia, and it was three years before I went up to Jerusalem."

Harmony with Acts

The word "immediately," in the sixteenth verse, requires perhaps a word of comment. "When God was pleased to reveal His Son to me," Paul says, "immediately I conferred not with flesh or blood, nor (to be specific, to take up the special form of dependence upon flesh and blood which the Judaizers allege against me) did I go up to Jerusalem to those who were apostles before me, but I went away into Arabia." Does the word "immediately" go with the negative part of the sentence only, or also with the positive part? Does Paul mean to say, "What I did not do immediately after my conversion was to go up to Jerusalem"; or does he mean to say, "What I did immediately after my conversion, instead of going up to Jerusalem, was to go away into Arabia"?

If the latter view is correct, then a difficulty might at first sight seem to arise when we compare this narrative with the one in the Book of Acts. In Acts, it is said that after Paul's conversion and the ensuing three days of blindness Paul "was with the disciples in Damascus some days, and immediately he preached Jesus in the synagogues, that this is the Son of God." If Paul "immediately" preached Jesus in the synagogues, how could he at the same time have "immediately" gone away to Arabia?

The difficulty is not, however, by any means insuperable. Of course, it disappears altogether if Paul's "immediately," in Gal. 1:16, goes only with the negative part of the sentence that follows; for in that case Paul would be saying that he did not immediately go up to Jerusalem, but he would not be saying how soon the journey to Arabia occurred. But even if the "immediately" goes—grammatically at least—with the positive as well as with the negative part of the sentence, still the passage can be understood perfectly well in harmony with the Book of Acts.

"After my conversion," Paul says in effect, "what was it that immediately followed? Certainly it was not any visit to Jerusalem. There was indeed a journey away from Damascus in those early days, but it was a journey *away from* Jerusalem—to Arabia—not *to* Jerusalem." The real point of the sentence is to deny that there was a journey to Jerusalem during those early days; it is not to establish the exact moment of the journey to Arabia. As has been well said by someone—in a place that we are unable to lay our hands on for the moment—when Paul uses the word "immediately" in connection with the journey to Arabia, he is thinking not in terms of days or of hours but of journeys. His journey at that time was not to Jerusalem but to Arabia.

Thus even if the word "immediately" goes with the positive as well as with the negative part of the sentence, still a brief period of preaching in Damascus after the conversion and before the journey to Arabia is not excluded. The journey to Arabia, which is not mentioned in Acts, may, therefore, be regarded as having taken place after the preaching activity mentioned in Acts 9:20. It may be remarked in passing, however, that other hypotheses may be advanced, and have been advanced, as to the place where the journey to Arabia is to be inserted in the outline provided by the Book of Acts.

One important result already emerges from a consideration of this question. We observe already, namely, that the author of Acts has not made use of the Epistle to the Galatians in the construction of his narrative. The very difficulties which face us in our effort to put the two accounts together really constitute an important argument in favor of the early date and independent historical value of the Book of Acts. A later writer, composing his narrative at a time when information about Paul's life had become scanty, and being driven, therefore, to use the scattered autobiographical passages in the Pauline Epistles, would have made the harmony between his narrative and that in the Epistles altogether easy. Difficulties in the harmonizing of two narratives, on the other hand, arise when the narratives, no matter how trustworthy they may be, are independent of each other. It is really a fact of enormous importance for the defence of Luke-Acts, and not for the attack upon it, that differences of opinion arise, and may legitimately arise, as to the way in which the narrative in Acts is to be put together with the narrative in Galatians in the construction of as complete an account as possible of the life of Paul.

Arabia

Paul went away, he says, into Arabia. By "Arabia" he means, no doubt, the country of the Nabatean kings, of whom the one who was reigning at this time was Aretas IV. Since that country extended almost to the gates of Damascus, it is not necessary to suppose that he made a long journey into the great peninsula which we now commonly speak of as "Arabia." His journey may have been long or it may have been short; we simply do not know how long it was.

Moreover, we do not know how long a time Paul spent in Arabia. We only know that the time was less than three years; for Paul tells us that three years after the conversion he went up from Damascus to Jerusalem, and we learn from Acts 9:20, 22, 23 that some of that period was spent in preaching in Damascus.

So far as what Paul tells us in Galatians is concerned, we might suppose that the stay in Arabia lasted only (say) a few weeks. Let it not be objected that so short a stay would not have been thought worthy of mention; for the importance of the journey to Arabia in Paul's argument is found not in the journey itself but in the contrast in which it stands with a journey to Jerusalem, which Paul is concerned to deny.

One consideration, perhaps, points to a somewhat longer stay in Arabia. It appears in the fact mentioned in Acts 9:26, that when Paul finally went up to Jerusalem the disciples there were afraid of him. Would they have been afraid of him if the three years since his conversion had been spent almost exclusively in his preaching (in a place so near as Damascus) of that faith which formerly he had laid waste? Is not their fear of him better explained if he had spent a large part of the time since his conversion in the remote region of Arabia?

This consideration, though it has some weight, is scarcely conclusive; and the wisest thing for us to do is to say frankly that we do not know how large a proportion of the three years was spent in Arabia and how large a proportion in Damascus.

Meditation or Preaching

What did Paul do when he was in Arabia? Two answers to this question have been given. Some have thought that he carried on a preaching activity there; others have thought rather that he engaged in meditation upon the implications of the wonderful new conviction that had come into his life through the appearance to him of the risen Christ. If we had to choose between these two views, we should certainly choose the second. Even if Paul preached in Arabia, he certainly did not neglect meditation and prayer; he was not like some modern pastors who are "too busy" to engage in intellectual and spiritual preparation for their sermons. Indeed, even in the later busy period of his life, when the care of all the churches rested upon him, Paul always gives evidence of being a man of thought as well as a man of action. Indeed, he was a man of action because he was a man of thought; his wonderful life-work, which has changed the entire history of the world, was possible only because of great convictions meditated upon in the depths of his soul.

Happy would it be for the Church if we had more preachers like Paul in this respect today! There is a tremendous bustle in the lives of the typical preachers and pastors of the present time, but a singular lack of power. Perhaps one reason is that the preachers in question are neglecting to have recourse to the springs of power. Real preaching is born in long and laborious study of the Word of God and in the agony of the preacher's soul.

Paul may have engaged in preaching activity in Arabia; but we are inclined to think that the time which he spent there was predominantly a time of meditation and prayer, and of the study of the Old Testament Scriptures (which never ceased to be for Paul the authoritative Word of God) in the light of the wonderful new revelation that he had received from Christ.

The Place of Paul's Conversion

Certain it is that after the stay in Arabia he "returned again to Damascus." The form of expression here is not without importance. Paul has not told us so far where the conversion took place. The Book of Acts says it took place near Damascus; but the Book of Acts is under fire in modern criticism. The tendency of certain modern skeptical historians is to keep Paul as far as possible from Palestine and from those who had known Jesus during His earthly ministry. Thus a few of these historians have even denied that Paul ever was in Jerusalem prior to his conversion. Such denial of course is possible only on the basis of a thoroughgoing rejection of the testimony of Acts. Thus if it had been only the Book of Acts that places the conversion of Paul near Damascus, the narrative in Acts would hardly have escaped criticism at this point. Rather might the historians to whom we have referred have been inclined, in defiance of Acts, to place the conversion of Paul at a point far more conveniently remote from Palestine than Damascus was. But as a matter of fact Paul himself, in Galatians, one of the universally accepted Epistles, says that after his conversion he "returned again to Damascus." If he "returned" to Damascus, he must have been there before, and the conversion must have taken place in or near that city. Thus the assertion of Acts as to the place of the conversion is incidentally confirmed. We may well surmise that if Paul had had occasion to give other details many more elements in the narrative in Acts would similarly have been confirmed.

Paul and Peter

Three years after the conversion, Paul went up from Damascus to Jerusalem. The manner of his departure from Damascus was remarkable. According to his own account in II Cor. 11:32,33, as well as according to the account in Acts 9:23-25, he escaped from his enemies by being lowered through the wall of the city in a basket.

He went up to Jerusalem, he tells us in Galatians, "to make the acquaintance of Cephas"—calling Peter, here as usually, by the Aramaic name of which "Peter" is a translation—and he remained with him fifteen days. We cannot be sure of all that occurred within that fifteen-day period. But one thing can be said with some confidence—Paul did not neglect the opportunity of listening to what Peter had to tell concerning the words and deeds of Jesus. When Paul speaks, as he does in Galatians, of his apostolic independence, of the fact that he has not received his gospel from the original apostles or from any other mere men, he does not mean that he was indifferent to factual information which came to him by ordinary word of mouth from those who had been with Jesus when He was on earth. Much of such information had already come to him before his conversion; for the public ministry of Jesus was not a thing done in a corner, and Paul was intensely interested in it, though only as an enemy. But after the conversion the fund of such information would be enormously increased, not only through Paul's contact with humble Christians in Damascus, but also, and particularly, when he came into personal contact with the chief of Jesus' intimate disciples. The incidental way in which Paul writes in his Epistles here and there about events in the life of Jesus or elements of His teaching shows clearly not only that such incidental references proceed from a far larger store of knowledge which he possessed himself, but also that they are parts, chosen as need arose, of a store of information which he had given to the churches in his initial teaching.

Paul and Jesus

What Paul does mean, when he says that he received his gospel not through a man but through Jesus Christ, is that neither Peter nor any other disciple of Jesus made him a Christian by taking him and leading him, through instruction or persuasion, to see that his hostile view of what he had heard about Jesus was false and that really this was the Messiah and the Saviour. That conviction—that new attitude toward the information which he had received—came, Paul says, from Jesus Himself, when He appeared to him on the road to Damascus; and directly from Jesus, moreover, not through Peter or any other mere man, did he receive his commission to preach that gospel of the truth of which he had thus become convinced. To some extent at least, Paul had heard the gospel even before his conversion. But it was not that hearing of the gospel which made him an apostle. What made him an apostle was the direct impartation of the gospel to him by Jesus Christ, partly confirming the truth of what he had already heard, but partly also leading him, no doubt, into a new fulness of truth.

To make Paul indifferent to the details of Jesus' life, to make him indifferent to what he heard from Peter and others about what Jesus had said and done, is to interpret certain passages in Galatians with entire disregard, not only of the Book of Acts, but also of certain other passages in Paul's own Epistles. In particular, it is to neglect the important passage, I Cor. 15:3-8, where Paul appeals, in support even of the central fact of the resurrection, not only to his own testimony but also to the testimony of Peter and of the Twelve and of the five hundred brethren who saw the risen Christ. And in I Cor. 15:11 Paul says in the clearest possible manner that his gospel was the same as that of the original apostles. "Whether, therefore," he says, "it be I or they, so we preach and so ye believed."

Surely it is a mere caricature of New Testament exegesis if we represent Paul as saying to Peter, during those fifteen days which he spent with him three years after the conversion, when Peter quite naturally started to tell him something about his intercourse in Galilee with the Lord: "Stop, Peter; you must not tell me anything that you heard Jesus say or saw Jesus do while He was with you on earth, because if you do you will impair my apostolic independence." On the contrary, the two men of course spoke of those wonderful events of which Peter was the best possible eyewitness; and it is natural to surmise that it was during that fifteen-day visit that Paul "received" the precious summary of the death, burial, resurrection and appearances of Christ which he reproduces in I Cor. 15:3ff. No doubt he had already learned in Damascus some or all of what appears in that summary; but authoritative confirmation of it—perhaps even the summary formulation of it which we have in the passage just mentioned—was in all probability received from Peter during that important first visit of Paul to Jerusalem after the conversion. Certainly it did not at all make Paul a disciple of Peter, as the Judaizers apparently said he was; it did not impair in the slightest his independent apostolic authority or overthrow the thesis, which he is establishing in this first great division of this Epistle, that he was an apostle not from men nor through a man but through Jesus Christ and God the Father who raised Him from the dead.

X. PAUL AND THE JERUSALEM CHURCH

"Then after three years I went up to Jerusalem to make the acquaintance of Cephas, and I remained with him fifteen days; but another of the apostles I did not see—only, I saw James the brother of the Lord. Now as to the things that I

am writing to you, behold, before God, I lie not. Then I went into the regions of Syria and of Cilicia. And I was unknown by face to the churches of Judaea which are in Christ. Only, they were hearing: 'He who formerly persecuted us is now proclaiming as a gospel the faith which formerly he laid waste'; and they glorified God in me" (Gal. 1:18-24, in a literal translation).

Was James an Apostle?

Last month we began the discussion of this first visit which Paul made to Jerusalem after his conversion. He went there, he says, to make the acquaintance of Peter, and he remained with him fifteen days. It was no doubt an important period in his life, but hardly long enough to make him the kind of mere disciple of Peter that the Judaizing opponents said he was. And as for the other apostles, upon whom, as well as upon Peter, the Judaizers might have held him to be dependent, he did not see them at all. Only, he did see James, the brother of the Lord.

It is a question whether Paul does or does not here call James an "apostle." The phrase which we have translated "only," in the sentence "Only, I did see James," means "except." If so, it might seem at first sight as though Paul does call James an apostle. If he says, "I saw no other of the apostles except James," that seems certainly to imply that his meeting with James was an exception to the general assertion that in addition to Peter he saw no other of the apostles; in other words, it seems to imply that James was an apostle.

As a matter of fact, however, the Greek phrase meaning "except" is sometimes used to introduce an exception to something that is more general than that which has actually been mentioned. So in Matt. 12:4, it is said of the shewbread: "Which it was not lawful for David to eat, nor for those who were with him, but only for the priests." Here the phrase which we have translated "but only" is the same phrase as that which we have translated "only" in our passage in Galatians. If we translated it "except" in the passage in Matthew, we should arrive at a thought which is clearly not intended. If we translated: "Which it was not lawful for David or those with him to eat *except* for the priests," that would imply that there was a company of priests among those who were with David at that time—which is clearly not the meaning. Rather is the underlying thought, to which the phrase that we are discussing introduces an exception, the thought that "it was not lawful for *anyone* to eat the shewbread." Of that general principle, the thought that has actually been *expressed* before—namely, that it was not lawful for David and his company to eat the shewbread—is only one particular instance. The phrase meaning "except" follows after the particular instance, although according to our ways of thinking it belongs rather with the more general principle.

So in our passage, Paul's mention of his meeting with James, even if James was not an "apostle," was in the nature of an exception to the assertion, "Another of the apostles I did not see." If Paul had let that assertion stand without the exception, and had defended himself in doing so on the ground that strictly speaking James was not an "apostle," he would have been engaging in something like a quibble, because even if James was not an "apostle" he was one of the pillars of the Jerusalem Church, dependence upon whom on the part of Paul would have established the Judaizers' point just as much as would dependence upon one of the "apostles." So here again, as in the passage which we cited from Matthew, the Greek phrase introduces an exception—only, it is an exception to something a little more general than what has actually been stated in the preceding words. It is here an exception to what is the underlying sense of the preceding passage—namely, "Another of the Jerusalem leaders upon whom the Judaizers say I am dependent I did not see at the time of that first visit."

Of course what we have said about the Greek phrase in question does not mean that the use of the phrase shows that Paul does *not* call James an apostle; it only means that the use of the phrase does not show that he *does* call James an apostle. It is open to us to translate the words either: "Another of the apostles I did not see except James," or "Another of the apostles I did not see—only, I did see James."

The question which of these two translations is correct will have to be decided on the basis of considerations that are not found in this passage itself.

The Three Persons Named James

When those considerations are attended to, it seems probable that the latter of the two translations is to be preferred. Certain it is that the James whom Paul mentions here was not among the twelve apostles.

The opinion has, indeed, sometimes been held that the "brethren of the Lord," of whom James was one, were cousins of Jesus, the word "brethren" being used in a broader sense than that in which we use the word in English; and that these "brethren of the Lord" are to be identified with persons of the same names who appear in the lists of the twelve apostles. But this opinion depends upon certain rather doubtful combinations, and seems to be opposed by the fact that specifically in the Gospel according to John (John 7:5) and by implication also in the Synoptic Gospels the brothers of Jesus are represented as not believing on Him during His earthly ministry, and certainly are not clearly designated in any way as being among His intimate disciples.

Thus the identification of "James the brother of the Lord" with the "James the son of Alphaeus" who appears among the Twelve must no doubt be rejected. Hence we have in the New Testament three persons who bore the name of "James." They are (1) James the son of Zebedee, who was martyred in A.D. 44 in accordance with the twelfth chapter of Acts, (2) James the son of Alphaeus, of whom scarcely anything is known except that he was one of the twelve apostles, and (3) James the brother of the Lord, who is mentioned here in Galatians.

James the Brother of the Lord

This James the brother of the Lord seems, as we have just observed, not to have been a disciple of Jesus during the public ministry. But, according to I Cor. 15:7, he was granted a special appearance of the risen Lord, and it is natural to surmise that, as in Paul's case, this appearance of the risen Lord to him was the means by which he was converted. With the other brothers of Jesus he was no doubt in the little company of men and women who met in the upper room in Jerusalem after the Ascension and before the day of Pentecost (Acts 1:14). In Acts 12:17 he appears in a position of leadership in the Jerusalem Church; for Peter, after his release from prison, is represented as saying to the company in the house of Mary the mother of John Mark: "Go shew these things to *James,* and to the brethren" (Acts 12:17). In Acts 15:6-29 he appears as presiding over the deliberations of the Jerusalem Church at the time of the "Apostolic Council"; and in Gal. ii. 1-10, in a passage which, as we shall see, probably refers to that same event or to events taking place at that same time, he is mentioned before the apostles Peter and John. In Acts 21:18-25, referring to the time of Paul's last visit to Jerusalem, James appears in a similar position of leadership.

When these passages are carefully read, it seems clear that James was specifically the head of the local Church in Jerusalem, whereas the twelve apostles had more general duties which increasingly took them on missionary or pastoral journeys outside of that city.

We learn from Josephus, the Jewish historian, that James was killed by the Jews in A. D. 62, after the death of the procurator Festus and before his successor had arrived in Palestine.

This James the brother of the Lord was the writer of the General Epistle of James, which is in the New Testament. The Epistle was no doubt written at an early time, prior to the controversy with the Judaizers and to the "Apostolic Council" of Acts 15:1-29: for its teaching about faith and works exhibits the most beautiful harmony of thought with Paul's teaching; and the writer would no doubt have avoided that superficial appearance of contradiction of Paul which has sometimes been a source of difficulty to devout readers of his Epistle if he had been writing after the terminology had become fixed, as it was no doubt fixed in the course of the controversy with the Judaizers.

"Unknown by Face to the Churches of Judaea"

Such was the only one of the pillars of the Jerusalem Church whom, in addition to Peter, Paul met during his first visit to Jerusalem after his conversion. It is now time for us to return to the account of that visit which Paul gives us in Galatians.

"As to the things which I am writing to you," he says, "lo, the fact that I am not lying stands in the presence of God"—and hence, since it is in God's presence, it is entirely true. Apparently the Judaizers had misrepresented the facts about that visit to Jerusalem, and so Paul is compelled to set the Galatians right about the matter by this strong asseveration. "God knows," he says, "that I am telling you the truth: I went up to Jerusalem not at once, but three years after my conversion; the only ones of the leaders that I saw were Peter and James; and I was with Peter only fifteen days."

"Then," he continues, "I went into the regions of Syria and of Cilicia; and I was unknown by face to the churches of Judaea which are in Christ. Only, they were receiving the report: 'He who persecuted us formerly is now proclaiming as a gospel the faith which formerly he laid waste.' And they glorified God in me."

Great stress has been laid by certain modern scholars upon the words, "I was unknown by face to the churches of Judaea which are in Christ." If, it is said, Paul was unknown by face to the churches of Judaea, at the time of his departure from Jerusalem, he must have been unknown by face to the church at Jerusalem, since Jerusalem is in Judaea. Therefore, the argument continues, during that first visit to Jerusalem he must have been in hiding, seeing Peter and James, but by no means becoming acquainted generally with the Jerusalem disciples. This representation, it is said, is contradictory to the account in Acts 9:26-30; 22:17-18. According to the Book of Acts, Paul was by no means in hiding when he was in Jerusalem during his first visit there after his conversion, but went in and out in Jerusalem and preached to the Greek-speaking Jews. Thus it is maintained by the scholars to whom we have referred that Acts is quite incorrect in its account of that visit of Paul to the Jerusalem Church.

Was Paul in Hiding in Jerusalem?

But surely this attack upon the trustworthiness of Acts is based upon a totally unjustifiable interpretation of the one verse, Gal. 1:22. Paul has just said that he was in Jerusalem; then he says that he was unknown by face to the churches of Judaea. Is not the natural meaning simply that he was unknown by face to the churches of Judaea generally with the one obvious exception of the city that he has just mentioned? Surely I might say today, in speaking about my acquaintance with Presbyterian churches, that I know the churches of Philadelphia, but cannot say that I know the churches of Pennsylvania. It requires only a little goodwill and common sense to interpret Paul's words here in similar fashion.

Moreover, there is some evidence that in the language of that time "Jerusalem" was sometimes definitely distinguished from "Judaea," the capital city possessing such a unique importance that the name of the district could be used to designate the rest of the district in distinction from the capital. That usage appears clearly in Mk. 3:7f., where it is said that there followed Jesus a great multitude from Galilee and from Judaea *and* from Jerusalem. Here Jerusalem is not included in Judaea, but Judaea and Jerusalem are coördinated as two distinct things.

At any rate, whether we appeal to this special usage or not, it is surely much more natural to interpret Paul as meaning that he was unknown to the churches of Judaea generally, exclusive of Jerusalem, than to derive from the passage the very adventurous notion that he had spent his time in Jerusalem during that first visit somewhere in hiding in a back room of Peter's house. If Paul had meant that he went away from Jerusalem without having seen the church that was in that city, surely it would have been natural for him to say that much more plainly; surely it would have been more natural for him to say, after recounting his meeting with Peter and James: "But I remained unknown by face to the church that was in that city." When he says merely, "I was unknown by face to the churches of *Judaea*," he seems to indicate rather plainly that he did not have the much more definite and much more noteworthy fact to mention, that he did not even see the church at Jerusalem itself.

Where Were the Apostles?

Perhaps it may be objected that if we interpret Paul as meaning merely that he was unknown to the churches of Judaea outside of Jerusalem, we are making him say something that had no point in his argument. What possible importance was there, it may be asked, in the question whether he did or did not see obscure country churches in Judaea? Surely the question under dispute was the question whether he had or had not come under the domination of the Jerusalem apostles. Jerusalem, therefore, it is said, was the place where his relationships became important in his argument, and therefore when he says "Judaea" it is primarily Jerusalem, the chief city of Judaea, that he has in mind.

This objection, far from being decisive, only calls attention to the most probable explanation of the whole matter. In all probability, the apostles, at the time of Paul's first visit to Jerusalem, were already engaged in the missionary and pastoral labors in Judaea in which we know that they did engage at an early time, in accordance with the direction of our Lord that they should be witnesses unto Him "in Jerusalem and *in all Judaea* and Samaria" (Acts 1:8). Therefore it became very much to the point in Paul's argument for him to deny acquaintance with those Judaean churches. Since many of the apostles were in those churches, he could not clear up the matter of his relations with the apostles without mentioning those churches. "At that time," says Paul, "I went up to Jerusalem and there saw Peter and James; but as for the churches in the country of Judaea—lest anyone should say that it was there, rather than in Jerusalem, that I became a disciple of the apostles—I did not even see those churches at all."

This hypothesis, that many of the apostles were in the Judaean churches at just that time, is not established by direct testimony. But it is very probable, not only because it is in harmony with all that we know of the movements of the apostles, but also because it serves to explain two things in Paul's account. It serves, in the first place, to explain why he met only Peter and James in Jerusalem. Those were the only ones of the leaders whom he met, not because he was in hiding when he was in Jerusalem, but because the others were out of the city, engaged in missionary and pastoral labors in the Judaean churches. In the second place, the hypothesis explains, as we have just seen, why he mentions the Judaean churches at all. Since many of the apostles were in those churches, it became important for him, when he was showing how limited his contact with the apostles was at that early time, to say that those churches knew him only from hearsay.

Let it be observed that Paul's lack of contact with most of the apostles at that time, and his lack of contact with the Judaean churches, did not indicate any suspicion of him on the part of those churches. On the contrary, he says that when they heard that he was preaching the faith which formerly he had laid waste—not some different faith, be it observed, but the same faith as that which had been proclaimed in Palestine from the beginning—they glorified God in him. In other words, they recognized that the Glory of God had been singularly manifested in the wonderful and blessed change that had been wrought in Paul.

What is Meant by "The Faith"?

It is a very interesting question what Paul here means by "the faith." We use the word "faith" in two distinct senses in English. Sometimes we designate by the word "the act of believing," and at other times we designate by it "the thing that is believed." We use the word in the former sense when we say that justification is by "faith," or when we call on men to have "faith" in Jesus. We use it in the latter sense when we speak of the Christian "faith" or the Reformed "faith" or the like.

In our passage, perhaps our first impulse is to take the word in the latter of these two senses; and certainly that sense fits admirably into the meaning of the passage. It yields a very good thought if we interpret Paul to mean: "They glorified God in me, when they heard that I was proclaiming as a gospel the message about Jesus Christ which formerly I was laying waste."

The only trouble is that it is doubtful whether this use of the word occurs elsewhere in Paul—at least in his earlier Epistles. It certainly occurs in the New Testament, as, for example, in the well-known passage in the third verse of the Epistle of Jude concerning "the *faith* which was once for all delivered unto the saints"; but whether it occurs in Paul's Epistles, and particularly in his earlier Epistles, is a disputed question.

Perhaps, therefore, contrary to our first impulse, we had better abide by the other meaning of the word in our passage; perhaps we had better take the word as meaning, as it commonly does in Paul, "the act of believing." In that case, Paul would here mean to say: "They glorified God in me when they heard that I was proclaiming as a gospel—that is, that I was commending to men as the appointed means of salvation—that trust in Jesus Christ which I was formerly endeavoring, by my persecutions, to root out of men's minds and hearts."

But even if the word be taken in this sense, Paul certainly does not mean that he proclaimed the act of believing as a means of salvation because of its psychological effect, apart from the thing that *was believed,* namely the gospel message. Such a thought, common though it is in the Church today, is just about as far from the teaching of the Apostle Paul as anything that could possibly be imagined. When Paul speaks of his work in proclaiming as a gospel that trust in Jesus Christ which unites men to Him, we may be sure that he thinks of that trust, not as working in itself, through its psychological effect, but as being valuable only because the message which was received by it was true. Thus if we should translate this passage: "When they heard that I was preaching as a gospel that message about Jesus Christ, that 'faith' which consists of what is believed when He is received as Saviour," we might be technically wrong, but we should not be departing, after all, very far from the essential meaning of the passage.

XI. HARMONY OF ACTS AND GALATIANS

"Then after fourteen years again I went up to Jerusalem with Barnabas, taking along also Titus; and I went up according to revelation; and I laid before them the gospel which I am preaching among the Gentiles, and privately before those who were of repute, lest perchance I should run in vain or should prove to have run in vain" (Gal. 2:1-2, in a literal translation).

Identification of the Second Visit

In last month's number we finished the discussion of Paul's first visit to Jerusalem after his conversion. It did not take place immediately after the conversion, but three years after, and in connection with it he saw no others of the pillars of the Jerusalem Church except the Apostle Peter and James the brother of the Lord, while with the Judaean churches outside of Jerusalem he had no contact at all. He was with Peter, moreover, only fifteen days.

Then he went away into the regions of Syria and of Cilicia. The Book of Acts tells us, more specifically, that he went to Tarsus, his birthplace, the chief city of Cilicia, and then was brought by Barnabas to Antioch, the chief city of Syria, to engage in the important work which was going on in that city after the gospel had been preached by certain Jewish Christians of Cyprus and Cyrene to the Gentile population.

"Then," says Paul, "after fourteen years again I went up to Jerusalem." What does he mean by "after fourteen years"? Does he mean fourteen years after the visit to Jerusalem which has just been mentioned, which visit in turn was three years after the conversion (Gal. 1:18), so that the total period between the conversion and this visit now to be narrated would be seventeen years; or does he mean fourteen years after the conversion—that is, eleven years (fourteen minus three) after the first visit? It is very difficult to answer this question; but the former view is perhaps slightly more probable.

With what visit mentioned in the Book of Acts is this visit narrated in Gal. 2:1-10 to be identified? Our first impulse might be to say that since it is the second visit mentioned in Galatians it is to be identified with the second visit mentioned in Acts.

The second visit mentioned in Acts was the "famine visit" of Acts 11:30; 12:25. Agabus came from Jerusalem to Antioch and prophesied a famine. To relieve the distress which this famine brought or would bring to the brethren in Judaea, Barnabas and Paul were sent up to Jerusalem with the gifts of the Antioch Church; and after the fulfilment of their commission they returned to Antioch (Acts 11:30; 12:25). Was this the visit which is to be identified with the one narrated in Gal. 2:1-10?

Chronological Considerations

Chronology does not quite interpose a decisive objection to the identification. The famine visit, it is true, is mentioned in the Book of Acts in close connection with the death of Herod Agrippa I, which occurred, as can be established from Josephus, the Jewish historian, in A.D. 44; and since Paul says (according to what we have just held to be the more probable interpretation of Gal. 2:1) that the visit narrated in Gal. 2:1-10 took place seventeen (three plus fourteen) years after the conversion, identification of this Gal. 2:1-10 visit with the famine visit would seem to put Paul's conversion in A.D. 27 (forty-four minus seventeen), which is clearly too early, since it would be earlier than the crucifixion of Jesus.

But, in the first place, it is not clear that the famine visit took place just in A.D. 44. It is true, the Book of Acts does mention the death of Herod Agrippa I, which took place in A.D. 44, between the mention of the journey of Paul and Barnabas to Jerusalem (Acts 11:30) and the mention of their return from Jerusalem to Antioch (Acts 12:25). But that may be merely because at the point where the author (by the mention of the journey of Paul and Barnabas from Antioch to

Jerusalem) brings the Antioch thread of his narrative into connection with the Jerusalem thread, he feels the need of bringing the Jerusalem thread up to date by the mention of events like the imprisonment of Peter and the death of Herod Agrippa I, which may have taken place some time before the point where the two threads of narrative are brought together. Thus it is possible that the famine visit of Paul and Barnabas to Jerusalem may have taken place not just in A.D. 44, but as late as A.D. 46.

Even so, however, it might seem as though that famine visit can hardly be identified with the visit of Gal. 2:1-10, since this visit of Gal. 2:1-10 took place seventeen years after the conversion and if we subtract seventeen from forty-six we shall get a date (A.D. 29) which is clearly too early for the conversion of Paul.

Inclusive Method of Reckoning?

This argument is not, however, quite decisive. In New Testament times an inclusive method of designating periods of time was often used. By this inclusive method, which counts both the year in which a period begins and the year in which it ends, 1933 would be "three years" after 1931. Thus "three years" in such designations would sometimes mean what we should call two years or even less; it would mean one full year and parts of two other years.

If Paul is using this method, then the "fourteen years" of Gal. 2:1 may be what we should call thirteen years, and the "three years" of Gal. 1:18 may be what we should call two years; so that if the visit of Gal. 2:1-10 be identified with the famine visit, and the famine visit be put not in A.D. 44 but in A.D. 46, we should obtain as the date of the conversion forty-six minus thirteen minus two, or A.D. 31—which, although uncomfortably early, is not quite impossible.

Moreover, it is by no means certain that Paul is reckoning the "fourteen years" of Gal. 2:1 from the first visit rather than from the conversion. Quite possibly what he means to do is to contrast the first visit, which occurred only three years after the conversion, with the Gal. 2:1-10 visit, which occurred fourteen years after that same event. If so, we should be obliged (on the assumption that the visit narrated in Gal. 2:1-10 is to be identified with the famine visit, and that the famine visit occurred in A.D. 46), to subtract only fourteen (or, with the inclusive method of reckoning, thirteen) from forty-six to get the date of the conversion, which would thus be A.D. 32 or 33—both quite possible dates. Indeed, we might even put the famine visit as early as A.D. 44, the actual year of the death of Herod Agrippa I, and still not obtain a prohibitively early date for the conversion.

It remains true that chronological considerations do on the whole favor the identification of the visit narrated in Gal. 2:1-10 with some visit later than the famine visit; but what we have just maintained is that they do not actually preclude identification with the famine visit, if other considerations make that identification natural.

Identification with the Apostolic Council

Perhaps the chief argument against the identification with the famine visit is to be found in the marked similarity between what is recorded in Gal. 2:1-10 and what is recorded in Acts about a visit other than the famine visit—namely, the visit at the time of the "Apostolic Council" of Acts 15:1-39. One of the similarities holds also, indeed, with reference to the famine visit as well as with reference to the Apostolic Council—Barnabas is represented in both places as being present with Paul. But other features are found only in Acts 15:1-39 and not in Acts 11:30; 12:25. In both Acts 15:1-39 and Gal. 2:1-10, the circumcision of Gentile converts is under discussion, and in both the result is the same—namely, approval of the position taken by Paul.

This argument for the identification of the event of Gal. 2:1-10 with that of Acts 15:1-39 and against the identification with the event of Acts 11:30; 12:25 is not, indeed, quite decisive. Even if Paul had discussed the matter of Gentile freedom privately with the pillars of the Jerusalem Church (as Gal. 2:1-10 may be interpreted to mean that he did discuss it), there would still be room, some years later, for a public pronouncement against the Judaizers like that which is recorded in Acts 15:1-39. Nevertheless, as we read Gal.

2:1-10 in comparison with Acts 15:1-39, it cannot be denied that our first impression is that they refer to the same event. That is at least the *prima facie* view of the matter.

In the following discussion, this *prima facie* view will be adopted provisionally in order that we may see how it works in detail. We shall endeavor to see how Gal. 2:1-10 and Acts 15:1-39 fit in together on the assumption that they refer to the same event. The momentous implications of this whole comparison will appear more clearly in the sequel.

The Famine Visit Not Mentioned?

Just at the beginning, we encounter what is often regarded as a serious difficulty. Paul says, after he has narrated his first post-conversion visit to Jerusalem, "Then after fourteen years again I went up to Jerusalem." Could he have passed over unmentioned a visit to Jerusalem that took place in that interval, as we are compelled to hold that he has done if we identify the visit narrated in Gal. 2:1-10 with the Apostolic Council and hold that the famine visit had taken place in between?

This question is often answered in the negative, and either one of two conclusions is drawn from that answer. Some of those who hold that Paul could not have passed over the famine visit here without mention draw the conclusion that this visit of Gal. 2:1-10 is itself the famine visit, and that the identification of it with the Apostolic Council of Acts 15:1-39, which we have adopted provisionally, must be given up after all. Others, insisting still on the identification of this visit with the Apostolic Council, draw the conclusion that the famine visit never occurred at all, and that therefore the information in Acts 11:30; 12:25 is incorrect.

But is the assumption upon which these two conclusions are based so well grounded as the advocates of it suppose? Is it true that Paul would have been obliged to mention the famine visit if it had really occurred between the first visit and the one narrated in Gal. 2:1-10?

At first sight, it might seem as though that were the case. In this passage, it might be said, the Apostle Paul is tracing in the most careful way his relations with the Jerusalem Church, by way of answer to bitter opponents who would have been quick to seize upon the slightest weakness in his argument. He has just narrated his first visit to Jerusalem with careful attention to detail and with asseveration of his complete accuracy. He has dealt with all possibilities of contact with the original apostles, in order that the Judaizers might not be able to say that he has left anything out. In Jerusalem, he is careful to tell us, he saw only Peter and James, and he did not visit the Judaean churches at all. Could he possibly lapse so soon from this completeness and carefulness of statement as actually to omit mention of a second visit to Jerusalem? Would not the Judaizers have been quick to seize upon so significant an omission? Would they not have said that there, at that second visit, which Paul (as they would have charged) was afraid to mention, was to be put the meeting with the Jerusalem leaders which showed Paul to be no independent apostle but a mere disciple of those whom Jesus had originally chosen?

The Transition in Paul's Argument

This argument, plausible though it may seem at first sight, is not decisive. It ignores the fact that there is a transition in Paul's argument between the first chapter and the second chapter of Galatians.

In the first chapter, Paul is arguing that at the beginning of his Christian life there was not even such *contact* with the original apostles as could have made him a mere disciple of theirs. To how late a period in Paul's life would this exhibition of lack of contact with the apostles have to be continued? Only, it seems natural to say, to the point where Paul was already well launched upon the preaching of his gospel. But that point was surely reached some time before the time of the famine visit, supposing the famine visit to have taken place as the Book of Acts says it took place.

What did Paul do when he was in or near Tarsus between the time when he left Jerusalem three years after his conversion and the time when Barnabas brought him to Antioch? Surely he preached there; and in all probability both the Galatians and the Judaizing opponents knew that that was the case, so that all the original readers of the Epistle to the Galatians would understand that when Paul says in Gal. 1:21 that he went to the regions of Syria and of Cilicia that meant that at that time he was launched very definitely upon the preaching of his gospel.

But if he preached his gospel before he had the kind of contact with the original apostles which could have made him a disciple of theirs, he could not have derived his gospel from them. Therefore, when in the Epistle he has traced his life up to the point where he was fairly launched upon the preaching of his gospel, the first part of his argument is over, and it no longer remains necessary for him to trace in any such detail the subsequent history of his relations with the Jerusalem leaders.

Conference With the Apostles

He proceeds, therefore, in the second chapter, to an entirely different argument. The point of this new argument is that when the original apostles, the very men to whom the Judaizers appealed, finally did have a conference with Paul about the content of his gospel, they took completely Paul's view of the matter, admitted gladly that Paul needed no endorsement from them and his gospel needed no addition, gave him the right hand of fellowship, and recognized the fact that his gospel had already been given him, without any mediation of theirs, by God Himself.

It is true, Paul is careful to say when this important conference took place. It took place, he says, fourteen years after the first visit (or, by another interpretation of his words, fourteen years after the conversion). But the point of this mention of the time of the conference visit is not to show that it was after an interval of so many years during which Paul had made no visits to Jerusalem, but rather to show that the first real conference with the original apostles, at which the content of Paul's gospel was discussed with them, did not take place at the first visit after the conversion, as apparently the Judaizers said that it did, but at a visit many years later.

The "after fourteen years" of Gal. 2:1 stands, therefore, in relation to the "after three years" of Gal. 1:18. "The first contact of any kind that I had with the original apostles," says Paul, "took place three years after the conversion; and the first real conference with them at which they expressed themselves about my gospel took place fourteen years later still."

The Apostles and the Famine Visit

Rightly regarded, therefore, Paul's argument does not demand that the famine visit should be mentioned, supposing it took place prior to the visit recorded in Gal. 2:1-10, unless it involved the important event of a real conference between the original apostles and Paul regarding the content of Paul's gospel and an expression of opinion by the original apostles about that gospel and about Paul's right to preach it.

But it is very improbable, from the account of the famine visit in Acts, that that visit, if it did really take place, involved anything of the kind. It is said in Acts 11:30 that the gifts were sent to the "elders" at Jerusalem; no mention is made of apostles as being there: and, indeed, it is quite possible that at the time of the persecution by Herod Agrippa I and for a time after his death the apostles were all out of the city. James the brother of the Lord was, indeed, no doubt there; but still, if the apostles were away, there would be no real opportunity at that time for the kind of pronouncement upon Paul's gospel which Paul would have been obliged to mention at this point in his argument in Galatians.

We must remember, moreover, that in the first two chapters of Galatians Paul is not constructing an argument which would hold against all possible objections, but rather is meeting specific objections of the Judaizers. Apparently it was that first visit to Jerusalem which they had seized upon for their purposes. Paul was obliged, therefore, to set them right in detail about that visit. But if the famine visit gave them so little color of support that they had not even tried to bring it forward, then Paul was not obliged to mention it in his argument, and his omission of mention of it before Gal. 2:1 does not prove either that the visit narrated in

Gal. 2:1-10 is to be identified with it or that the Book of Acts is in error in representing it as having occurred.

XII. PAUL AT JERUSALEM

"Then after fourteen years again I went up to Jerusalem with Barnabas, taking along also Titus; and I went up according to revelation; and I laid before them the gospel which I am preaching among the Gentiles, and privately before those who were of repute, lest perchance I should run in vain or should prove to have run in vain" (Gal. 2:1, 2, in a literal translation).

"According to Revelation"

We have seen that this visit of Paul to Jerusalem is to be identified either with the "famine visit" of Acts 11:30; 12:25 or (more probably) with the "Apostolic Council" of Acts 15:1-39.

Paul says that he went up "according to revelation." If he is speaking of the famine visit, then possibly the "revelation" that he mentions is to be identified with the revelation that was brought to the church at Antioch through Agabus' prophecy of a famine (Acts 11:28), although it must be confessed that the context in Galatians suggests a revelation given directly to Paul rather than a revelation given through some other person.

Such a revelation given directly to Paul is almost certainly intended if the visit here spoken of is the one at the time of the Apostolic Council. There was trouble at Antioch: the Judaizers demanded that the Gentile converts should be circumcised; and the Antioch Church sent Paul and Barnabas up to hold a consultation about the matter. But this external occasion for Paul's going to Jerusalem does not at all exclude a divine revelation given directly to him. He was urged by the church to go; but the question whether he should comply with this request was decided, he says, by direct revelation from God. Here, as elsewhere, his apostolic independence was preserved.

Private and Public Conferences

"And I laid before them," Paul continues, "the gospel which I preach among the Gentiles." There is no formal antecedent for the pronoun "them"; but when it is said, "I went up to Jerusalem and laid before them the gospel," every reader will understand that the word "them" designates the members of the church in Jerusalem.

There is serious doubt as to how the following words should be translated—whether they should be translated "and privately before those who were of repute," or "privately, I mean, before those who were of repute." Either translation is possible.

If the former translation be chosen, Paul is distinguishing a general conference with the Jerusalem Church from another conference which he held with the leaders. "I went up to Jerusalem," he says (according to this interpretation), "and laid my gospel before the church generally; and in addition I laid it, in a private conference, before the leaders."

If the latter translation be chosen, Paul is merely defining a little more closely the way in which he laid his gospel before the church. He did so, he says (according to this interpretation), by taking the leaders as the representatives of the church. "I went up to Jerusalem," he says, "and laid before them the gospel which I am preaching among the Gentiles—privately, I mean, before those who were of repute."

The question which of these two interpretations is right is not so important as might at first sight be supposed.

The former interpretation, it is true, does bring a confirmation of the Book of Acts which is lacking in the second. The Book of Acts tells us plainly that there was a general meeting of the Jerusalem Church at which Paul and Barnabas recounted their work among the Gentiles and at which Peter and James spoke. Such a public meeting, or such public meetings, of the Jerusalem Church would be directly mentioned by Paul according to the former of the two interpretations of Gal. 2:2—according to the interpretation which makes Paul say: "I laid my gospel before them (the Jerusalem Church) *and* privately before those who were of repute."

But public meetings of the church are not really excluded by the other interpretation, which makes Paul say: "I laid my gospel before them (the Jerusalem Church)—privately, I mean, before those who were of repute." Only, in this case Paul would not in this verse be *mentioning* those public meetings, but would merely be singling out for mention the thing that was important for his immediate purpose—namely, the private conference between him and the leaders.

"Those Who Were of Repute"

Paul says that he laid his gospel privately before "those who were of repute." The persons designated "those who were of repute" are, as verse 9 tells us, James the brother of the Lord and Peter (Cephas) and John. But why are they designated "those who were of repute"?

The same phrase occurs at the end of verse 6; and in verses 6 and 9 it occurs in the fuller forms, "those who were reputed to be something" and "those who were reputed to be pillars." Why does Paul repeatedly use in this passage so unusual a designation of the leaders of the church in Jerusalem?

Certainly the use of the phrase cannot mean that Paul is casting despite upon the Jerusalem leaders; he cannot possibly mean that they were only *reputed* to be something, or only reputed themselves to be something, whereas in reality they were of no great importance at all. Any such view as that is refuted in the clearest possible way by other passages in which Paul speaks of these men with the utmost respect—particularly by I Cor. 15:3-11, where he appeals to their witness to the risen Christ and says that it was the same gospel that was preached both by them and by him. Why then does he use this unusual phrase?

Possibly he does so because he is taking the phrase from the lips of his Judaizing opponents. The phrase sometimes designates in Greek "the notables"; far from being derogatory to the persons to whom it is applied, it is in such passages used as an honorable title. Possibly the Judaizers used it in such a way in their attempt to cast discredit upon Paul; possibly they said that the real men of repute, the real men of reputation, were Peter and the other apostles in Jerusalem and not the upstart Paul. If so, it is possible that Paul is here saying to them in effect: "You say that the real men of reputation are Peter and the other original apostles: well, if they are, why do you not listen to their acceptance of me as an apostle whose authority is independent of, and equal to, their own?"

A Difficult Situation

However, that suggestion can never rise above the level of conjecture. It is quite possible that Paul is using the phrase of his own motion and not as a phrase coined by his opponents. We must remember that Paul found himself in a rather difficult situation when he began to recount the events of Gal. 2:1-10. At first sight, it might seem as though the very fact that he felt it necessary to appeal to what the original apostles had said indicated a certain subordination. Why, it might be asked, if he was really independent of the Jerusalem leaders, did he find it necessary to appeal to their endorsement?

It is this impression, perhaps, which Paul is guarding against by the phrase "those who were of repute." These men really were something very important indeed—namely, apostles of Jesus Christ with a commission equal to Paul's own. But it was not their real importance, great as it was, which made it necessary for Paul to go up and lay his gospel before them. Rather was it merely the importance which—quite rightly, it is true—was attributed to them by others. "My right to be an apostle," Paul is saying, "is not due to any commission or any endorsement which the original apostles gave me. Great though they were, I do not need to appeal to their greatness to establish my apostleship; for my apostleship came to me directly from Christ. The only reason why I appeal to them is to stop the propaganda of the Judaizers: they are the men whom the Judaizers recognize and whom the Judaizers hold to be generally recognized; and therefore, when *they* accepted me as an apostle independent of themselves, surely the Judaizers and all affected by the Judaizers ought to listen."

The Purpose of the Conference

"I laid my gospel before the Jerusalem leaders," Paul says, "and privately I laid it before those who were of repute, *lest perchance I should run or should prove to have run in vain.*" Here again two interpretations, and consequently two translations, are possible. The Greek words just translated "lest perchance" may also mean "with the question whether perchance"; and if they mean this here, an excellent sense results. "I laid my gospel before them," Paul, in accordance with this interpretation, would say, "with the question whether I were running or had run in vain."

Of course, the question was not necessary for Paul's own sake: Paul knew perfectly well, without being told by the original apostles, that the gospel which he had preached was true and that his labor had by no means been in vain when he had preached it. But he asks the question to stop the propaganda of the Judaizers. He says to the pillars of the Jerusalem Church: "You have been appealed to by the Judaizers against me. Well, here is the gospel that I have preached and here is the way in which I have preached it. Will you not examine it and tell these Judaizers and all who may be disposed to listen to them whether in preaching that gospel I have or have not been running in vain? I know perfectly well what you are going to say; for you and I have been commissioned by the same Christ to preach the same gospel. But I need your testimony to put a stop to those who have falsely appealed to you against me."

Was the Church Divided?

Unquestionably this translation gives an excellent sense, and we are somewhat tempted to adopt it. But since there is in the New Testament no other use of the Greek words in this way as introducing an indirect question, and since these same words are used in another passage in this very Epistle (Gal. 4:11) as meaning "lest perchance," we shall probably have to stick to the meaning "lest perchance" here also. Thus Paul says: "I laid my gospel before them, lest perchance I should run, or should prove already to have run, in vain."

By that he does not mean at all that he could not continue to preach his gospel with a good conscience no matter what the original apostles or any other man should say about it. He had been entrusted with it directly by Christ, and the commission thus received could not be invalidated by any human authority whatsoever. But what he means is that in actual practice the Judaizers are interfering seriously with his work; they are drawing men away from his gospel. Unless that Judaizing propaganda is stopped, his labor among the Gentiles will to a certain extent be in vain—not in vain because his gospel would be any less true than it was before, but because of the practical results of the false teaching. These Judaizers appealed to the original apostles against Paul. That appeal constituted a serious menace. Paul himself knew, indeed, that it was a false appeal. Christ had commissioned him; but He had also commissioned the original apostles, and it was impossible that the two commissions should be in contradiction. But if the Gentile converts, through the propaganda of the Judaizers, really came to believe that the original apostles were opposed to Paul, a serious situation obviously would result. Those original apostles were really apostles, and Paul himself recognized that fact. So long as the Gentiles were allowed to think that these apostles were hostile to Paul, a serious contradiction seemed to be introduced into the apostolic witness. Until that contradiction was shown to be non-existent, the work of preaching the gospel was seriously hindered. To show that the contradiction was non-existent, Paul went up to Jerusalem and laid his gospel before the very authorities to whom the Judaizers appealed. The glorious result of this step will be discussed in the subsequent issues of *Christianity Today*.

XIII. FALSE BRETHREN AND A TRUE GOSPEL

Then after fourteen years again I went up to Jerusalem with Barnabas, taking along also Titus; and I went up according to revelation; and I laid before them the gospel which I am preaching among the Gentiles, and privately before those who were of repute, lest perchance I should run in vain or should prove to have run in vain. But not even Titus who was with me, being a Greek, was compelled to be circumcised. But on account of the privily brought in false brethren, who came in privily to spy out our liberty which we have in Christ Jesus, in order that they might bring us into bondage—to whom not even for an hour did we yield by way of subjection, in order that the truth of the gospel might remain with you (Gal. 2:1-5, in a literal translation).

The Case of Titus

The first part of this passage has been treated in the last two articles. We noticed last month that Paul conferred with the leaders of the Jerusalem Church not because he needed to receive any commission from them or through them (since his commission came to him directly from Christ), but in order to stop the propaganda of the Judaizers, who had falsely appealed to the original apostles against Paul. The same thing will become even clearer through our present study.

"But not even Titus who was with me," says Paul, "being a Greek, was compelled to be circumcised." The Judaizers at Antioch—supposing our provisional identification of the event of Gal. 2:1-10 with the Apostolic Council of Acts 15:1-29 to be correct—had demanded that *all* Gentile converts be circumcised. "But as a matter of fact," Paul says, "not even the Gentile Titus who was there with me in Jerusalem itself, the very centre of Judaism, was compelled to be circumcised. In his case at least, venturing as he did into the holy city, compromise might have seemed to be in place. But as a matter of fact there was no compromise at all. Not even he was circumcised, to say nothing of the Gentiles who were out in the Gentile world."

What does Paul imply by the word "compelled"? Does he mean that the pillars of the Jerusalem Church demanded that Titus be circumcised, but that he (Paul) simply refused to accede to their demand? Certainly he does not mean that. If it had come thus to a breach between him and the Jerusalem leaders, the "right hand of fellowship," which he mentions in verse 9, would have been impossible. What is much more probable is that the Judaizers demanded the circumcision of Titus but the leaders agreed with Paul in refusing to do as they asked. However, we must not attempt to read too much between the lines. All that Paul clearly tells us is that his going up and laying his gospel before the leaders of the Jerusalem Church did not necessitate even the circumcision of Titus, a Gentile who was right there with him in Jerusalem itself.

False Brethren

"But," Paul continues, "on account of the privily brought in false brethren. . . ." The grammatical structure of what follows is exceedingly difficult. The words, "on account of the privily brought in false brethren," constitute a prepositional phrase. A prepositional phrase is usually adverbial; it usually modifies a verb. At any rate, it makes no sense by itself. If I meet a man on the street and say to him simply, "On account of the privily brought in false brethren," he naturally thinks that something has interrupted me, and that I was going on to tell him something that *happened* or that ought to happen on account of those false brethren.

Now the trouble is that Paul seems to use the prepositional phrase here in just such a disconnected way. It is true, a good many words follow the propositional phrase in the rest of verse 4 and in verse 5. But these words are all of them in two relative clauses; and these relative clauses do not complete the meaning of the prepositional phrase, but are simply adjectives modifying the noun "false brethren" within the prepositional phrase. The skeleton of the verses is: "But on account of the privily brought in false brethren, who came in privily, to whom we did not yield for an hour. . . ." It will at once be seen that the sentence, provided it be regarded as beginning with verse 4, is never brought to completion. Paul does not tell, as he would have had to tell in order to complete the sentence, what happened on account of the privily brought in false brethren. There is no verb for the prepositional phrase to modify.

A Broken Sentence?

In view of this difficulty, a number of commentators say simply that verses 4 and 5 constitute an "anacoluthon"—that is, Paul begins a sentence which he breaks off before it is completed, such long and such weighty relative clauses having been brought in as modifiers of the noun in the initial prepositional phrase that that phrase is never given the verb that it was originally intended to modify. If this view of the structure be correct, opinions may differ as to what Paul was intending to say when he began the sentence. Probably he was intending to tell something of the trouble or discussion which arose in the Jerusalem Church on account of the Judaizers' contention that Titus should be circumcised. But inasmuch as he has already, in one of the relative clauses modifying the noun in the prepositional phrase, told what the upshot of the discussion was—namely that he did not yield for a moment—he does not pedantically go back to review the discussion itself. Instead, he breaks the sentence off with a kind of impatience and goes on to something else.

An anacoluthon is not always a defect in style. Sometimes it may express very well the writer's feeling of impatience; sometimes it is more impressive, because of what it does not say, but only leaves the reader to supply, than the most regular sentence-structure would be. It is used in some passages very effectively by Paul.

But this particular anacoluthon, if anacoluthon it be, is of a rather unusual kind. It is not surprising, therefore, that many commentators have sought to avoid finding it in the passage. That can be done, if at all, only by taking the prepositional phrase, "on account of the privily brought in false brethren," with something that *precedes*, so that verse 4 would not begin a new sentence at all.

A Test Case

Some, for example, have supposed that the prepositional phrase modifies a verb "was circumcised," to be supplied from the preceding sentence. "Not even Titus," these expositors would make the passage mean, "was *compelled* to be circumcised; but it happened—that is, Titus was circumcised—on account of the privily brought in false brethren."

This interpretation must certainly be rejected. Paul could hardly have circumcised the Gentile Titus at Jerusalem; for that would have been a desertion of his great principle. It would have been totally different from the circumcision of the half-Jew Timothy at Lystra (Acts 16:1-3). Titus presented a test case; and to have yielded with regard to him would certainly seem to involve betrayal of the cause. Moreover, if Paul *had* yielded, surely he would have been obliged to explain his action in far clearer terms than would then be found in Gal. 2:3-5; he could hardly have said simply: "Not even for an hour did we yield by way of subjection."

A far more likely suggestion is that which regards not the circumcision of Titus, but the non-circumcision of him, as the thing which is explained by the prepositional phrase at the beginning of verse 4—the thing which took place "on account of the privily brought in false brethren." "Not even Titus," Paul would say in accordance with this interpretation, "was compelled to be circumcised; and that—namely, the non-circumcision of Titus—was on account of the privily brought in false brethren." In other words, if the false brethren had not been there, Titus might have been circumcised; but their general contention about the Gentile converts made the question about Titus a test case, so that yielding even in that case became impossible.

This interpretation also must be pronounced improbable. In the first place, it may well be doubted whether Paul would ever have agreed to the circumcision of Titus even if the Judaizers had not been there; and, in the second place, the supplying of the idea of non-circumcision with the prepositional phrase is very unnatural and very unlikely to occur to any ordinary reader.

An Explanatory Phrase?

Much more worthy of consideration than either of these two interpretations is that which regards the prepositional phrase, "on account of the privily brought in false brethren," as "epexegetical"—we trust that the readers of *Christianity*

Today will pardon us for the use of a grammatical term occasionally if we promise not to do it too often—as epexegetical, we say, of the words "compelled to be circumcised" in the preceding verse. The connection would then be: "Not even Titus . . . was compelled to be circumcised—compelled to be circumcised, I mean, on account of the privily brought in false brethren." The prepositional phrase at the beginning of verse 4 would thus merely define a little more closely the kind of compulsion which is being denied in verse 3, the kind of compulsion which the Judaizers desired but which as a matter of fact was not carried out.

This interpretation gives an excellent sense, and possibly it is correct. The only question is whether the prepositional phrase can be understood as epexegetical of a word or phrase in what precedes without some clearer indication than Paul actually gives us in the text. The repetition of the word or phrase of which the added phrase is epexegetical—in this case the words "compelled to be circumcised"—is perhaps as much required in Greek as it is in English. We were obliged to repeat the words "compelled to be circumcised" in order to make the meaning clear in English. Would not Paul have been obliged to repeat them if that was the meaning that he had intended in the Greek?

An Unusual Interpretation

These difficulties in the interpretations so far considered lead us to consider another interpretation, which, it must be confessed, has met with scarcely any favor from the commentators. According to this interpretation, the prepositional phrase, "on account of the privily brought in false brethren," modifies not any word or phrase in what immediately precedes but the verbs in verses 1 and 2; and what Paul is explaining by the prepositional phrase is the thing that most required explanation—namely, his going up to Jerusalem and laying his gospel before the leaders of the Jerusalem Church. "I went up to Jerusalem," Paul would be saying if this interpretation is right, "and laid my gospel before the leaders. That might look like subordination on my part. But as a matter of fact it involved no subordination or compromise at all. So little did it involve compromise that not even Titus who was right there with me in Jerusalem had to be circumcised. On the contrary, it really happened—that is I went up to Jerusalem and laid my gospel before the leaders—not on my account, as though I needed endorsement from anyone, but on account of the privily brought in false brethren, whose propaganda needed to be stopped by a word from the very leaders to whom they themselves appealed."

This interpretation is for the most part rejected with scant consideration by modern commentators, on the ground that the verbs with which it connects the prepositional phrase lie too far back to be in the mind of the reader when the prepositional phrase is read. But the force of this argument is weakened when one sees that those verbs in verses 1 and 2 express the main point of the passage, and the point which was most open to misunderstanding. By denying the circumcision of Titus in verse 3, Paul has stated what his going up to Jerusalem and laying his gospel did *not* involve; it is therefore quite in order for him to tell, as he does according to the proposed interpretation of verses 4 and 5, what those actions *did* involve.

The Dangers of Originality

It is only with very great diffidence that we propose an interpretation which, while not at all original with us, has met with general rejection. The Bible has had many readers during the past nineteen hundred years; many minds have applied themselves to the interpretation of it. Where our mind differs from almost all the others, we are usually inclined to suspect that it is our mind that is wrong, and not the mind of so many wiser and more learned men. We are sometimes amazed at the sublime confidence with which modern expositors or translators put forward idiosyncrasies of their own in the interpretation of the Scriptures as though they stood as firm as Holy Writ itself. A man can sometimes apply criticism very profitably to himself before he applies it to others.

All that we can say is that the interpretation just proposed does seem to commend itself to us anew whenever we come back to a fresh reading of this much discussed passage. We are very far indeed from thinking that it is certainly correct, and have not even ventured to incorporate it in the translation at the beginning of this article.

Fortunately the three interpretations which we have designated as possible—unlike the two decisively rejected ones—are very similar in their ultimate implications. Whether (1) Paul begins at verse 4 a new sentence which he breaks off in an anacoluthon, or whether (2) he is simply defining a little more closely the kind of compulsion which might have been exerted in the case of Titus but as a matter of fact was not carried through, or whether (3) he is explaining further his action in going up to Jerusalem and laying his gospel before the leaders—an action capable of much misunderstanding —in any case, Titus was not circumcised and would not under any circumstances have been circumcised.

Having thus considered as best we can the general structure of verses 4 and 5, we turn now, very briefly, to certain details in those verses.

Plain Language

Paul here calls the Judaizers "false brethren," and the meaning of that term is clear. "Brother" in Paul's Epistles means "fellow-Christian," and thus a "false brother" is a man who claims to be a Christian or is thought to be a Christian and yet is not, or does not show himself by his present actions to be, a Christian at all. It is not a pleasant term, but the reason why it is not a pleasant term is that the thing that it designated was not a pleasant thing. These Judaizers might have seemed to a superficial observer to be true disciples, but in their heart of hearts, Paul seems to mean, they were Pharisees rather than disciples of Jesus Christ. They were depending upon their own works for salvation, and according to the apostle Paul a man cannot posssibly do that if he is to be saved. So Paul calls them false brethren. Unlike the leaders of the modern Church the apostle Paul believed in calling things by their true names.

These false brethren were "brought in secretly" and "came in secretly." The notion which we have translated by the word "privily" or "secretly" is not definitely expressed in the words which Paul uses, but it seems rather clearly to be implied. What Paul means is that these men came into a place where they did not belong.

Into what place were they "brought in" and into what did they "come in"? Our first impulse might be to say, "Into the Church in general," these words being thus merely explanatory of the term "false brethren." But it is natural to give the words a more special reference; it is natural to take them as referring to the action of the Judaizers in coming into the Church at Antioch. Certainly that action as it is described in Acts 15:1 is most aptly designated by these words of Paul. This reference of the words—at least of the word translated "came in privily"—is practically certain if our suggested interpretation of the phrase "on account of the privily brought in false brethren" be correct. In that case, the coming of the false brethren into the Antioch Church would clearly be designated as the occasion for Paul's going up from Antioch to Jerusalem.

Christian Liberty

The liberty which these Judaizers came in to spy out was particularly the liberty of the Gentile Christians, which Paul can call "our liberty" because he shares it with them. But at bottom it was a liberty possessed by all Christians whether Jews or Gentiles. It was the liberty which a man has when he gives up the vain effort to establish his own righteousness before God and trusts only in the atonement which Christ accomplished on the cross.

That liberty was being attacked by the Judaizers when they asked the Gentile converts to keep the ceremonial law. But it is also being attacked in the modern Church when men seek by their own efforts to attain salvation by exhibiting "the spirit of Jesus" in their lives. Now as always true liberty is to be obtained only when a man depends for his salvation unreservedly upon the grace of God.

To the demands of the Judaizers, Paul says, "we yielded not even for an hour by way of subjection, in order that the truth of the gospel might remain with you."

No inferences can legitimately be drawn from these last words with regard to the time when the Galatian churches were founded. Even if they were founded after that conference with the Jerusalem leaders of which Paul is writing in our passage, still Paul's action at that conference could be said to have been taken in order that the truth of the gospel might *remain* with them; since that action was taken for the benefit of Gentile converts generally, not only those who had already been won but also those who might be won afterwards. Moreover, the Greek words may possibly be translated, "in order that the truth of the gospel might remain *for you*" or "unto you," rather than "with you." The phrase does not prove indeed that the Galatian churches had not been founded before the conference, but it also does not prove that they *had* been founded then. It sheds no clear light, one way or the other, either upon the question of the destination of the Epistle (to North or South Galatia) or upon the question of the identification of the conference (with the famine visit of Acts 11:30; 12:25 or with the Apostolic Council of Acts 15:1-29). Those questions will have to be decided, if they can be decided at all, on the basis of other evidence.

XIV. PAUL'S COMMISSION AND ITS IMPORTANCE TO US

"But from those who were reputed to be something—of whatever sort they were, it makes no difference to me; God does not accept the countenance of a man; for to me those who were of repute added nothing, but, on the contrary, when they saw that I had been entrusted with the gospel of the uncircumcision just as Peter with that of the circumcision (for He who had worked for Peter unto the apostleship of the circumcision had worked also for me unto the Gentiles), and when they recognized the grace that had been given me, James and Cephas and John, those who were reputed to be pillars, gave to me and Barnabas the right hand of fellowship, that we should go unto the Gentiles, and they unto the circumcision—only, that we should remember the poor, which very thing also I was zealous to do" (Gal. 2:6-10, in a literal translation).

Another Broken Sentence

In the immediately preceding verses, which were treated in last month's issue of *Christianity Today,* Paul has spoken of the Judaizers and of his refusal to yield to them regarding the test case of Titus. Those verses constitute in some sort a digression; and the apostle now returns with verse 6 to the point at which he has broken off. He has told us in verse 2 that he laid his Gospel before the leaders of the Jerusalem Church. Now he tells us what they said to him in reply. With the words "from those who were reputed to be something," contrasting as these words do the leaders of the Church with the Judaizers of whom he has just spoken, the Apostle takes up the interrupted thread of his narrative.

We observed last month that verses 4 and 5, in the opinion of many expositors, constitute an "anacoluthon"—that is, Paul begins a sentence which he breaks off without completing it in any grammatical way. There, however, the anacoluthon is of such an unusual kind, if it really does exist, that many scholars have sought to avoid it by joining the verses to the preceding sentence.

In our passage, on the other hand, there is an anacoluthon which is altogether natural and easy. Paul was intending, when he began the sentence, to say, "From those who were reputed to be something I received nothing"; but after the words, "from those who were reputed to be something," several explanatory clauses intervene; the sentence is broken off; and Paul expresses in a different form the thought which he had in his mind. Instead of saying, as he had at first intended to say, "From those who were reputed to be something I received nothing," he expresses exactly the same thought by saying, "Those who were reputed to be something added nothing to me."

The Main Point

The only question is whether the word which we have translated provisionally by the conjunction "for" in the last clause of verse 6 really means "for" or is merely resumptive of the broken thread of the sentence.

If it means "for," it gives a reason for the words, "of whatever sort they were it makes no difference to me," or for the words, "God does not receive the countenance of a man." Paul would thus mean to say: "Whatever advantages the Jerusalem leaders possess, it makes no difference to me; for to me at least (whatever others may have received from them) they added nothing, since my gospel had already been given me by Christ." Or else, he would mean: "God does not accept the countenance of a man; for this general principle is illustrated in the present case by the fact that I, who had so little advantages compared with those of the Jerusalem leaders, needed to receive nothing from them."

If either of these two interpretations be right, the whole weighty series of clauses beginning with the word "for" in the last clause of verse 6 and extending to the end of verse 10 is introduced in support of a parenthetical assertion. But what is thus introduced in support of the parenthetical assertion is also the main point of the whole passage, so that in content, though not in form, Paul has completed what he started out to say, and any further grammatical completion of the sentence would have been pedantic and unnecessary.

However, the word which we have provisionally translated "for" is also sometimes used in Greek merely to resume the broken thread of a sentence, as we in English use the words, "I say," or the like. If this be the use of the word here, then the passage is to be translated: "But from those who were reputed to be something—of whatever sort they were, it makes no difference to me; God does not accept the countenance of a man—to me, I say, those who were of repute added nothing. . . ."

Fortunately it does not make much difference which meaning is to be attributed to the word; it does not make much difference whether it introduces a reason for what stands in the parenthesis or resumes the thread of the sentence after the parenthesis is completed. In either case, the sentence is grammatically incomplete, but in either case Paul fully completes the expression of the thought that he had in mind when he began.

Former Privileges and Present Authority

So much for the general grammatical structure of the sentence. When we come now to the details, we can pass over without further comment the phrases, "those who were reputed to be something" and "those who were reputed to be pillars." Those phrases were sufficiently dealt with in the December issue of *Christianity Today*.[1] They do not, as we there observed, indicate indignation against the original apostles, but only indignation against the Judaizers who had falsely appealed to the original apostles against Paul.

At the beginning of the parenthesis in verse 6, there is serious question about the meaning of one word. The word which we have translated by the suffix "-ever" in the phrase "of what*ever* sort they were"—thus regarding it merely as imparting a somewhat more indefinite tone to the "of what sort"—may also mean "formerly" or "once upon a time." If the meaning "formerly" or "once upon a time" is to be attributed to the word here, then the clause means: "Of what sort they *formerly* were makes no difference to me"; and we have a clear allusion to the advantages which James and the original apostles possessed during the earthly ministry of Jesus, when the apostles were intimate disciples of Jesus, and when James, though not a disciple, was bound to the Lord by close human ties. No doubt the Judaizers had emphasized those former advantages of the Jerusalem leaders. "Paul," they had no doubt said, "is an upstart and a newcomer, whereas Peter and the others have long been bound to Jesus in the closest possible way." In opposition to that argument, Paul would be saying (if the word in question does mean "formerly" here): "Of what sort the Jerusalem pillars were formerly—during the earthly ministry of Jesus—makes no difference to me."

Certainly that interpretation of the word yields an excellent sense, and it may be correct. But it is quite possible also that the other interpretation is right, and that the word merely makes the "of what sort" a little more indefinite.

Even, however, if this latter interpretation be adopted, even if the word be taken to mean "-ever" and not "formerly,"

---
[1] See xii. Paul at Jerusalem (Editor's Note).

there is still probably an allusion, though in this case not so definite an allusion, to the advantages which the original apostles and James the brother of the Lord enjoyed during the earthly ministry of Jesus. Even if Paul says merely: "Of whatever sort James and Peter and John were, it makes no difference to me," still he is alluding to advantages which those three men enjoyed in the opinion of the Judaizers, and prominent among such advantages was no doubt the former close association of those men with Jesus when He was on earth.

Man's Person and God's Grace

In the next clause, Paul indicates the underlying reason why it made no difference to him how great the Jerusalem apostles were. The reason was that God had already given him all the authority that he could in any case have received from them; God does not, in the disposal of His favor, regard the outward advantages of this man or that; His grace runs counter to all human expectations; and so He had given to Paul, the enemy, a commission which made him independent even of what James or Peter or John could give.

The expression, "to accept the countenance of," which occurs in this clause, is formed in imitation of a phrase of the Hebrew Bible meaning "to lift up the countenance of." In the New Testament, it is used in a distinctly unfavorable way, meaning "to look upon the outward advantages of," "to show partiality because of the high position of the one with whom one is dealing." "No such partiality," says Paul, "is to be attributed to God; high worldly position means nothing to Him; He puts down the mighty from their seats and exalts them of low degree; and so He bestowed His favor upon me, the persecutor, as much as upon those whom all in the Church regarded highly as the original friends of Jesus."

Paul does not mean that the long association of the original apostles with Jesus was a matter of no importance; on the contrary, he regarded it no doubt as a blessed privilege. But what he does mean is that the Judaizers were wrong in thinking that such privileges of the original apostles set limits to the divine grace. "God's ways are not man's ways," Paul means to say. "To human eyes it might have seemed as though the original apostles alone could be true apostles of Jesus Christ. They had been with Jesus when He was on earth; they were looked up to—and rightly—in the Church. But God's grace broke through all such human calculations. The Lord Jesus appeared to me after apparently the series of the appearances had been closed; I, the persecutor and the enemy, was made to be an apostle equal to the apostles whom all in the Church revered."

A Possible Misunderstanding

We observe here again, as we have observed before, that Paul's appeal to the pillars of the Jerusalem Church was capable of being misunderstood. When a man appeals to another for endorsement, the natural inference might seem to be that he is appealing to a higher instance, to the source from which he regards his authority as being derived. Was not Paul confessing, then, by his appeal to the original apostles, that his authority was derived from them; was he not saying to the Judaizers, in effect: "You say that I am not an apostle; well, I *am* an apostle because the pillars of the Jerusalem Church sent me out; they constitute surely the highest authority, and if *they* commissioned me, my commission is valid indeed"?

Such an understanding of the appeal to the Jerusalem leaders, plausible though it might seem at first sight, is exactly what Paul is most concerned to deny. His concern to deny it will explain a number of the peculiarities of Gal. 2:1-10, and will refute many of the false inferences that have been drawn from those peculiarities.

It will explain, for example, as we have already observed, the use of the peculiar expressions, "those who were of repute," "those who were reputed to be something," "those who were reputed to be pillars," as referring to James and Peter and John. By these expressions Paul does not mean to say that these men were not really *"something,"* were not *really* "pillars," but were only reputed to be such. On the contrary, he shows in the plainest possible way, by his references to them elsewhere (and indeed, for that matter, in this very passage), that he recognized them as true witnesses of the risen Christ and as men who had a high commission in the Church. What he does mean is that it was not their real importance, but only the importance attributed to them by the Judaizers, that caused him to appeal to them in this particular connection. If he had appealed to their real importance, that would have meant that he had received his authority from them; it would have been equivalent to saying: "Accept me as an apostle because James and Cephas and John were so great as to be able to transmit authority to me."

For exactly the same reason, Paul says, in the passage with which we are now dealing: "Of whatever sort they were, it makes no difference to me." Taken out of the context, these words might seem to betoken an unbrotherly indifference, on the part of Paul, to those who had been apostles before him; but in the context they indicate nothing of the kind.

Paul and the Original Apostles

From many points of view, it did make a very great difference to Paul what the original apostles were; it made a great difference to him, for example, that they were true witnesses of the risen Christ, and in I Cor. 15:3-8 he tells us that he appealed to their witness in his basic teaching in the churches. But from the particular point of view which is determinative in this particular passage in Galatians, it made no difference. Here it was not a question of factual detail about the life of Jesus on earth, nor of additional testimony to the resurrection which would impress those who had not yet been won to Christ. In such matters Paul undoubtedly received much from the original apostles, who had lived so long with Jesus on earth. But here it is a question of Paul's apostolic authority—not whence he received this piece of information or that regarding Jesus, but whence he received his commission as an apostle. With regard to that question, he did not need to appeal to the original apostles or to any man; he did not need to say: "I am an apostle because James and Cephas and John were so great as to be worthy channels through which my apostleship could be transmitted to me." In fact, that is just what he is anxious *not* to say.

What he is anxious here to say is that the greatness of these men had nothing whatever to do with the matter in hand; his apostleship did not come to him through any man, but directly from Christ; and so no man's greatness—not even the greatness of the original apostles of Jesus — had anything whatever to do with its invalidation. He appeals, therefore, to the original apostles not because of their real greatness—which he did not at all deny—but because of the greatness that was attributed to them by the Judaizers. The Judaizers had appealed to them in a falsely exclusive way, as though they were the only ones who had a right to speak. "Well," says Paul, "let the Judaizers be refuted out of the mouths of the men to whom they themselves have appealed. James and Cephas and John did not give me a commission at the Jerusalem conference. On the contrary, they recognized the fact that I had already been commissioned in complete independence of them; they did not say: 'You are worthy, Paul, and therefore we send you out henceforth to preach'; but they said: 'God has already bestowed His grace upon you; you are already preaching the same gospel as that which we preach, and you have received that gospel in the same way, directly from the Lord Jesus Christ; go forward in your sphere as we go forward in ours, that Christ may be preached unto every creature.' "

Why Paul Contended

Was Paul engaging in an unworthy contention when he insisted so strenuously upon his complete independence; was he animated by unworthy jealousy when he guarded so carefully, in our passage, against any thought that it was the real greatness of the original apostles to which he was obliged to appeal as though his commission came in slightest measure from them?

The answer is, most emphatically, "No." Paul was not contending for himself when he contended for his apostolic independence; he was contending for Christ's little ones of all ages, and for the countless multitudes who have received the gospel through his written and spoken words. He was contending—in ultimate import—for the right of the eighth chapter of Romans, and all the other glorious chapters of the Pauline Epistles, to stand in Holy Scripture; he was contending for the wonderful symmetry and completeness of God's Word. Unless the Epistles of Paul be truly apostolic, they should be excluded from the Bible; and if they were excluded, what a sadly mutilated Bible we should have!

No, Paul was not contending for himself when he contended for his apostolic independence, but he was contending for the One who gave him his apostleship, and for the Church whom that One purchased by His precious blood.

The claim of Paul to apostolic independence, so zealously guarded in the Epistle to the Galatians, does, it is true, place before us a sharp alternative. If the claim was justified, then Paul is to be received today, as always, with the love and gratitude of the Church; but if the claim was not justified, then he deserves much of the opprobrium which has been heaped upon him by an unbelieving world.

Attempts are sometimes made to evade the issue. Attempts are sometimes made to find good in Paul and yet reject his apostolic claims.

We need not wonder that those attempts are made. Similar attempts are made in the case of a greater One, in the case of the Lord Jesus Himself. Jesus came forward with stupendous claims. Men reject those claims today, and yet seek to retain Jesus as the moral ideal of the race. They will not take Him as their Lord and their God; yet they are pleased to admire Him as the leader of mankind into a higher life.

But all such attempts to avoid the issue are vain. In reality, Jesus is everything or nothing. He is either God come in the flesh, as He claimed to be, or else He is unworthy of the admiration of men. Is it really sufficient to give Him the polite admiration that the Church is graciously bestowing upon Him today? "Let the dead bury their dead," He said to a half-hearted disciple when He was on earth. His claims are equally stupendous today. Reject His claims, and you make Him unworthy even of that measure of devotion which He is receiving from modern men.

A somewhat similar alternative faces us when we consider Paul. He too advanced stupendous claims. His claims were, indeed, infinitely less than the claims of Jesus; he certainly never presented himself as God; he never presented himself as a supernatural person. But though he did not present himself as a supernatural person, he did present himself as one who had a supernatural commission.

Men have tried to evade the issue presented by such a claim. They have tried to push the claim into the background in the account which they give of the life of Paul. They have made excuses for the apostolic consciousness of Paul as they have made excuses for the Messianic consciousness of Jesus; they have tried to show that it was psychologically necessary in that age, that it was the temporary form in which Paul expressed an abiding experience. They have tried to admire Paul the man, after they have ceased to believe that he was, in the sense in which he meant the word, an apostle of Jesus Christ.

But all such efforts are vain. These "Liberal" historians, with their polite excuses for Paul, are farther perhaps from the truth about him than are the radicals who, attending to his stupendous claims, abhor him and all his works. Paul refuses to be placed in the mould in which men try to place him today. Unless his commission was supernatural in the high sense in which he represented it as being, unless it was totally different in kind from the commission of ordinary Christians or the greatest of the saints of the historic Church or the greatest of religious geniuses, then he was a mere visionary and enthusiast, and all his defence against his detractors in Galatia and elsewhere was but the work of an overwrought and irascible man. But if the Lord Jesus really appeared to him on the road to Damascus and made him, not by any human agency but in very presence, an apostle instead of an enemy, then his defence of his apostleship was defence not of himself but of his Lord, and then, too, his Epistles are part of God"s holy Word, not one whit inferior in authority to the words which Jesus spoke when He was on earth.

XV. "THE APOSTOLIC DECREE"

"But from those who were reputed to be something—of whatever sort they were, it makes no difference to me; God does not accept the countenance of a man; for to me those who were of repute added nothing, but, on the contrary, when they saw that I had been entrusted with the gospel of the uncircumcision just as Peter with that of the circumcision (for He who had worked for Peter unto the apostleship of the circumcision had worked also for me unto the Gentiles), and when they recognized the grace that had been given me, James and Cephas and John, those who were reputed to be pillars, gave to me and Barnabas the right hand of fellowship, that we should go unto the Gentiles, and they unto the circumcision—only, that we should remember the poor, which very thing also I was zealous to do" (Gal. 2:6-10, in a literal translation).

No Addition to Paul's Gospel

Last month we treated the beginning of this momentous sentence in which Paul tells of the result of the Jerusalem conference, and we showed what the structure of the sentence is. Paul began the sentence as though it were to be in the form, "From those who were reputed to be something I received nothing"; but then, after the intervention of several very weighty parenthetical clauses, he concludes it in the form, "To me those who were of repute added nothing."

We must now consider this latter utterance, which, in the course of modern criticism, has been one of the most discussed utterances in the whole of the New Testament.

The meaning of the word which we have translated "added" is fixed by the preceding context. Paul says in verse 2: "I laid before them the gospel which I am preaching among the Gentiles." The word translated "added" here in verse 6 is in the Greek exactly the same word as the word translated "laid before" in verse 2, except that here in verse 6 it has prefixed to it a preposition meaning "in addition." What Paul is saying, then, is this: "I laid my gospel before them; and they laid nothing before me in addition. They had nothing to add to my gospel, but recognized it as true and complete and as having been given to me by God."

Thus what Paul is denying in verse 6 is that the pillars of the Jerusalem Church made any additions to his gospel; and that is all that he is denying. A clear recognition of that fact would have saved a vast amount of error in the modern study of the New Testament.

Acts and Galatians

Failing to recognize that fact, or failing to understand its implications, many modern critics of the New Testament have found in Paul's words, "They added nothing to me," in Gal. 2:6, a contradiction between the Pauline Epistles and the Book of Acts.

The Book of Acts, these critics insist, in the account which it gives of this meeting between Paul and the Jerusalem Church, says that the Jerusalem leaders did "add" something very important — namely, "the Apostolic Decree" of Acts 15:20, 23-29; 21:25. The Book of Acts, according to these critics, says that the Jerusalem Church, while not requiring the Gentile converts to be circumcised and to keep the whole of the ceremonial law, did require them to keep a part of the ceremonial law; it did require them not only to refrain from the sin of fornication, but also to refrain from "things offered to idols and from blood and from things strangled" (Acts 15:29). Thus, according to the Book of Acts, say these critics, a compromise was effected at the Jerusalem conference; circumcision was not required—in that Paul's position was endorsed—but, on the other hand, Paul's teaching was modified to the extent that certain portions, at least, of the ceremonial law were imposed upon the Gentile converts. Could there be, these critics ask, any clearer example of an addition to Paul's teaching? Paul said, "Believe in Christ and you do not need to keep the ceremonial law"; the Jerusalem Church said, "Believe in Christ and, while you do not need to keep all of the ceremonial law, you do need to keep certain particularly necessary parts of it."

A Critical Lever

In Galatians, say these critics, any such compromise is entirely excluded; in Galatians, Paul says of the Jerusalem leaders, "They added nothing to me." In Acts, on the other hand, say these critics, Paul is represented as submitting tamely to a compromise, which certainly does involve a modification of, or addition to, his gospel. Thus Acts is found by these critics to be in conflict with Galatians. But if so, Acts must be wrong; since scholars of all shades of opinion recognize Galatians as being a genuine epistle written by an eyewitness and therefore true. But if Acts is wrong at this point, where it can be tested by comparison with a recognized authority, then—so the argument runs—it is presumably wrong elsewhere as well, and the whole account which it gives of the apostolic Church is discredited. But the Third Gospel evidently was written by the same author as the author of Acts; therefore, if Acts is discredited, so is the Third Gospel; and since the Third Gospel gives essentially the same account of the life of Christ as do the First and Second Gospels, their account also is discredited; and thus the entire New Testament account of the events at the basis of the Christian Church is shown to be unhistorical.

Such is the reasoning when it is reduced to its simplest terms. Of course, many other considerations are adduced against the New Testament books; but such is the importance of these words, "They added nothing," in the whole discussion that it may be said with a rather high degree of truth that it was at this point that modern negative criticism of the New Testament applied its lever to throw the entire edifice of historic Christianity to the ground.

But is the lever rightly applied? Is the Book of Acts really in contradiction with the Epistle to the Galatians at this point?

There are three ways in which that question may be answered in the negative—three ways in which Acts and Galatians may be shown to be in harmony with respect to the Apostolic Decree.

Galatians Before the Council?

In the first place, it may be held that the Epistle to the Galatians was written before the Apostolic Council, according to the hypothesis which was discussed in the November, 1931, number of *Christianity Today*,[1] and that the meeting with the Jerusalem leaders which Paul describes in Gal. 2:1-10 was entirely different from, and earlier than, the "Apostolic-Council" meeting of Acts 15:1-29. Obviously if the Epistle to the Galatians was written before the Apostolic Council, Paul could not in Galatians mention a decree which the Council *afterwards* passed; and the silence of Galatians about the Decree would show only that when Galatians was written the Decree had not *yet* been passed; it would not show that the Decree was not afterwards passed, and passed exactly in the way which the Book of Acts describes.

Something is to be said for this way out of the difficulty; it is followed by certain noteworthy modern scholars, and it may possibly be correct. If it were the only way to avoid admitting a contradiction between Acts and Galatians, then we should be thoroughly justified, in accordance with scientific historical method, in adopting it, because there is a great weight of independent evidence to show that Acts was written by a companion of Paul who could not have been mistaken about so central a matter as the Apostolic Council. To treat that weight of independent evidence as though it did not exist, just because, on the basis of one of several possible ways of interpreting Gal. 2:1-10, Acts is in contradiction with Paul is not merely contrary to the Christian Faith, but is contrary to the sound scientific methods of study which are constantly employed in other fields of historical research.

The Text of the Decree

The second possible way of showing Gal. 2:6 to be in harmony with Acts 15:29 is to adopt the reading of the so-called "Western text" at Acts 15:20, 29; 21:25. The text or wording of the Book of Acts can be shown to have been handed down in the Church at an early time—say, in the second

---
[1] See xi. Harmony of Acts and Galatians (Editor's Note).

century—in two different forms. One was the form, called by modern scholars the "Neutral text," which has been preserved for us in our two earliest and best New Testament manuscripts, the Codex Vaticanus and the Codex Sinaiticus, together with a number of other less important documents. The other was the form, called by modern scholars the "Western text," which has been preserved for us especially in one Greek manuscript, the Codex Bezae, and, with varying degrees of clearness, in certain remnants of the "Old Latin" translation of the Book of Acts and in certain quotations from the Book of Acts in early Christian writers.

Now the Western text at Acts 15:20, 29; 21:25 omits the word meaning "what is strangled" or (as it appears in 15:29) "things strangled." If the Western text is right in this omission, then what the Gentile converts were told to refrain from, according to the Book of Acts, was "things offered to idols [or "pollutions of idols," as it is in Acts 15:20], blood and fornication." If this short text, without "what is strangled," is correct, what is the meaning of the Decree? The answer to that question depends largely upon the meaning of the word "blood." "Blood," as a thing to be refrained from, may mean one of two things: (1) it may mean the *shedding* of blood, or murder; or (2) it may mean the *eating* of blood, or disobedience to the Mosaic food-law which forbids the eating of meat with the blood in it.

This second meaning seems to be fixed for the word "blood" if the word meaning "what is strangled" is included in the Decree as it is included by the Neutral text; or, at least, if "what is strangled" is included in the text, then, whatever be the meaning of "blood," the Decree does contain a direction about foods, since a prohibition of "what is strangled" can only mean a prohibition of the eating of what is strangled.

If, however, the word translated "what is strangled" be omitted, then "blood" may mean the shedding of blood or murder, and the three things prohibited in the Decree may be simply the three deadly sins; idolatry ("things offered to idols" or "pollutions of idols"), murder ("blood") and fornication. But if the ceremonial element was thus absent from the Decree, the Decree did not constitute any addition to

Paul's gospel, since Paul of course had told his converts as clearly as anyone else had done that they must refrain from these three deadly sins. Indeed, the negative part of the Decree, like the positive part, would be a way of rebuking the Judaizers and of agreeing with Paul. "You have been told by the Judaizers," the Jerusalem Church would be saying to the Gentile converts, "that you must be circumcised and must keep the ceremonial law; but, as a matter of fact, all the things that you need to refrain from are sins like idolatry, murder and fornication." According to this view, the prohibition of idolatry, murder and fornication would be only a particularly forcible way of saying that the abstinence from other things which was insisted upon by the Judaizers was *not* required.

But the Western text of the Book of Acts, upon which this solution of the problem is based, is usually incorrect, and in all probability it is incorrect here. A few noteworthy modern scholars have, indeed, adopted the Western text of the Decree, and the decision with regard to it is not perfectly easy; but on the whole the solution which it provides for the problem of Acts and Galatians is to be regarded as inferior to either of the other two.

The Best Solution

On the whole, the best solution is the one which we must now consider—namely, the one which admits that Gal. 2:1-10 and Acts 15:1-29 refer to the same visit of Paul to Jerusalem and that the Neutral text of the Decree is correct, but insists that the Decree, rightly interpreted, did not constitute an addition to Paul's gospel and so did not need to be mentioned by Paul at Gal. 2:6.

What was the real meaning of the Apostolic Decree according to the Book of Acts? Was it a part of the gospel, or was it something entirely different; were its prohibitions something to be added to faith in Christ as among the conditions of salvation, or was their purpose of entirely different kind?

The answer to this question, and the key to the whole problem, is probably to be found in Acts 15:21. In that verse,

James the brother of the Lord, immediately after advocating the Decree with its four prohibitions, goes on to say: "For Moses from ancient generations has in the several cities those who proclaim him, being read in the synagogues every Sabbath."

Various interpretations, indeed, have been proposed for this much discussed verse. But surely the most natural interpretation is that which makes James here give a reason for the four prohibitions in the Decree by pointing to the fact that there are many Jews in the cities to which the Decree is to be sent. "There are many Jews in those cities," says James; "they hear the law of Moses read in the synagogues every Sabbath; from the reading of the law they come to abhor especially certain things in Gentile life; and in order to win them the Gentile disciples of Jesus ought to refrain from those things."

So interpreted, the observance of the four prohibitions in the Decree was to be regarded not as necessary to salvation but only as a means of avoiding offence in certain mixed communities where there were many Jews. Not being necessary to salvation, it was not an addition to Paul's gospel; and not being an addition to Paul's gospel, it is not excluded by Paul's words in Gal. 2:6. "I laid my gospel before them," says Paul, "and they made no addition to it." These words of Paul remain true even if the Apostolic Decree was issued by the Jerusalem Church.

Was there a Compromise?

But could Paul ever have agreed to such a measure, even if it was intended in the way that we have just indicated? Could he have agreed to such a method of avoiding offence to the Jews?

About one hundred years ago, the scholars of the so-called "Tübingen school" were ready with their answer. "Of course Paul could never have done any such thing," they said. "Paul was no compromiser or time-server; he would have insisted on full Gentile freedom without any concessions to Jewish narrowness; and when the Book of Acts represents him as agreeing to such concessions the Book of Acts clearly is wrong."

But the general trend, at least, of subsequent scholarship is somewhat away from such a conclusion as that. The plain fact is that there are in the Pauline Epistles themselves, the very authorities to which the Tübingen scholars appealed, elements which show that on occasion Paul was perfectly ready to advocate exactly the kind of concession to Jewish feeling that is advocated in the Apostolic Decree. In I Cor. 9:20, for example, Paul says that he became to the Jews as a Jew, in order that he might gain Jews, and that he became to those who were under the law as under the law (though not being himself under the law), in order that he might gain those who were under the law. It would be difficult to imagine a more complete agreement than that passage contains with the purpose of the Apostolic Decree as it is explained in James' words in Acts 15:21.

The truth is that where no principle was involved, where it was only his own convenience that was at stake, Paul, the heroic and uncompromising defender of Christian liberty, was the most concessive of men. One thing is clear—he would never have agreed to the Apostolic Decree if it had been, as it is often represented as being, a "compromise." Paul was no compromiser either at Jerusalem or anywhere else. If the prohibitions of the Apostolic Decree had been intended as being necessary to salvation, they would have been an addition to Paul's gospel, and Paul would never have agreed to them in the world. But if they were merely an effort to win the Jews in mixed communities to the Lord Jesus Christ by avoiding unnecessary offence under certain special circumstances, they were quite in accord with Paul's practice, and Paul could well have accepted them in the sense in which they were meant

The Limited Address

It should be observed that this Decree, according to Acts 15:23, was not addressed to Gentile converts everywhere, but only to those in "Antioch and Syria and Cilicia." It is true, that Paul did, according to Acts 16:4, give the Decree over to converts in certain cities not in Syria or Cilicia but in the southern part of the Roman province of Galatia; and it is true that in Acts 21:25 James, in his reference to the Decree, does not mention the geographical limitations of the address. But these observations cannot obscure the significance of the fact that the Decree was formally addressed by the Jerusalem Church only to the converts in Antioch and Syria and Cilicia. It was not a piece of formal legislation for all Gentile converts everywhere—if it had been, Paul might well have been less ready to accept it—but it was a direction given, in view of certain special conditions, to certain mixed communities in Antioch and Syria and Cilicia, where, presumably, there were many Jews and where the congregations were probably in a relation to the Jerusalem Church much closer than that which prevailed in distinctly Pauline churches.

The outstanding fact, however, about the Apostolic Decree which shows it to be in harmony with Galatians is not the limitation of its address but the fact that it was not an addition to Paul's gospel; it was not an addition to what he had said about the way of salvation. Paul had said: "Believe on the Lord Jesus Christ, and thou shalt be saved quite apart from the works of the law." The Jerusalem leaders said: "That is entirely right; we have nothing to add to it; salvation is, as Paul has told you, by faith alone and not by faith *and* works."

This great result of the Jerusalem conference was not invalidated at all by the solution which the Apostolic Decree found for the problems of certain mixed communities, where there were many Jews whom both Paul and the original apostles desired to see won for Christ.

The foregoing treatment of the Apostolic Decree must be regarded only as a summary. For a fuller treatment the reader is referred to the book by the same writer, *The Origin of Paul's Religion*, where also the entire comparison between the Book of Acts and the first two chapters of Galatians is treated in greater detail than in the present series of expository studies.

Next month we shall turn to easier matters, and shall be able to make much more rapid progress.

XVI. THE RIGHT HAND OF FELLOWSHIP

"But from those who were reputed to be something—of whatever sort they were, it makes no difference to me: God does not accept the countenance of a man; for to me those who were of repute added nothing, but, on the contrary, when they saw that I had been entrusted with the gospel of the uncircumcision just as Peter with that of the circumcision (for He who had worked for Peter unto the apostleship of the circumcision had worked also for me unto the Gentiles), and when they recognized the grace that had been given me, James and Cephas and John, those who were reputed to be pillars, gave to me and Barnabas the right hand of fellowship, that we should go unto the Gentiles, and they unto the circumcision—only, that we should remember the poor, which very thing also I was zealous to do" (Gal. 2:6-10, in a literal translation).

One Gospel Given to Both

In the last number of *Christianity Today,* we showed that when Paul says in Gal. 2:6, "For to me those who were of repute added nothing," he is not excluding such an action as the issuance of the so-called "Apostolic Decree" with its four prohibitions as recorded in Acts 15:20, 29; 21:25. That discussion involved the whole difficult question of the relation between Acts and Galatians, and of the identification, with one or another of the visits recorded in Acts, of the visit to Jerusalem which Paul records in Gal. 2:1-10.

This month we turn to somewhat easier matters and can make more rapid progress.

"But on the contrary," Paul continues (after the momentous words discussed last month), "when they saw that I had been entrusted with the gospel of the uncircumcision just as Peter with that of the circumcision. . . ."

It is very important here to observe the tense of the verb "had been entrusted." What the leaders of the Jerusalem Church recognized was not that Paul was then being entrusted with the gospel of the uncircumcision, not that he was worthy to be entrusted with it by their instrumentality, but that he had *already* been entrusted with it, in complete independence of them, by God.

By speaking of "the gospel of the uncircumcision" and (by implication) of "the gospel of the circumcision," Paul does not mean to say that there were two different gospels, one to be preached to Gentiles and the other to be preached to Jews. Such an interpretation is excluded by the "right hand of fellowship" which, according to verse 9, the Jerusalem pillars gave to Paul and Barnabas; it is also expressly excluded by I Cor. 15:11, where Paul says, "Whether it were I or they, so we preached and so ye believed." What Paul means, and what the Jerusalem leaders recognized, is that it was the same gospel that was everywhere proclaimed, but that to Paul had been entrusted the special duty of preaching that gospel to Gentiles, and to them the special duty of preaching it to Jews.

How did they "see" that Paul had been entrusted with the gospel? It is natural to think in this connection of the glorious results of Paul's preaching of the gospel out in the Gentile world; and the Book of Acts tells us that Paul and Barnabas recounted in Jerusalem "how great things God had done with them" (Acts 15:4) and "how great signs and wonders God had done through them among the Gentiles" (Acts 15:12). No doubt that was one kind of evidence that convinced the Jerusalem leaders that Paul had really been entrusted with the gospel. But there is no reason why we should not also include among the evidence that convinced them the immediate impression that they received when Paul told them what his gospel was.

One God Working for Both

At any rate, we are told in the next verse that at least one reason why they were convinced that Paul had been entrusted with the gospel was that God had worked for him as He had worked for Peter. "For He who had worked for Peter unto the apostleship of the circumcision had worked also for me unto the Gentiles." It is not very important to ask whether the working of God here referred to was the working in the hearts and lives of the hearers, giving effect to the gospel that

Paul preached, or the working of God in Paul himself, making him powerful in the preaching of the gospel. Probably both kinds of working are included. At any rate, the Jerusalem leaders saw that it was the same gospel that had been preached by Peter and by Paul, because the same God had worked for both.

"And when they had recognized the grace that had been given me. . . ." The Jerusalem leaders saw that the divine favor rested upon Paul. No doubt they saw it partly through the marvellous effects of his preaching in the Gentile world. But here, at least, even if we should not do so in verse 7, we ought probably to think also, and perhaps primarily, of the immediate impression which the Jerusalem leaders received from Paul. They were convinced, by their immediate contact with him there in Jerusalem, that the divine favor had been bestowed upon him to make him what they so plainly saw him to be.

"James and Cephas and John, those who were reputed to be pillars, gave to me and Barnabas the right hand of fellowship." James the brother of the Lord is here put first, although he was not one of the Twelve Apostles, because he was the head of the Jerusalem Church and so seems to have presided over its meetings. These men are here called "pillars" by a natural figure of speech which has come, through the influence of this passage, into our common parlance, in which we speak of "pillars of the Church."

The Meaning of "Fellowship"

The pillars of the Jerusalem Church gave to Paul and Barnabas the right hand of fellowship. The word "fellowship" is derived from a word meaning "common"; a man has "fellowship" with another, in accordance with the usage of this word, when he has something in "common" with him. But it is perfectly clear from the context what it was that the Jerusalem leaders had in common with Paul, and what they recognized that they had in common with him when they extended to him and Barnabas the right hand of fellowship. They had the gospel in common with him. By extending to him the right hand of fellowship, they indicated that they and he were both engaged in preaching the same gospel of the same Lord.

The word "fellowship" is a fine, rich word; it is the same word as that which appears in the "Apostolic Benediction" at the end of the Second Epistle to the Corinthians, where Paul writes of the "communion" of the Holy Ghost. There is no reason whatever for weakening its meaning in our passage in Galatians.

Much mischief has been wrought in the interpretation of the Bible by making the interpretation of what is clear fit a doubtful interpretation of what is obscure. So in the Epistle to the Galatians some men have read a great deal between the lines. They have interpreted the puzzling phrases, "those who were reputed to be something," "those who were reputed to be pillars," to mean that Paul was in permanently strained relations with the original apostles; and then, on the basis of that very doubtful view, they have proceeded to explain "the right hand of fellowship" to mean merely that the Jerusalem leaders on the one hand and Paul on the other made a cold agreement to disagree, a cold agreement to keep apart from each other in order that quarreling might be avoided. As a matter of fact, what is abundantly clear about this passage—a passage in some respects obscure—is that the Jerusalem leaders and Paul did *not* make a cold agreement to disagree, but that they gave each other the right hand of fellowship and said thereby that they were all engaged in preaching the same gospel of the Lord Jesus Christ and that neither group of them could do without the other.

The So-Called "Division of Labor"

The pillars of the Jerusalem Church, Paul says, "gave to me and Barnabas the right hand of fellowship, that we should go to the Gentiles and they to the circumcision." In the Greek, there is no verb at all in this purpose clause; it reads merely, "that we to the Gentiles, they to the circumcision." Some verb no doubt has to be inserted in English; but the Greek is more general, and yet more forcible. "We to the Jews, you to the Gentiles"—such was the way in which the Jerusalem leaders summed up the guidance of God in sending out laborers into His harvest in those days.

Grievous errors have often arisen in the modern understanding of this "division of labor." It has been represented as though its purpose were largely negative—to prevent Paul from trespassing upon the field of the original apostles, and to prevent the original apostles from trespassing upon the field of Paul. So the question has been asked by some modern scholars whether the meaning of the division was geographical or ethnological—that is, whether Paul was to preach in Gentile *countries* and the original apostles in the Jewish *country*, Palestine; or whether Paul was to preach to Gentiles, wherever they might be found, even in Palestine, and the original apostles were to preach to Jews wherever they might be found, even in Gentile countries. The suggestion has even been made that Paul understood the division in one way and the original apostles in the other, Paul understanding it geographically and the original apostles ethnologically, so that when Peter came to Antioch he was doing right according to *his* understanding of the arrangement (since there were some Jews at Antioch) but wrong according to Paul's understanding (since Antioch is not in Palestine).

But the very raising of such questions shows a complete misunderstanding of the right hand of fellowship which the Jerusalem leaders gave to Paul. As a matter of fact, the so-called "division of labor" between Paul and the original apostles was not, strictly speaking, a division of labor at all; its purpose was not negative; it was not meant at all as a limitation of the field of one party or of the other; it did not mean that Paul was not to preach to Jews or that Peter was not to preach to Gentiles; it did not mean that Paul was not to preach in Palestine or that Peter was not to preach outside of Palestine. But it meant that so far, according to the plain meaning of God, Paul had been sent predominantly to the Gentiles and the original apostles to the Jews; and that, therefore, unless both Paul and the original apostles continued their work, the cause would suffer. "Neither of us," said the Jerusalem leaders, "can do without the other, you and we are both preaching the same gospel; but we are needed to preach it to the Jews and you and Barnabas are needed to preach it to the Gentiles. It is all Christ's work; and in the future prosecution of the work, among both Jews and Gentiles, both by your instrumentality and by ours, we all have fellowship."

"Remember the Poor"

There was one express exception to the division of labor (if we may call it such) between the Jerusalem leaders and Paul. "We to the Gentiles," says Paul, "they to the circumcision—only, that we should remember the poor." By "the poor" is meant, of course, the poor of the Jerusalem Church. "God has sent you to the Gentiles," said the Jerusalem leaders; "but do not be so exclusively an apostle to the Gentiles as to forget our poor people here in Jerusalem."

It is very important to observe that this exception, introduced by the word "only," is not an exception to the assertion in verse 6, "To me those who were of repute added nothing." If it were an exception to that assertion, then the omission of all mention of the Apostolic Decree would, despite what we said last month, become very strange. If the inculcation of care for the Jerusalem Church was an exception to the general assertion, "They added nothing to me," then surely the inculcation of the four prohibitions of the Apostolic Decree would also seem to be an exception, and Paul would probably have been obliged to mention that exception as much as the other. In other words, if Paul meant to say, "They added nothing to me except that I should remember the Jerusalem poor," then the words, "they added nothing," would probably not be interpreted (as we interpreted them last month) merely as denying an addition to Paul's gospel, but would have to be taken in a much broader sense, as denying any communications addressed by the Jerusalem leaders to Paul; and in that case it would seem strange that Paul does not mention the Apostolic Decree as an exception along with the inculcation of relief for the Jerusalem poor.

As a matter of fact, however, it is quite impossible to take the words, "only, that I should remember the poor" (verse 10), with the words, "they added nothing." Those words lie four verses back (in verse 6); and it is of course as plain as day that what verse 10 is actually to be taken as presenting an exception to is the division of labor which has been mentioned in the immediately preceding verse. "You to the Gentiles, we to the Jews," said the Jerusalem leaders to Paul. "That is the general division of labor which so far seems to have been established by the guidance of God. But there is one matter at least where we hope you will not take the division too strictly even now—to say nothing of any guidance of God which may be given to both of us in the future. There is one matter concerning the Jews in which we need the help of you, the Apostle to the Gentiles, even now. We hope you will not forget our poor of the Jerusalem Church."

Paul took very seriously indeed that call for help. He says here in Galatians, "which very thing also I was zealous to do"; and in I and II Corinthians and Romans it becomes evident that the collection for the Jerusalem poor was very much on his heart.

XVII. CONSEQUENCES VERSUS TRUTH

"But when Cephas came to Antioch, I withstood him to the face, because he was condemned. For before certain men came from James; he ate with the Gentiles; but when they came, he withdrew and separated himself, fearing those who were of the circumcision. And there dissembled together with him also the rest of the Jews; so that even Barnabas was carried away with their dissembling. But when I saw that they were not walking straight according to the truth of the gospel, I said to Cephas before them all. . ." (Gal. 2:11-14a, in a literal translation).

A Vacillating Policy

In the last number of *Christianity Today*, we finished our exposition of Gal. 2:1-10, which passage, it will be remembered, presents the second of Paul's arguments in defence of his apostolic independence. The first argument (in Gal. 1:11-24) was that his conversion was not brought about by human persuasions or teaching but by the immediate act of Christ, and that even after his conversion he had not had the early or extended contact with the original apostles which the Judaizers' notion of his dependence upon them would require. His second argument (in Gal. 2:1-10) was that when he did discuss his gospel fully with the Jerusalem leaders they took his view, not the Judaizers', about the matter and recognized that his gospel was the same gospel of Christ as the gospel which they preached, and that it had already been given to him, without their instrumentality, by divine commission. Now, in Gal. 2:11-21, Paul presents the third and last of his arguments for his apostolic independence. So independent was he, he says, that on one occasion he could even oppose the chief of the original apostles himself.

"But when Cephas came to Antioch," says Paul, "I withstood him to the face, because he was condemned." It is not necessary to ask *by whom* Peter "was condemned"; Paul means that his very act condemned him. When he says that he "was condemned," that is only a more forcible way of saying that he was worthy of condemnation.

Certain Men From James

"For before certain men came from James," says Paul, "he ate with the Gentiles; but when they came, he withdrew and separated himself, fearing those who were of the circumcision." In interpreting the phrase "from James," extreme views should be avoided. The phrase seems to mean more than that these men came from Jerusalem—as it would mean if "James" were merely used intead of "Jerusalem" because James was the head of the Jerusalem Church. But the opposite error is much more serious. It is a great mistake to jump to the conclusion, as some have done, that these men were sent by James with the express purpose of accomplishing what their coming did as a matter of fact temporarily accomplish—namely, the withdrawal of Peter and other Jewish Christians from table-companionship with Gentiles in the Antioch Church. Perhaps all that we can surmise is that these men had stood in some way closer to James than did the generality of the Jerusalem Church. But what their connection with him was, and whether they had any kind of commission from him at all when they went to Antioch—these questions can probably never be answered. It is important in such cases not to read too much between the lines.

We cannot even be perfectly sure that these men are blamed by the Apostle Paul. Their coming to Antioch had an unfortunate effect, but whether they intended it to have that effect is by no means clear.

Separation From The Gentiles

After the coming of these men, Peter "withdrew and separated himself" from the table-companionship in which he had previously engaged with the Gentile members of the Antioch Church. The tense of the verbs may indicate that the process of withdrawal was a gradual one; possibly Peter at first merely made his table companionship with the Gentiles less frequent than it had been before; possibly we are meant to understand that he entered upon a policy of withdrawal rather than that there was any sudden or definite break.

He acted in this manner, Paul says, because he feared "those who were of the circumcision." This latter phrase might be taken as designating "those the starting-point of whose life was circumcision," "the advocates of circumcision"; but here it is perhaps better just to take it as meaning "Jews." Of course, the particular Jews who are meant are the men who came from James. Peter withdrew and separated himself because he feared to allow his table-companionship with Gentiles to continue in the presence of those Jews.

To understand such conduct on the part of Peter, it is necessary to envisage the situation somewhat more clearly than is sometimes done. At that time, the Church had not yet abandoned the work of offering the gospel to the Jewish people as such. The gospel was to be offered, as even Paul intimates (Rom. 1:16), "to the Jew first, and also to the Greek." So at the conference described in Gal. 2:1-10 we need not suppose that Paul asked the Jewish Christians in Jerusalem to cease circumcising their children or to cease attendance upon the Temple. These things were not, indeed, regarded as being necessary to salvation either by the original apostles or by Paul, and the Gentile Christians were expressly exempted from them; but the Jerusalem Christians, for the time at least, continued to observe them. Any final abandonment of them on the part of the whole Church was left to the further guidance of God.

Paul did not, therefore, demand that Peter or other Jewish Christians should relinquish, for the present at least, their Jewish manner of life, especially if (in accordance with Paul's principle of becoming all things to all men, I Cor. 9:19-22) it seemed necessary for the winning of the non-Christian Jews. But a strict Jewish manner of life involved, or was thought to involve, avoidance of table-companionship with Gentiles. If, therefore, Peter had never entered into such table- companionship, it is not altogether clear that Paul at that time would have urged him to do so.

The Order Of Events

At this point, however, a difficulty seems to arise. Was not the very purpose of the four prohibitions of the Apostolic Decree (Acts 15:20, 29; 21:25) to make table-companionship, as well as other kinds of companionship, possible between Gentile Christians and Jewish Christians in mixed churches? Was not the very notion of the Decree that the Gentile Christians were to avoid certain particularly abhorrent things, especially in the sphere of foods, in order to avoid giving offence to their Jewish brethren? Could the difficulty at Antioch, then, ever have arisen if the Apostolic Decree had been passed? Would not all that have been settled if the Decree was only observed?

Such considerations, especially when taken in connection with those mentioned when we were dealing with Gal. 2:1-10, have led some modern scholars to reject the identification of the meeting described in that passage with the Apostolic Council of Acts 15:1-29 and to adopt the identification with the "famine visit" of Acts 11:20; 12:25. The order of events, these scholars think, then becomes perfectly easy to understand. First, the leaders of the Jerusalem Church agreed with Paul in holding, against the Judaizers, that the Gentile Christians did not need to be circumcised, and gave to Paul and Barnabas the right hand of fellowship (Gal. 2:1-10).

But—say the advocates of this view—there were many things that were not settled at that time. It was not contemplated that Jewish Christians should give up their Jewish manner of life. What, then, should be done in mixed churches where Jewish Christians and Gentile Christians lived together? How could the Jewish Christians possibly maintain their Jewish manner of life and at the same time hold companionship, especially table-companionship, with such Gentiles? These questions—so the hypothesis continues—gave rise to the trouble at Antioch. Peter at first solved the problem in the interests of the unity of the Church. He relinquished the strictness of his Jewish manner of life in order to hold table-companionship with his Gentile brethren. But then, fearing those who came from Jerusalem, he went back on his decision and withdrew from such table-companionship. Finally, however, the whole matter was settled—according to the hypothesis which we are now considering—by the Apostolic Council of Acts 15:1-29. That Council solved the problem of mixed churches by decreeing that the Gentile Christians, while not observing the whole ceremonial law, should refrain from certain particular things which would give the most poignant offence to their Jewish fellow citizens.

There is no question but that this reconstruction of the order of events is in some respects very attractive. But there are also serious difficulties about it; and we do not think, in particular, that it is rendered necessary by Gal. 2:11-21. Even if the Apostolic Decree had already been passed before the time dealt with in this passage, still there may have been strict Jews in the Church who thought themselves required to avoid table-companionship with Gentiles even if the Gentiles observed the four prohibitions of the Decree, so that even after the Apostolic Council there was room for such a situation as that which this passage describes.

A Policy Of Concealment

"And," Paul continues, "there dissembled together with him [Peter] also the rest of the Jews, so that even Barnabas was carried away with their dissembling." The Greek word translated "dissembling" in this passage is the word from which our English word "hypocrisy" comes. But it does not necessarily involve anything like such sharp condemnation as the English word does. The English word means "pretending to be better than one really is," while the Greek word means merely "playing a part," "making an incorrect impression," no matter in what particular way or with what particular motive the incorrect impression is made.

What Paul means is that Peter and Barnabas and the other Jewish Christians were concealing their real principles out of fear of those who had come from James. They had seen clearly that in the new era ushered in by the redeeming work of Christ it was God's will that already the strictness of the Mosaic Law (or of the current interpretation of its implications) should be relaxed to permit full fellowship between Jewish Christians and Gentile Christians in mixed churches. They had ordered their lives accordingly. Yet now, in the presence of these men from Jerusalem, they were acting as though their principles were of a different kind. Their present conduct did not correctly express their convictions. To characterize such conduct, Paul uses a word of which there is no exact translation in English. It was certainly not "hypocrisy," and even "dissembling" is too strong.

The Danger Of "Splitting The Church"

Yet, despite such explanations, we can see clearly that the situation was serious enough. What poignancy of sorrow lies behind Paul's words: "Even Barnabas was carried away with their dissembling!" Barnabas, the man who had introduced Paul to the leaders of the Jerusalem Church (Acts 9:27), who had later (Acts 11:25) brought him from Tarsus into that very Gentile work at Antioch to which he was doing so much harm by his present conduct—even Barnabas was carried away by a miserable policy of concealment and compromise!

Moreover, the situation was not only painful but exceedingly delicate and dangerous. Paul had against him not only Barnabas and the entire Jewish Christian part of the Antioch Church, but also the chief of the Jerusalem apostles, the chief of the original Twelve who had been chosen by the Lord

Himself. Surely such a situation demanded the utmost caution; one false move, and the Church would be "split." No doubt such considerations might have been presented to Paul at Antioch, as they are presented to the evangelical minority in the Presbyterian Church of the present day. But Paul did not think much of them. He was not an adherent of the fashionable modern policy of unanimous reports; he did not believe in settling the affairs of the Church in secret committee chambers, and in concealing the underlying differences by pages of verbiage like that produced by the Commission of Fifteen appointed by our General Assembly of 1925. He would have nothing whatever to do with the policy of concealment and compromise. What he did do is presented in sharp, clear fashion in his own words. "But when I saw," he says, "that they were not walking straight according to the truth of the gospel, I said to Cephas *in the presence of all.* . . . " (italics not Paul's, but ours; but we doubt whether Paul would disagree with our use of them).

The Truth Of The Gospel

Why did Paul take such a dangerous step as that, and why do supposedly evangelical leaders refuse to take such steps today? The answer is given by the phrase, "according to the truth of the gospel." Peter's conduct was not in accordance with the gospel. That was enough for Paul. Regardless of consequences, he was obliged to speak out. He withstood Peter to his face; he rebuked him before them all.

The difference between Paul and many ostensibly evangelical leaders in the Presbyterian Church today may be put very briefly. These ostensibly evangelical leaders consider consequences; Paul considered truth.

There is no question which kind of conduct has the blessing of God. Under the present policy of concealment and compromise, evangelicalism is becoming weaker and weaker in the Presbyterian Church and in the other churches of today; under Paul's brave policy of withstanding to the face and of speaking out, the apostolic Church went on to conquer the world.

XVIII. THE POWER OF EXAMPLE

"But when I saw that they were not walking straight according to the truth of the gospel, I said to Cephas before them all: 'If thou being a Jew livest as the Gentiles do and not as do the Jews, how is it that thou art compelling the Gentiles to Judaize?' " (Gal. 2:14, in a literal translation).

How Much Was Addressed to Peter?

In the last article, we discussed the beginning of the incident at Antioch. At first, Peter held table-companionship with the Gentile Christians; but then, fearing the disapprobation of certain men who had come from James, he was withdrawing from such companionship. By such conduct he was concealing his true principles; and he was not acting in accordance with "the truth of the gospel." Paul spoke out boldly in opposition. Putting all consideration of consequences aside, he withstood Peter to his face in the presence of the whole Church.

Today we begin to study what he said to Peter. But where does the speech to Peter end? Some have supposed that it ends with verse 14, so that all that Paul reports of what he said to Peter is the one sentence: "If thou being a Jew livest as the Gentiles do and not as do the Jews, how is it that thou art compelling the Gentiles to Judaize?" In that case, the rest of the second chapter of the Epistle is simply a comment by Paul to the Galatians setting forth the reasons for his attitude at Antioch.

But surely such a view of the passage is unnatural. The brief sentence which we have just quoted from verse 14 is very abrupt if it is all that Paul gives us of the speech which he made to Peter: the reader inevitably expects that more of that speech will be reported; and since the words that follow are very natural on Paul's lips in his address to Peter, it is altogether probable that they are a part of that address. There is no clear break in the discourse until we come to the beginning of Chapter III, where, with the words "O foolish Galatians," Paul seems to mark the point where he turns from the report of what he said to Peter at Antioch to that which he is now saying directly to the Galatian Christians.

No doubt the report of Paul's Antioch speech is not intended to be anything like a verbatim report; it is the substance of what he said that the Apostle is here calling to mind. No doubt also he is thinking, before he gets through the report, more of the present effect of his words upon the Galatian Christians than of their effect upon Peter long ago at Antioch. What he had said to Peter at that time was essentially the same thing as that which he now desires to say to the Galatians. Hence Gal. 2:11-21 forms a transition between the first main division of the Epistle, in which Paul meets the attack upon his independent apostolic authority, and the second main division, in which he defends the content of his gospel. The very heart of Paul's gospel is set forth in the passage with which we begin to deal this month.

What Is Meant by "Live"?

"If thou," says the Apostle in his report of what he said to Peter at Antioch, "livest as the Gentiles do and not as do the Jews, how is it that thou are compelling the Gentiles to Judaize?" What does Paul mean by the word "livest" in this sentence? Some think that the word is used in its high, special sense, to designate that life in communion with God, that life that is life indeed, which the Christian has in Christ. Paul would then be saying to Peter: "If thou hast thy new life, thine eternal life, in the same way as the way in which the Gentiles have it—that is, not by earning it through the works of the law but by receiving it through the free grace of God—how is it that thou art compelling the Gentiles to try to get that true life in an entirely different way from the way in which thou hast got it thyself?" This interpretation may possibly be correct.

Another interpretation, however, is also possible—the interpretation which takes the word "livest" in a more ordinary sense. According to this interpretation, Paul would simply be saying: "If thou being a Jew livest as the Gentiles do—that is, if thou hast taken it as the fixed habit of thy manner of life to relinquish the keeping of the ceremonial law—how is it that thou art compelling the Gentiles to keep that ceremonial law?" At first sight, an objection might seem to arise against this view from the present tense of the verb "livest." Was Peter living at that time as the Gentiles do; was it not just because he was *not* living as the Gentiles do, but rather was living as the Jews do, that he was being blamed by Paul? But the objection is not serious. Paul may mean by the present tense of the verb merely that the fixed principle of Peter's manner of life was to live as the Gentiles do, even though there might be temporary aberrations from that principle as was the case when those men came from James. Peter had lived in a Gentile manner before; and the presumption was that he would live in a Gentile manner again. Why then, Paul would be saying, does he conceal that fixed principle of his life by pretending in the presence of those men from Jerusalem to be a strict Jew?

How Peter Influenced the Gentiles

The question between these two ways of understanding the word "livest" is difficult to decide. In either case, it is fairly clear what Paul means when he says that by withdrawing from his former table-companionship Peter was "compelling" the Gentiles to Judaize. The compulsion referred to was not physical compulsion; and it was not even the compulsion of any definite command or advice. Rather it was the compulsion which Peter was exerting by his example. He had accustomed those Gentile Christians to table-companionship with him. Then he withdrew from them because they did not keep the ceremonial law. Would they not draw the inference that if they were Christians they were Christians only of a second rank? If they wanted to continue the companionship which they had enjoyed with the chief of the original apostles of their Lord, they must apparently do as the Judaizers had told them to do—be circumcised and keep the law of Moses. We can understand how powerful such considerations must have been; they would lend much weight to what the Judaizers had always said.

But if the Gentiles yielded to such considerations, that would mean that they were putting trust in their own works as being necessary to the obtaining of merit with God. And that would mean, according to Paul, that they had fallen from grace and that Christ would profit them nothing.

A Peril to Men's Souls

We shall never understand the situation unless we see that for a Gentile Christian to keep the ceremonial law was a very different thing, according to Paul, from a Jewish Christian's keeping of it. If, indeed, a Jewish Christian's keeping of it meant that the Jewish Christian regarded it as necessary to salvation—necessary in supplement to faith in Christ—then a Jewish Christian's keeping of it would be just as bad, according to Paul, as a Gentile Christian's. But the point is that a Jewish Christian's keeping of it did not necessarily mean that, whereas a Gentile Christian's necessarily did.

A Jewish Christian might keep the ceremonial law on the ground that the gospel was still being offered to the Jewish people as such, and that therefore the time had not yet come when the corporate identity of the people should be broken up. But if a Gentile Christian kept the ceremonial law, then, since that ran counter to all national custom and to all ordinary considerations of policy, it could scarcely mean anything else than that it was regarded as being necessary to salvation—as being necessary in order that a man should belong to the people of God. It could scarcely be regarded otherwise—or, to put the thing more cautiously, it *would* as a matter of fact, under the circumstances that then prevailed, scarcely be regarded otherwise—than as a meritorious work which a man needed to perform in order to win the favor of God. But if it was so regarded, then, according to Paul, it was contrary to the very heart of the gospel of Christ. A man who tries to earn his salvation, or to do anything towards earning it, has, according to Paul, done despite to the free grace of God.

It was into such a deadly error that Peter's conduct was leading the Gentile Christians at Antioch. If Peter had never begun to hold table-companionship with those Gentile Christians, it is not at all certain that Paul would ever have blamed him. Paul did not demand—for the present at least—that the Jewish Christians of Jerusalem should give up their Jewish manner of life. But when Peter had once accustomed the Gentile Christians to hold table-companionship with him, then his withdrawal from such table-companionship would tend to lead them to seek a continuance of their table-companionship with him by keeping the ceremonial law. And that would mean, for them, the adoption of a principle of justification by works and not by faith alone.

XIX. JUSTIFICATION BY FAITH

"We are by nature Jews and not sinners of the Gentiles; but, knowing that a man is not justified by the works of the law but only through faith in Christ Jesus, even we believed in Christ Jesus, in order that we might be justified by faith in Christ and not by the works of the law, because by the works of the law no flesh shall be justified" (Gal. 2:15-16, in a literal translation).

Not Even Jews Were Justified by Works

In last month's issue of *Christianity Today*, we discussed the beginning of Paul's report of the speech which he made to Peter at Antioch. "If thou," Paul had said to Peter, "being a Jew, livest as the Gentiles do and not as do the Jews, how is it that thou art compelling the Gentiles to Judaize?" Peter himself did not on principle keep the ceremonial law; his principles led him to abandon it on occasion. Yet by the force of his example at Antioch he was leading the Gentile Christians to keep it. Such conduct was inconsistent. Surely a Jew, if anyone, would make it the principle of his life to keep the ceremonial law; and if even a Jew abandoned it, certainly it was unreasonable for him to lead the Gentiles to keep it.

This thought is developed further in the passage which we now consider.

"We," Paul said to Peter, "are by nature Jews and not sinners from among the Gentiles. We Jews, if any men, would rely upon the law; unlike the Gentiles, we did not need to acquire whatever benefits the law conferred by abandoning our own people and by uniting voluntarily with the people of Israel; on the contrary, we were Jews *by nature;* we were not 'sinners,' in the old, Jewish sense of the word which divided men into the two classes of 'Jews' and 'sinners' and equated the Gentiles with the latter; we had, from our birth on, whatever righteousness the law could give."

"Yet we gave up all that," Paul continued in his address to Peter, "in order to obtain our salvation in exactly the same way as that in which it was obtained by those despised 'sinners' of the Gentiles." "But, knowing that a man is not justified by the works of the law but only through faith in Christ Jesus, even we believed in Christ Jesus, in order that we might be justified by faith in Christ and not by the works of the law, because by the works of the law no flesh shall be justified."

The Meaning of the Word "Justify"

Here we have the first occurrence in the Epistle to the Galatians of the momentous verb "to justify." Does that verb mean "to make righteous" or "to declare righteous"? At the very root of evangelical Christianity, as over against the Roman Catholic view, is the conviction that the word means not "to make righteous" but "to declare righteous."

The question might seem to be settled (to say nothing of other passages) by Rom. 3:4, where, in a quotation from Ps. 51:4, *God* is said to be "justified" — "in order that Thou mightest be justified in Thy words and mightest prevail when Thou art judged." Obviously God cannot be "made righteous," but He can be "declared righteous" or "recognized as righteous." It is, therefore, surprising indeed to find Professor Edgar J. Goodspeed, in his "American Translation" of the New Testament, actually translating the word that means "justify" by "make upright"! It would be difficult to imagine a rendering which more completely fails to get the meaning of the Pauline word.

In saying so, we can appeal not merely to Protestant tradition, but to the overwhelming weight, it is safe to say, of modern opinion. Many modern scholars who are as far as possible from holding, for themselves, to Paul's doctrine of justification by faith do at least recognize the fact that it *was* Paul's doctrine; and it may no doubt be said that in his incorrect rendering of the word "justify" Professor Goodspeed is placing himself in opposition to modern grammatico-historical exegesis just as much as to the very roots of the Christian faith.

Plainly, then, the word "justify" in Paul's Epistles means "declare righteous," "pronounce righteous," and not "make righteous." God's act in "justifying" the sinner is—if we may use a theological term—a "forensic" act. That is, it is an act that is analogous to the act of a judge in pronouncing a sentence of acquittal upon a prisoner at the bar.

Justification and the "Modern Mind"

No doubt the entire forensic aspect of salvation, the entire question how a sinful man can become right with God, is highly distasteful to the "modern mind," as indeed it is distasteful to the unregenerate mind of sinful man in all ages. "We will have nothing to do," men say, "with these juridical notions of God, which represent God as a stern judge pronouncing sentence upon mankind; rather will we think of Him only as a loving Father and as the source of life."

The reason why the forensic aspect of salvation is so distasteful to the "modern mind" is perfectly plain. It is distasteful because it involves a profound view of sin as transgression of the law of God. Men no longer believe today in a law of God; the only law that they will recognize is a law that a man imposes upon himself. Sin they regard—if they are willing to use at all the antiquated word—as merely imperfection. They will have nothing to do with the idea of guilt. It is no wonder that they will not think of God as Judge.

But whatever modern men may think of the forensic aspect of salvation, it is perfectly clear that Paul thought a great deal of it. Modern men may not be interested in the question how a sinful man who has disobeyed God's command and come under the dreadful penalty of God's law may yet stand before God's judgment seat; but it is at least clear that Paul was supremely interested in it. In removing it from great passages in Paul's Epistles, by the translation of the word "justify" by the very modern expression "make upright," Professor Goodspeed is making the Epistles more palatable to modern men; but he is closing his eyes to what the Epistles really contain. Whether we like it or not, the fact does remain that the Apostle Paul was supremely interested in the question how a sinful man can become right with God and that he answers that question by the great doctrine of justification by faith alone.

Justification by Faith Alone

"Knowing," says Paul, "that a man is not justified by the works of the law, but only through faith in Christ Jesus . . . ." The Greek phrase which we have here translated "but only" means, in itself, "if not" or "unless" or "except." Can we then translate it "unless" or "except" in this verse? Most assuredly we cannot do so. We should then make Paul say, "A man is not justified by the works of the law except through faith in Christ Jesus"; and that would mean that if a man has faith in Jesus to help the works of the law out, he can be justified by the works of the law after all; it would mean that, while a man is not justified by works alone, he is justified by works and faith taken together. Thus faith would become merely the means by which a man's works become effective for salvation.

But that was almost exactly the view of Paul's opponents, the Judaizers. Certainly, therefore, Paul cannot mean to give expression to it here as his own view; and indeed he contradicts it in the clearest possible way in the latter part of this very sentence, where he places being justified by the works of the law in sharp opposition to being justified by faith.

Evidently, therefore, Paul is here using the phrase meaning "if not" or "except" in the sense which we discussed in the October, 1931, number of *Christianity Today*[1] — the sense, namely, in which the phrase introduces an exception to a general proposition of which what has actually been expressed in the preceding sentence is merely one specific instance. Here the phrase introduces an exception to the general proposition, "A man is not justified at all"; and Paul means to say, "A

---

[1] See x. Paul and the Jerusalem Church (Editor's Note).

man is not justified at all except through faith in Christ Jesus." But the general proposition is not actually expressed in what precedes; it is merely implied in the specific instance of it that "a man is not justified by the works of the law." Luther, therefore, was quite justified in holding this passage to teach the doctrine of justification by faith *alone*.

"Even we," says Paul, "believed in Christ Jesus, in order that we might be justified by faith in Christ and not by the works of the law, because by the works of the law no flesh shall be justified." It is not quite clear whether Paul has a specific Old Testament passage in mind in the last clause of this sentence, "because by the works of the law no flesh shall be justified." Possibly he is thinking of Ps. 143:2. But even if he has no specific Old Testament passage in mind, the Hebraistic phrase "no flesh" and the Hebraistic form of the sentence (which cannot be brought out in an English translation) show rather clearly that he is basing his proposition upon the whole teaching of the Old Testament. "You and I," said Paul to Peter, "believed in Christ Jesus, in order that we might be justified by faith in Christ and not by the works of the law, because in general the proposition stands firm on the basis of the Old Testament that no man is justified by the works of the law." If we ask how Paul showed in detail that the Old Testament teaches that general proposition, we need only turn to such a passage as Gal. 3:10-12.

XX. THE PERIL OF INCONSISTENCY

"But if in seeking to be justified in Christ we were found, ourselves also, sinners, is Christ a minister of sin? God forbid! For if the things which I tore down, these things again I build up, I show myself to be a transgressor. For I through the law died to the law that I might live to God" (Gal. 2:17-19a, in a literal translation).

The General Sense

In the last two articles in this series we have been considering the speech which Paul made to Peter at Antioch. "You and I," said Paul to Peter, "were Jews by nature; we had all the advantages which the law could give. Yet we relinquished our confidence in all those advantages, so far as the attainment of salvation was concerned, by seeking our salvation in exactly the same way as that in which it is to be sought by despised Gentile 'sinners' — namely, by the free grace of Christ received by faith alone."

At that point, an objection might arise from the Jewish point of view; and the objection is taken up incidentally and by implication at the beginning of the passage which we study this month.

It is rather a difficult passage. But difficult though it is in certain details, the general thought of it does seem to be fairly clear. That general thought may perhaps be paraphrased as follows: "We Jews, when we became Christians, gave up seeking justification through the law; we became just as much 'sinners' (in the old Jewish sense of the word, which divided humanity into the two classes of (1) Jews and (2) sinners), as the Gentiles. But it was Christ who led us to take that step. If so, if Christ led us to become 'sinners,' how shall we avoid the conclusion that Christ was one who led us into sin? Only by recognizing that that Jewish distinction between 'sinners' and Jews is invalid. We must not set it up again. If we do set it up again, then we do charge Christ with being a helper in sin. Christ led us to become 'sinners' in that Jewish sense of the word. If that sense is right, then, since Christ led us to become 'sinners,' He led us into sin."

A Difficult Connection

So much for the general thought. We must now consider briefly one or two details.

The first difficulty concerns the connection of the sentence, "For if I build up the things which I tore down I show myself up as a transgressor." That sentence is introduced by "for"; it gives thus a reason for something that precedes. But the words immediately preceding are "God forbid" (literally, "May it not be"). Our first impulse would be, then, to regard the "for" clause as giving a reason for the "God forbid." The sense of the "God forbid," when it is taken together with the question which it answers in the negative, is:

"No, Christ is not a helper in sin." If, then, the "for" clause gives a reason for that negative assertion, we get the following: "Christ is not a helper in sin; for if I build up the things which I tore down I show myself to be a transgressor." But that hardly seems to make sense. It is very difficult to see how the sentence introduced by "for," so understood, gives any reason for, or has any logical connection with, the preceding clause.

The connection could, indeed, be established if we could introduce the word "only" into the clause introduced by "for." Then we should have the thought: "Christ is not a helper in sin; for only if I build up what I tore down do I show myself to be a transgressor and thus show Christ to have led me into transgression by leading me to tear it down, whereas, on the other hand if I stand by the step which I have taken I do not confess that it was wrong for me to take it and so do not confess that Christ led me into sin when He led me to take it."

This interpretation yields a perfectly good thought. But the trouble with it is that in order to adopt it we have to insert the all-important word "only," the word upon which the whole interpretation hangs.

How Vacillation Dishonors Christ

It seems better therefore, to say that the sentence introduced by "for" does not give a reason for the "God forbid"—does not give a reason for Paul's negative reply to the question, "Is Christ a helper in sin?"—but rather explains how Paul came to raise that blasphemous question. No doubt it would have been more coldly logical to postpone the negative answer to the question—to postpone, that is, the "God forbid"—until the question itself has been thoroughly explained. But the Apostle Paul, though always logical, is not coldly or pedantically logical; and so here, when he raises the blasphemous question, "Is Christ a minister of sin?," he prefers first to brush that blasphemous question aside with his indignant "God forbid," before he explains how that question ever could arise. We get, then, the following sense for the passage: "If in giving up the law as a means of salvation we became 'sinners,' is Christ a helper in sin? You will agree with me, Peter, in rejecting any conclusion so blasphemous and absurd; you will agree with me in brushing that conclusion aside with an emphatic 'God forbid.' But let us look at that matter a little more closely. That blasphemous conclusion does follow by an inevitable logic, Peter, from your vacilating conduct. If, by your example in refusing table-companionship to Gentile Christians, you build up that view of the law as a means of salvation which when you trusted in Christ you tore down, you confess that you did wrong in tearing it down; and, since Christ led you to tear it down, you confess that *He* did wrong, you confess that He was your helper in an act of sin."

Tearing Down and Building Up

So much for the question regarding the connection of the sentence introduced by "for" with what precedes. Another question has been asked about this passage. What is meant by the "transgression" which is referred to in verse 18? Two opposite views have been held.

According to one view, the "transgression" is the initial act of Paul and Peter and other Jewish Christians in turning their backs upon any thought of the law as a means of salvation. According to the other view, the "transgression" is not the tearing down, but paradoxically enough, the building up.

Let us consider the second of these views first. According to this second view, Paul is expressing the paradoxical thought that in this particular case, unlike what usually prevails, it is a transgression to build a thing up. That paradoxical thought becomes clear, say the advocates of this interpretation, when verse 18 is taken in close connection with the words "through the law" in verse 19. "In this particular case," Paul would be saying, "I would become a transgressor of the law in building up the law as a means of salvation, because it was through the law that I died to the law; since the law commanded me to tear the law down as a means of salvation, I would become a transgressor of the law—paradoxical though it may seem—in going back upon that initial act by building the law up again."

This interpretation has the advantage that it exhibits a good and close connection between verse 18 and verse 19; according to it, the "for" at the beginning of verse 19 is made to introduce a reason for what immediately precedes. What is perhaps even more important, it relieves us of our previous difficulty regarding the "for" sentence in verse 18; it makes it possible for us to take that "for" sentence, after all, as a reason for the immediately preceding "God forbid," and relieves us from the necessity, which we had previously felt ourselves to be under, of making the "for" of verse 18 jump back of the "God forbid" to the question with which the "God forbid" is an answer. Thus, if we can adopt this identification of the "transgression" with the building up, even what we have already said about verses 17 and 18 will have to be abandoned, and the whole passage will be understood as follows: "If we became 'sinners' when we gave up the law as a means of salvation, is Christ, who led us to take that step, a helper in sin? No, He is not a helper in sin; for in this particular case, unlike ordinary cases, it was not a sin to tear the thing down; the law itself commanded us to tear it down, so that Christ, in leading us to tear it down, did not lead us to be transgressors of the law; on the contrary, we became transgressors of the law if, going back upon what Christ led us to do, we build the law up."

The Right View About the "Transgression"

Despite the advantages of this interpretation, despite the close logical connection which, unlike the other interpretation, it shows between every clause and the immediately preceding clause, it must probably be rejected. The trouble is that verse 18—"For if the things which I tore down these things again I build up, I show myself to be a transgressor"—is worded as though it were a general and obvious proposition, and most emphatically not as though it were meant to express a paradoxical exception to that general proposition. If Paul had meant that in this particular case that general proposition does not hold, but on the contrary it is the building up and not the tearing down that is the "transgression," why did he not make clear in some way—in verse 18 itself—that he is talking about the particular case and not about the general proposition? As a matter of fact, verse 18 is put in the most studiedly general form, and no ordinary reader would take it in any other way than simply as expressing the obvious thought that if just after tearing a thing down I proceed to build it up again, I confess thereby that I did wrong in tearing it down; I confess that my tearing it down was a transgression.

We, therefore, despite the temptation offered by the view just discussed, are inclined to stick to our previous interpretation of the connection between verse 17 and verse 18. The "for" in verse 18 does, we still hold, go back of the "God forbid"; it does not give a reason for this negative answer to the question, "Is Christ a minister of sin?," but it explains how that question came to be raised.

What, then, on this view of verse 18, is the meaning of the "for" at the beginning of verse 19? We have rejected the close connection between this verse and the immediately preceding verse. What shall we put in place of that connection? For what does the "for" at the beginning of verse 19 introduce a reason? We answer that it introduces a reason for the general thought of verses 17 and 18. "Away," says Paul, "with all this inconsistency which confesses that we did wrong in giving up the law as a means of salvation and which thereby confesses that Christ did wrong in leading us to do it. I for my part will have nothing to do with such inconsistency; I broke with the law (as a means of salvation) not temporarily but for ever; I *died* to it, that I might live to God."

If there is any proposition in what precedes which we must single out as being that for which the "for" of verse 19 introduces a reason, it must be, we suppose, the "God forbid" of verse 17. "Christ is not a minister of sin," says Paul; "for, in opposition to all vacillating policy which would make Him a minister of sin, I for my part stand firmly by the decision which He led me to make; I for my part *died* to the law, as He led me to do, in order that I might live to God."

At first sight, this might seem to be an artifical and unnatural treatment of the passage. The passage falls into four divisions, of which the last two are causal clauses introduced by "for": (1) "Is Christ a minister of sin?"; (2) "God forbid!"; (3) "For if I build up what I tore down I show myself to be a transgressor"; (4) "For I through the law died to the law." According to our interpretation, (3) refers not to (2) but to (1), and (4) refers not to (3) but to (2). At first sight, this business of making causal clauses give the reason, in each case, not for what immediately precedes but for something further back would seem to be unwarranted. The answer to the objection will be found if a man will just read the passage over again and take it as a whole. When he does that, he will see, we think, that the interpretation proposed does bring out the sense of what Paul was intending to say.

The Sin of Vacillation

At any rate, the difficulties of the passage do not obscure its profound meaning for the modern Church. Whatever interpretation be adopted as to details, the passage does set forth the danger—nay, the terrible sin—of inconsistency. If we merely go back upon what *we* have done, well and good. We are but weak and fallible men, and often we make mistakes. But if we go back upon what *Christ* led us to do, if we go back upon some decision of principle which we made for Christ's sake, then we are falling into a very dreadful sin.

How common that sin is in the modern Church; how common it is, in particular, in our Presbyterian Church in the U.S.A.! A man decides to take a stand for the gospel of Christ against that "other gospel" of doctrinal indifferentism which now dominates our Church. Then comes flattery from the ecclesiastical authorities; then comes Satan's voice about "peace and work" and about avoidance of contention, and about propagation versus defence and about making our message positive and not negative and about not alienating the support of moderate and peace-loving men in the Church and about teaching the truth and letting Church politics go. At first, the man resists the Tempter's voice. But as these shibboleths of unbelief continue to make their impact upon his soul, his evangelical ardor begins to wane. He begins to fear the ecclesiastical machinery; he begins to consider consequences rather than principle; he begins to withdraw and separate himself from those who bear the reproach of Christ.

Such vacillation is one of the greatest enemies of the evangelical cause today. One wobbly evangelical often does more harm to the cause of the gospel, and leads more of Christ's little ones astray, than do a dozen Modernists. God send us men of a different type, no matter how few they may be! God send us foursquare men, who give the cause their all! God send us men who will say, as over against the "other gospel" now dominant in the Presbyterian Church: "I for my part will never go back upon a decision which Christ led me to take; I will never dishonor Him by confessing that what I did for His sake was sin; I have broken once and for all with that other gospel, which now dominates the Church, and I will never make common cause for one moment, in presbytery, General Assembly or theological seminary, with those who proclaim it."

XXI. THE NEW LIFE

"For I through the law died unto the law that I might live unto God. I have been crucified together with Christ; and it is no longer I that live, but Christ liveth in me. And the life which I now live in the flesh I live in the faith which is in the Son of God who loved me and gave Himself for me. I do not make void the grace of God; for if righteousness is through the law, then Christ died in vain" (Gal. 2:19-21, in a literal translation).

What Is Meant by "the Law"?

In the last number of *Christianity Today*, we discussed the connection of the first sentence in this passage with what precedes. The "for" of that sentence, we observed, introduces a reason for the main thought of the whole preceding passage, which main thought is: "Away with a miserable vacillation which would repudiate what Christ led us to do and would therefore imply that Christ is a minister of sin." "I," says Paul, "will have nothing to do with such vacillation; for I for my part, when I broke with the law, did so once and for all; I did not separate myself from the law merely in some temporary fashion, but I *died* to the law; my break with the law was as irrevocable as death."

In interpreting the words, "I died to the law," two errors should be avoided.

In the first place, when Paul speaks of "the law," he does not mean merely the ceremonial law, but he means the whole law of God as it is set forth in the Old Testament, including what modern men would call its ethical as distinguished from its ceremonial requirements. When the meaning of the term "the law" is limited to the ceremonial law, the real point of the Epistle to the Galatians is missed. That is the root error of Ernest DeWitt Burton, in his learned commentary on the Epistle. According to Burton — if we may summarize the thought in our language, not in his—Paul is contending in the Epistle to the Galatians for a view of the will of God which finds the true essence of God's will in great general principles, as over against an external or piecemeal notion of morality. There could scarcely be a more serious error. As a matter of fact, Paul is contending in this great Epistle not for a "spiritual" view of the law as over against externalism or ceremonialism; he is contending for the grace of God as over against human merit in any form. The particular form in which human merit was sought by the Judaizers in Galatia was an observance of the ceremonial law; but Paul's objection would have been essentially the same if the error had been of the form which appears in the religious "Liberalism" of our day. Salvation by character, salvation by our love for God, or (after the crass manner of "Abou ben Adhem") by our love for our fellowmen, salvation by "making Christ Master in the life," salvation by "complete surrender" —these are all just differing forms of the one central error which seeks salvation in human merit, and they all alike come under the condemnation of Paul's tremendous polemic in the Epistle to the Galatians.

But another error needs also to be avoided. If the interpretation which we have just mentioned attributes too little meaning to the words, "I died to the law," if it makes those tremendous words mean merely that a higher form of law is to be put in place of a lower one in order that human obedience to the law may attain merit with God, another interpretation is equally erroneous in attributing too *much* meaning to the words. We refer to the error of "antinomianism," which supposes that according to Paul the law of God, as it is set forth in the Bible, is no longer binding upon the Christian man.

That error is plainly contradicted by the Word of God, and in particular it is quite out of accord with the teaching of Paul in this Epistle. "They that do such things," says Paul in Gal. 5:31 after a very specific catalogue of sins, "shall not inherit the Kingdom of God"; and the same stern teaching appears everywhere in the New Testament. No, Christianity, according to the Apostle, is not a way for a man to free himself from the requirements of God's law.

The Ceremonial Law

There was, indeed, a part of the law as set forth in the Old Testament which was no longer binding in the new dispensation—the part, namely, that consisted in the law's ceremonial requirements. The reason why the ceremonial law was no longer binding is set forth fully in the Epistle to the Hebrews. It was not because the ceremonial requirements were not true commands of God; it was not because disobedience to those requirements, in Old Testament times, was anything other than a deadly sin; it was not because increasing religious insight showed that those ceremonial requirements had been unnecessary after all. But it was because those requirements, though of divine authority, were temporary; they were expressly intended by God for the time before the coming of Christ. They were shadows of good things to come; and when that which they foreshadowed had appeared, the shadows were done away.

In Galatians, there is just a hint of this explanation of the ceremonial law; it is found in Gal. 4:1-11, where Paul does seem to treat the old dispensation as being a preliminary, though divinely ordered, period, when man's worship of God was still bound to external things. But in most of the Epistle the ceremonial law is not separated from the rest of the law of God as the Old Testament sets it forth. Paul is not here dealing with the question of ceremonialism versus "spiritual" worship (to make use of the word "spiritual" in a very modern and very un-Pauline way); he is dealing with a far profounder question — the question of human merit versus divine grace. The particular form in which merit was being sought in Galatia was an observance of the ceremonial law; and Paul takes that particular form as the object of attack, without specifically pointing out its relation to other forms. But his words apply, and apply with crushing force, against those other forms; in particular, they apply against the entire non-doctrinal, "practical" trend of the religion of the modern Church. That non-doctrinal, "practical" religion is just one form of the very ancient error that human goodness is sufficient to make a man right with God.

This great verse, in other words, must be interpreted in the light of its context; and when it is so interpreted its meaning becomes perfectly clear. "When I became a Christian," says Paul in effect, "I ceased to seek my salvation from my own obedience to the law of God; in that sense, at least, I died to the law; my connection with it, as a means of obtaining merit with God, was forever done away."

The Substitutionary Death of Christ

What does Paul mean by the words "through the law," when he says: "I through the law died to the law"? How did the law itself cause Paul to die to the law?

At first sight, that question might seem to be answerable by an appeal to Gal. 3:24, where the law is said to have been a schoolmaster to bring men to Christ. Without a clear revelation of God's will, men might have comforted themselves by an appeal to their own goodness; but the law of God as set forth in the Old Testament revealed, or ought to have revealed, to men their utter hopelessness as sinners in the sight of God, and so led, or ought to have led, them to accept the free salvation offered by Christ. The law, in other words, led men, by its clear revelation of what God requires, to relinquish all claim to salvation by their own obedience. In that sense, surely, Paul could say that it was "through the law" that he died to the law. The law made the commands of God so terribly clear that Paul could see plainly that there was no hope for him if he appealed for his salvation to his own obedience to those commands.

This interpretation yields a truly Pauline thought. But the immediate context suggests another, and an even profounder, meaning for the words. The key to the interpretation is probably to be found in the sentence, "I have been crucified together with Christ," which almost immediately follows. "The law," Paul probably means, "caused me to die to the law, because the law, with its penalty of death upon sin (which penalty Christ bore in our stead) brought Christ to the cross; and when Christ died I died, since He died as my representative." In other words, the death to the law of which Paul here speaks is the death which the law itself brought about when it said, "The soul that sinneth it shall die." Christ died that death, which the law fixes as the penalty of sin, when He died upon the cross; and since He died that death as our representative, we too have died that death; the penalty of the law is for us done away because that penalty has been paid in our stead by the Lord Jesus Christ. Thus our death to the law, suffered for us by Christ, far from being contrary to the law, was in fulfilment of the law's own demands. We are free from the penalty of death pronounced by the law upon sin not because we are rebels against the law, but because the penalty has been paid by Christ.

The Christian Life

The death of which Paul speaks in this verse is followed, he says, by a new life. "I through the law died to the law, that I might live unto God." The connection which existed between me and the law when I was still liable to the law's penalty of death is done away now that Christ has died in my stead; the law has nothing more to say against a man after its penalty has been paid. But this death to the law is, according to Paul, followed by a new life; and that new life is lived in communion with God and for the glory of God.

It is interesting to observe how intimately the two aspects of salvation are connected in this great passage. In the

Epistle to the Galatians, Paul is dealing primarily with what the theologians call the "forensic" aspect of salvation—he is dealing, in other words, with the question how, despite the guilt of sin, the sinner is freed from that guilt and becomes right with God. But this forensic aspect of salvation is intimately connected with the "vital" aspect; the new and right relation to God as Judge always goes together with the new life which the sinner possesses after he has been made a new creature by the Spirit of God. The familiar hymn is quite true to Holy Scripture when it says:

"Be of sin the *double* cure,
Cleanse me from its guilt and power."

That new life unto God which the sinner comes to possess because of the death of Christ is further characterized as being the very life of the Saviour Himself. "It is no longer I that live," says Paul, "but Christ liveth in me."

These words, if they stood alone, might conceivably be taken in a mystical or pantheizing sense, as though Paul regarded the Christian life as consisting in a merging of the personality of the believer in the being of Christ. But Paul need not fear such an interpretation; for everywhere in his Epistles the relation between the believer and Christ is presented in a thoroughly personal way, as a relation between one person and another. Paul was no mystic—in the strict sense of that word.

But although Paul's words in this passage are certainly not to be taken in an impersonal, mystical sense, they should, on the other hand, certainly not be explained away. Christianity, according to Paul, is not the easy-going thing that is being mistaken for it today; it is not merely a new influence brought to bear upon a man; it is no mere introduction of a new motive into human conduct: but it involves a new life, and that new life, in its quality as well as in its source, is the life of Christ. Look at Christians, says Paul, and you see so many manifestations of Christ.

The Ground of Confidence

An obvious objection may be raised against that view of Christianity—the objection, namely, that it is not a fact. Are

Christians really leading such entirely new lives; is it perfectly clear that Christ is living in them? Are they not living in the same old world; and do they not exhibit themselves still some, at least, of the characteristics of that old world?

This objection is anticipated by Paul in the very next words. "The life which I now live in the flesh"—there is an admission which the Apostle makes. "I admit," says Paul in effect, "that I am still living under the same old conditions of life in this world, and that I am still struggling against the old temptations that are found also in a humanity untouched by the grace of God; yes, I am still living a life 'in the flesh.' But that life in the flesh is lived by faith: completion has not yet come; I am still struggling on in this world: but I have faith to believe that completion will surely come. And the ground of my faith regarding the future is found in what Christ has already done for me; I am confident that the One who loved me and gave Himself for me on the cross will bring to completion the work that He there began; I am confident that faith will one day give place to sight, that the utter newness of the life of believers, now partly hidden, will one day be plain for all to see."

"I do not make void the grace of God," says Paul in concluding the report of his speech to Peter; "for if righteousness is through the law, then Christ died in vain." The "for" here gives a reason for the use of the harsh word "make void" —" 'make void,' I say; for that is just the right word, since if, as the Judaizers say, justification comes even in part through our own obedience to the law, then Christ died in vain."

This verse is the key verse of the Epistle to the Galatians; it expresses the central thought of the Epistle. The Judaizers attempted to supplement the saving work of Christ by the merit of their own obedience to the law. "That," says Paul, "is impossible; Christ will do everything or nothing: earn your salvation if your obedience to the law is perfect, or else trust wholly to Christ's completed work; you cannot do both; you cannot combine merit and grace; if justification even in slightest measure is through human merit, then Christ died in vain."

XXII. THE CROSS OF CHRIST

"O foolish Galatians, who hath bewitched you, before whose eyes Jesus Christ was openly pictured as crucified" (Gal. 3:1, in a literal translation).

The Divisions of the Epistle

We have finished our consideration of the first main division of the Epistle, in which, in Gal. 1:11—2:21, Paul defends his independent apostolic authority over against the contention of the Judaizers that he was an apostle only through the mediation of those who had been apostles before him. Now we turn to the second main division, embracing the central portion of the Epistle from Gal. 3:1 to Gal. 5:12, in which Paul defends the *content* of his gospel of free grace as over against the Judaizers' contention that faith, in the attainment of salvation, must be supplemented by works.

But the divisions in the Pauline Epistles are not always easy to make; and so, in the present case, Paul's account of his meeting with Peter, which we have just been studying, belongs as much to the second main division of the Epistle as to the first. No doubt it is a part of the Apostle's defence of his independent apostolic authority: so independent was he, he says, that on one occasion he could even withstand the chief of the original apostles himself. But what he said to Peter on that past occasion at Antioch was the very thing that he wanted to say also now to those converts in the Galatian churches. So the passage Gal. 2:11-21 contains the very heart of that gospel of free grace which Paul is going on to defend in the following section of the Epistle.

How Did Peter Respond?

The fact that Gal. 2:11-21, especially in the latter part of the passage, contains what Paul was desiring to say now to the Galatians may help to explain why we are not told how Peter took the rebuke which was given him at Antioch and what the result of the scene was. The silence of the Apostle about this matter has seemed to some scholars to leave room for very serious conclusions as to the history of the apostolic age. If Peter had been convinced by Paul's argument, why did not Paul point in triumph to so gratifying a conclusion of the Antioch scene? The real result of the scene—so the contention of these scholars runs—must have been far less edifying, and what really resulted was a permanent breach or at least coolness between Paul on the one hand and the Jerusalem apostles on the other.

With regard to this well-known contention of the "Tübingen school" of New Testament critics, it may be said, in the first place, that the notion of a permanent conflict of principle between Paul and Peter is contradicted by passages, written long after this Antioch scene, in which Paul refers to Peter with the utmost respect (I Cor. 3:22; 9:5; 15:5): it is contradicted, in the second place, by the entire subsequent history of the Christian Church, which is quite incomprehensible if there was a permanent breach between the apostles at the beginning; it is contradicted, in the third place, expressly by I Cor. 15:11, where Paul distinctly says that his gospel was the same as that of the original apostles; finally, it is contradicted by the very passage, Gal. 2:11-21, which is appealed to most confidently in favor of it, since in this passage Paul insists that his *principles* were the same as Peter's and objects only to Peter's inconsistency in the application of those principles.

Why Paul Does Not Tell

But—to return to the immediate point under discussion—why does not Paul complete the story of the Antioch scene if the end of the story was as edifying as we have just tried to make it out to be; if Peter was really convinced by what Paul said to him at Antioch, why does not Paul say so in triumph in our Epistle?

Of course, it may be said, in general, in answer to such questions, that the Galatian readers probably knew many things that modern readers do not know; very probably they knew perfectly well that there was no permanent breach between Paul and Peter, so that it was not necessary for their attention to be called to that fact in this Epistle.

But something more definite can be said in explanation of Paul's silence regarding the outcome of the Antioch scene. The plain fact is that before the Apostle has finished his account of what he said to Peter at Antioch he is thinking far more of the present effect of his words upon the Galatian readers than of the effect of them long ago at Antioch. In the passage which we studied last month he has been upon the very heights; as the fine old eighteenth-century commentator, Bengel, remarked, the contents of that passage may be called "the sum and marrow of Christianity." Paul has been pouring out his very soul in that passage; he has been celebrating the glories of the Cross of Christ. For him to have returned after that passage to the details of what had happened at Antioch would have been almost pedantic. What he is thinking of as he pens those glorious words at the end of the second chapter of Galatians is the unspeakable grace of God contrasted with the fact that his beloved converts in Galatia have turned their back upon it and have done despite to the Cross of Christ. No wonder that he refrains from rehearsing pedantically what the Galatians probably already knew about the results of the Antioch scene; no wonder that, instead, he breaks out in the words, "O foolish Galatians, who hath bewitched you?" "You have had bestowed upon you all the marvels of the free grace of God; you have received new life through the Cross of Christ; yet you are making it all of none effect in order to try to earn by your own miserable works what Christ has purchased for you by His blood. Who hath bewitched you to make you turn your back upon so great salvation?"

The Missionary Preaching of Paul

"Who hath bewitched you," says Paul, "before whose eyes Jesus Christ was openly pictured as crucified." Here we have one of the precious references in the Pauline Epistles to the missionary preaching of the Apostle as distinguished from the instruction which he gave to Christian people. There are many things that we do not know about the missionary preaching of Paul, since the Epistles are addressed not to the unconverted but to Christians and since the Book of Acts gives us only brief examples of the Apostle's preaching to the unconverted world; but one thing we do know about it—we do know that at the very heart of it was the Cross of Christ. "The story of the crucifixion," Paul says in our passage, if we may paraphrase his words, "was made so vivid and so plain in my first preaching among you that it was as though a great picture of Christ on the cross were being held up before your eyes, or [if we adopt a different interpretation of the word that is figuratively used] as though a great placard were being held up before you with the words on it, 'Jesus Christ crucified.'"

Of course, this story of the Cross was not presented by the Apostle merely as an inspiring story of a holy martyrdom; but it was presented as something that had profound meaning for those to whom it was proclaimed. "Christ died for your sins," said Paul to those unconverted people in the Galatian cities.

Should Doctrine Be Preached to the Unconverted?

According to the tendency of religious work which is prevalent at the present day, Christian doctrine, including the central doctrine of the atonement, is to be presented to people, if at all, after rather than before they have been saved. The advocates of this method sometimes have kind things to say about doctrine; it is necessary, they admit, in its proper place. A man who has already entered upon holy living, some of them no doubt say, will go on to study his Bible and will attain an ever more correct view of Christ and of the meaning of Christ's death. But at the beginning all that, it is held, is unnecessary; at the beginning all that is needed is surrender of the human will. What a man needs to do first, it is thought, is to put away his sin by his own act of surrender; there is time enough later for doctrinal instruction.

Whether that non-doctrinal, anti-intellectualistic method of religious work is right or wrong, it may be observed at any rate that it is quite contrary to the New Testament from beginning to end. The New Testament does not, in the manner of these modern religious workers, offer a man salvation first and then preach the gospel to him afterwards; but it preaches the gospel to him first—with the blessed doctrine of the atonement at the center of it—and then, through his acceptance of that gospel, it brings salvation to his soul. It was to unconverted people that Paul preached in Galatia the message of the Cross of Christ; and when they accepted that message—that "doctrine"—they were saved.

XXIII. THE SPIRIT OF GOD

"This only I wish to learn from you: Was it by the works of the law that ye received the Spirit, or was it by the hearing of faith? Are ye so foolish? Having begun in the Spirit do ye now make an end in the flesh? Have ye suffered so great things in vain—if indeed it be in vain? He therefore who supplieth to you the Spirit and worketh miracles among you, doeth He it by the works of the law or by the hearing of faith?" (Gal. 3:2-5, in a literal translation).

The First Glorious Days

With the first verse of the third chapter of Galatians, which we studied in the last article in this series, Paul introduces the second main division of the Epistle, which contains his defense of justification by faith alone as over against the gospel—falsely so called—of the Judaizers, which offered justification by faith *and* works. Today we study the first of the arguments which Paul adduces in defense of his gospel.

It is a very simple argument indeed. "You received the Holy Spirit," says Paul, "by faith alone, before you ever heard of the teaching of the Judaizers, before you ever thought of trying to attain merit by keeping the law. But if you received the Spirit apart from the works of the law, what more can the works of the law possibly bring you? By the gift of the Holy Ghost God set the stamp of His approval unmistakably upon the gospel as it was originally proclaimed to you —the gospel which bade you trust to the Cross of Christ not for a part of your salvation but for all."

"This only I desire to learn from you," says Paul. He does not mean that the immediately following argument is the only one that he intends to adduce, but he does apparently mean that it would be sufficient even if it stood alone. "Just tell me this one thing," he means to say, if we may venture to explain his meaning by a modern colloquial usage: "How did you receive the Spirit—by faith alone or by works? If you will just answer me that one question, the Judaizers will be refuted then and there."

When Paul speaks of the "Spirit" in this connection, he is no doubt thinking, in part at least, of special or miraculous gifts of the Spirit of God such as those that are described in I Cor. 12—14; for he refers to those special gifts rather plainly in verse 5. Evidently the presence of the Spirit in the Galatian churches was not something that could be doubted. It could be made the basis of an argument because it did not itself need any argument to establish it. It was a perfectly clear and palpable thing.

But those special gifts were not the only marks of the Spirit's presence in the Galatian churches. Another mark of His presence was found in the changed lives of the Galatian converts. "Love, joy, peace, longsuffering, gentleness, goodness, faith, meekness, temperance"—these things, as well as prophecy, healings and the gift of tongues, were "the fruit of the Spirit."

There is one thing, however, which Paul does not mean by "the Spirit"; he does not mean what the Board of Foreign Missions of the Presbyterian Church in the U.S.A. apparently means when in a recent official statement it refers to "the spirit and principles of Christ." For "the spirit of Christ" in that vague sense there is small place in the gospel of Paul; what Paul means by the Spirit is not the "spirit of Christ," with "spirit" spelled with a small letter—not the spirit in this vague sense so over-emphasized by the unbelief of our day—but the Third Person of the blessed Trinity, the Holy Spirit of God.

How Was the Spirit Received?

"You received the Spirit," says Paul, "not by doing something but by hearing something; not by doing the things that the law commands but by hearing the gospel of the Cross of Christ. You received the Spirit by the hearing of faith"—

that is, by listening, not in indifference or in unbelief but in faith, to that story of the Cross of Christ. "Jesus Christ crucified was openly pictured before your very eyes in my missionary preaching. You simply listened to the story, and you received it in faith. You did not try to do anything to earn what Christ had already given you by His death. You said simply: 'Christ died there on the cross for me; He died to wipe away my sins; he died to make all well between God and me; I receive the gift and that is all.'" That is what Paul means by "the hearing of faith"—it is the hearing which faith renders to the story of the Cross of Christ.

"The result of that hearing," Paul says, "was plain. By that hearing, without merit, without works, without anything contributed on your part, you received the Spirit of God."

"But if you received the Spirit by faith alone, what folly to think that anything else is needed now! What folly to think that anything else is higher than the Spirit of God! Are ye so foolish? Having begun in the Spirit, do you now come to completion in the flesh?"

That is said, of course, from the point of view of Paul, not from the point of view of the Judaizers. The Judaizers would never have admitted that in advocating the keeping of the law of God, as a means of attaining God's favor in addition to what they had obtained from the Cross of Christ, they were advocating something that consisted in, or was dictated by, "the flesh." But Paul believed in calling things by their right names, not by the names applied to them by human pride. So, no matter what the Judaizers thought about it, he insists that in advocating attainment of merit with God by their works, they were asking the Galatian converts to follow a glorious beginning, when they received the Spirit of God by faith alone, by a miserable end when they would drop back to dependence upon that which is trusted in by unredeemed humanity. There may possibly be a secondary reference to the external character of those observances—especially circumcision—by which the Judaizers asked the Galatian converts to attain merit with God; but even if there is such a reference it should not be allowed to obscure for one moment the central observation that this Epistle is directed essentially not against ceremonialism in the interests of "spiritual" religion, but against human merit in the interests of divine grace.

Were the Galatians Persecuted?

"Have ye suffered so great things in vain?," Paul asks. But what things does he mean; what were the sufferings to which he here refers? The only answer, if we hold to the usual translation of this verse, can be that the sufferings here referred to were persecutions which the Galatian converts had been called upon to endure. We may surmise that they were persecutions instigated by the non-Christian Jews, persecutions which might have been avoided by the Galatian converts if they had not evoked the jealousy and ire of the Jews by insisting on the freedom of Gentile Christians from the ceremonial law. Paul says in Gal. 5:11 that if he were still preaching circumcision the "offence of the Cross" would be done away. So here, if the translation "suffered" be right in the question, "Have ye suffered so great things in vain?," Paul would apparently be meaning to say: "If you are now going to fall at last into a practice which would have avoided all these persecutions, what was the use of enduring the persecutions in the first place? It looks as though you had endured them in vain."

It is by no means certain, however, that the translation "suffered" is correct. The word which we have just translated "suffered" is in itself a neutral word—that is, it can be used to designate experiences either good or bad. But if it is taken as a neutral word here, the reference to persecutions is removed. Paul would be taken as saying not, "Have ye suffered so great things in vain?," but simply, "Have ye experienced so great things in vain?" In that case, all would be perfectly plain. The reference would of course simply be to the great experiences of the Spirit's presence of which Paul has just spoken and of which he continues to speak in the following verse. "You received glorious manifestations of the Spirit's presence," he would be saying, "before you ever heard of the Judaizers and before you ever thought of keeping the ceremonial law; you received them by faith alone. But did you receive them in vain? After God poured out upon you those signal manifestations of His grace as a result of the simple preaching of the Cross of Christ, are you now going to turn your back upon all that by having recourse to another gospel; despite those wonderful experiences of the Spirit's presence, received as a gift of God through faith, are you now going to try to earn by your own miserable works that which God has already showered upon you so richly; was it all in vain that God put the stamp of His approval so clearly upon the gospel of the all-sufficiency of the Cross of Christ; are you now going to desert that gospel after all for the 'other gospel' of the Judaizers?"

The only difficulty with this interpretation is that the word translated "experienced" usually (to say the least) means "suffered" unless there is some word with it to indicate plainly that it is used in a good or in a neutral sense. The bad sense, "suffered," though it did not necessarily belong to the word, is usually attached to it unless there is clear indication to the contrary.

On the whole, we are rather inclined to think that that indication is here plainly enough given in what precedes and follows. If the word means "suffer" here—if, thus, there is a reference to persecutions—that reference is entirely isolated in this Epistle. If, on the other hand, the word means "experience," then this verse is in perfect accord with what precedes and what follows; Paul would simply be continuing his appeal to the glorious manifestations of the Spirit's presence. He would be insisting that these manifestations would seem to be all in vain if the Galatian converts should now turn to some gospel different from that on the basis of which they had been so richly blessed by God.

The matter is, however, by no means certain. It cannot be denied that the verb is usually employed in the bad sense "suffer" unless there is some adverb with it; the possibility cannot be excluded, therefore, that there is, after all, in this verse an isolated reference to persecution. The verse involves an exegetical problem which may never be solved.

An Appeal to the Readers

At any rate, Paul does not allow his question, "Have ye experienced [or "suffered"] so great things in vain?," to stand without qualification. "If indeed it be in vain," he adds. Various interpretations have been suggested for this conditional clause. But it is best interpreted as a kind of appeal to the readers not to allow the painful supposition in the preceding question to stand even for a moment. "Have you experienced so great things in vain—if indeed it be in vain?" That is, Paul means to say: "I hope that the necessity even of putting the question may be done away; I hope you may cease to listen to the Judaizers and may return to the simplicity of the gospel of Christ; I hope that that dreadful supposition that those glorious experiences of the Spirit's presence were all in vain may at once be refuted by the heed which you give to my Epistle. 'In vain,' do I say? Oh, let it not be in vain, my brethren; let us at once put that supposition behind our backs, because you return at once to the gospel from which the Judaizers are trying to lead you away."

In the following verse, Paul summarizes the argument which he has just advanced in verses 2-4. "He, therefore, who supplieth to you the Spirit and worketh miracles among you, doeth He it by the works of the law or by the hearing of faith?"

So translated, the verse would seem to imply that the manifestations of the Spirit's presence had not yet been discontinued in the Galatian churches; despite the perilous condition of the churches, Paul would seem to be saying that God was still supplying the Spirit to them and was still working miracles among them. But the matter is by no means so clear in the Greek as it is in our provisional English translation. The verse may perhaps be translated: "He who *supplied* to you the Spirit and *worked* miracles among you, *did* He it by the works of the law or by the hearing of faith?" So interpreted, the verse would simply be referring to that first glorious time before the Judaizers had appeared on the scene. Or, finally, the time when God supplies the Spirit may simply not be in view. "He who supplieth to you the Spirit in general," Paul may mean, "without reference to the question whether He is still doing it, doeth He it in general, at any time that He may be found to do it, by the works of the law or by the hearing of faith?"

The words which we have translated "worketh miracles among you" may also be translated "worketh miraculous powers in you"; since the decisive word *dynamis*, "power," may be used in either sense. Obviously the difference is not important. In either case, the reference is to special gifts of the Spirit's presence—presumably like those which are mentioned in I Cor. 12—14.

So ends the first of Paul's arguments in defense of his gospel. It is a perfectly simple argument: "The Cross was proclaimed to you. You listened to the story and received it in faith, without attempting to add any merit of your own to what Christ had done for you when He died for your sins. The result was plain. You received the Spirit of God. But if you received the Spirit thus through faith alone, how can you possibly believe the Judaizers when they tell you that something in addition to faith is necessary if you are to be saved? What more can a man possibly have than the Holy Ghost? What surer sign of salvation can there be than His presence?"

XXIV. THE AUTHORITY OF THE BIBLE

"Just as Abraham believed God, and it was reckoned unto him for righteousness. Know, therefore, that those who are of faith, these are sons of Abraham. And the Scripture, foreseeing that God would justify the Gentiles by faith, proclaimed the gospel beforehand to Abraham, to the effect: 'In thee all the nations shall be blessed.' So then those who are of faith are blessed with believing Abraham" (Gal. 3:6-7, in a literal translation).

The Argument from Scripture

In the last number of *Christianity Today*, we considered the first of the arguments which Paul adduces in favor of the great central doctrine of justification by faith alone apart from all human merit. "You received the Holy Spirit, plainly manifested," the Apostle says, "by receiving in simple faith the story of the Cross, before you ever heard of the Judaizers or ever thought of trying to attain merit by your own observance of God's law. But if you received the Holy Spirit thus apart from the works of the law, what more can you possibly expect to have through your works; what can possibly be higher than the presence of the Spirit of God? Nay, in seeking to establish your own merit, you are doing despite to the Spirit of God, and are really descending from the Spirit to the flesh—to the things in which unaided humanity relies."

This month we turn to the second of Paul's arguments. It is the argument from Scripture, and to it Paul attaches here as always supreme weight. It was particularly important, of course, in dealing with the Judaizers: in their insistence upon observance of the ceremonial law they had no doubt appealed to the Old Testament against Paul; and it was important, therefore, for Paul to show that their interpretation of the Old Testament was wrong. But only the shallowest reading of the Epistles can possibly lead a man to think that the Apostle's appeal to the Old Testament was merely an argumentative device — useful in defeating the Judaizers but not valuable in the Apostle's own mind. Nothing could be further from the fact. As a matter of fact, to Paul as well as to our Lord Jesus Himself, the written Word of God was decisive in all controversy. People who make "the teachings of Christ" instead of the whole Bible the seat of authority in religion are doing despite to the teachings of Christ themselves; and people who make what they wrongly call "the living Spirit," in opposition to the written Word, an independent source of our knowledge of God are doing despite to that blessed Holy Spirit by whose gracious ministration the written Word has been given unto men. Let it never be forgotten that the real source of life for the Church is the holy Book; when the Church seeks life apart from the Book, as it is doing today, then it always faces, as it faces today, a terrible loss of power. If the Bible were rediscovered, as it was rediscovered at the time of the Reformation, we should have in the Church today the same new life as that which then set the world aflame.

The Promise to Abraham

It is not surprising, therefore, that Paul appeals here to the Scriptures of the Old Testament. They were authoritative in the Gentile churches from the very beginning just as much as in the Jewish churches.

"Just as Abraham believed God," says Paul, "and it was reckoned unto him for righteousness." The proof from Scripture joins so closely to that which has preceded that some modern editors place the paragraph division after this first verse instead of before it. "When the Holy Spirit was so plainly manifested in the Galatian churches, not on the basis of human merit, but simply on the basis of the grace of God received by faith, that," Paul says, "was in exact accord with what happened when Abraham became right with God not on the basis of works, not on the basis of his own merit, but through faith."

The Old Testament passage which Paul is here quoting is Gen. 15:6. In the fourth chapter of Romans he quotes the same passage and expounds it more fully; and, in general, the best commentary on this whole part of the Epistle to the Galatians is the fuller treatment of the same subject in Romans.

In Gen. 15:6, Abraham is represented as believing the promise of God that he should have numerous descendants—that his seed should be as the stars for multitude. But that was only one of the promises of God to him; and the Apostle rightly treats the promises as forming a unity. In the promise of a numerous progeny was included the blessed promise of that One of Abraham's descendants through whom the blessing should come to all mankind. Abraham believed the promise, and it was reckoned unto him for righteousness—that is, it was through his faith, not through any good works of his, that he was made right with God.

Christianity Not a New Religion

It is a great mistake to say that Christianity, as over against the old dispensation, was a "new religion"; indeed, it is a mistake to say that Christianity is *a* religion at all, among other religions. On the contrary, there is just one revealed religion, and the revelation that is at the basis of it is recorded in both the Old and the New Testament. The Old Testament saints were saved in just the same way as that in which the New Testament saints are saved—namely, by the death of Christ—and the means by which the Spirit of God applied to them the benefits of Christ's death was exactly the same as the means by which the same Spirit applies those benefits to Christians today—namely, faith. The Old Testament saints, like Christians today, received the gospel of the grace of God; and, like the New Testament saints, they received it by faith. The only difference is that the gospel was proclaimed to the Old Testament saints by way of promise, while to us it is proclaimed by way of narrative of what has already been done. Immediately after the Fall of man, the plan of God for salvation began to be executed—with the promise contained in Gen 3:15—and the men who are saved in accordance with that plan are not adherents of "a religion" among other religions; they are not men who have built upon a common human fund of "religion" certain special religions known as "Judaism" and "Christianity," but they are men to whom God has supernaturally revealed and supernaturally applied His saving work. That one revealed "religion" does not differ from the religions of mankind merely in degree; its supremacy does not consist even in being the one perfect religion as over against the imperfect ones; but it is different from the religions of mankind because, while they represent man's efforts to find God, this "religion" is built upon the sovereign and gracious and entirely unique act by which God found man and saved him from the guilt and power of sin.

The One Way of Salvation

To that marvellous unity and uniqueness of God's saving work both in the old dispensation and in the new, the Apostle Paul appeals in the passage now before us. "Know, therefore," he says, "that those who are of faith, these are sons of Abraham." Not those who are descended from Abraham by ordinary generation, not those who have united themselves to Abraham's descendants by circumcision and the keeping of the law of Moses, certainly not those who have tried—vainly—to attain merit with God by any kind of observance of God's law, but those who have the same faith as that which Abraham had are his true sons and the true heirs of the promises which God gave to him.

"And the Scripture, foreseeing that God would justify the Gentiles by faith, proclaimed the gospel beforehand to Abraham, to the effect: 'In thee shall all the nations be blessed.'" Here we have a reference to Gen. 12:3, the same passage being quoted in a speech of the Apostle Peter in Acts 3:25. When the Scripture said, reporting the words of God to Abraham, 'In thee shall all the nations be blessed'—that is, 'The blessing that is now pronounced upon thee, Abraham, shall be a blessing to all the nations'—when the Scripture said that, it said it in view of this fact which we now see before us, that God is pronouncing the Gentiles and not merely the Jews to be righteous through faith; now we see the fulfilment of that ancient promise of God.

"So then those who are of faith are blessed with believing Abraham." That is the conclusion of this first division of Paul's argument from Scripture. "Abraham was justified by faith, not by works," says Paul; "and those who are of faith, being his true descendants, share his blessing."

XXV. THE ATONEMENT

"For as many as are of the works of the law are under a curse; for it is written, 'Cursed is everyone who does not abide by all the things written in the book of the law to do them.' But that in the law no one is justified with God is clear, because 'the just shall live by faith'; but the law is not of faith but 'he who has done them shall live in them.' Christ redeemed us from the curse of the law by becoming a curse for us, because it is written, 'Cursed is everyone who hangeth upon a tree,' in order that unto the Gentiles the blessing of Abraham might come in Christ Jesus, in order that we might receive the promise of the Spirit through faith" (Gal. 3:10-14, in a literal translation).

The Curse of the Law

Last month we began to study Paul's argument from Scripture in defence of the great central doctrine of justification by faith alone. "Abraham was justified by faith, not by works"—so we summarized the Apostle's words—"and those who are of faith, being his true descendants, share his blessing."

This month we observe how the same thing is proved by an argument from the contrary. "It is those who are of faith who receive Abraham's blessing," says the Apostle in effect; "for certainly those who are of the works of the law do not; indeed, far from receiving a blessing, they receive only a curse—a curse from which Christ had to set them free before the blessing could ever possibly come to them" (verse 10-14).

Everyone who depends upon his own accomplishment of the works which the law prescribes is under a curse; "for it is written (Deut. 27:16), 'Cursed is everyone who does not abide by all the things written in the book of the law to do them.' " It is evident that one link is here omitted from the argument. "Everyone," Paul says, "who depends upon his own obedience to the law is under a curse; for the law pronounces a curse upon all who disobey." The argument depends, of course, altogether upon the assumption that no one has obeyed the law. If anyone had obeyed the law, then the curse which the law pronounces upon disobedience would not apply to him.

But this assumption is to Paul so much a matter of course that it does not need to be expressed. Some expositors, indeed, think that it *is* expressed—in the next verses, where Paul says that when the Scripture declares that "the just shall live by faith" it declares that the just shall not live by his works—in other words, that he has not really kept the law—since justification by works and justification by faith are mutually exclusive. But it is simpler, and, we are inclined to think, better, to say that the argument in verse 10 is complete in itself and that that argument depends on the unexpressed but obviously valid assumption that no one has really kept the law. The law pronounces a curse upon disobedience; no one has really obeyed; therefore all are under the curse.

Thus verses 11f. are best to be regarded as presenting a separate argument in defence of the thesis that everyone who depends upon his own works is under a curse. The first argument (verse 10) is that since the law pronounces a curse upon disobedience, and since all have disobeyed, therefore all are under the curse. The second argument (verses 11f.) is that since the Scripture says that a man is justified (and attains life) by his faith he cannot possibly be justified by his works, since being justified by faith and being justified by works are mutually exclusive.

Grace vs. Merit

"But that in the law [practically the same as 'by means of the law'] no one is justified before God is plain," because [as Scripture says, Hab. 2:4] 'the just shall live by faith.' But the law is not of faith [does not partake of the nature of faith], but [as Scripture says, Lev. 18:5] 'he who has done them [the commandments] shall live in [or 'by'] them.'" "These words, 'he who has done them shall live in them,'" Paul means to say, "describe the nature of the law. It requires *doing* something. But faith is the opposite of doing. So when the Scripture says that a man is justified by faith, that involves saying that he is *not* justified by anything that he does. There are two conceivable ways of salvation. One way is to keep the law perfectly, to *do* the things which the law requires. No mere man since the fall has accomplished that. The other way is to *receive* something, to receive something that is freely given by God's grace. That way is followed when a man has faith. But you cannot possibly mingle the two. You might conceivably be saved by works or you might be saved by faith; but you cannot be saved by both. It is 'either or' here not 'both and.' But which shall it be, works or faith? The Scripture gives the answer. The Scripture says it is faith. Therefore it is *not* works."

Such is Paul's argument. The law, far from bringing the blessing, brought only a curse. Far from being an aid to salvation, the law in itself was a stupendous obstacle to salvation. It was not merely that salvation had to be obtained in a way that was independent of the law. That is no adequate statement of the case. No, the stupendous obstacle which the law interposed against salvation had to be overcome before salvation could be obtained.

The obstacle was overcome by Christ. But how was it overcome? Paul now gives the answer, and in doing so he unfolds the inmost heart of the gospel.

"Christ Redeemed Us"

"Christ redeemed us," he says, "from the curse of the law by becoming a curse for us." The first question is whom he designates by "us." Does he mean all Christians; or does he mean Jewish Christians, who had previously been expressly under the curse of the Mosaic law and were now redeemed from that curse by Christ? On the whole, it is probable that he means the latter. In this Epistle, the distinction between Jews and Gentiles is very much in view; it had been insisted upon by the Judaizers; Paul is showing how it is done away in Christ. So here, when he says, "Christ redeemed *us* . . . in order that *unto the Gentiles* the blessing of Abraham might come in Jesus Christ," it seems rather clear that he is contrasting "us" with "Gentiles," so that by "us" he must designate not all Christians but only Jewish Christians.

This interpretation does not, however, do away with the application of this glorious text to all of us today. Nothing could be further from Paul's thought than to hold that although Christ redeemed Jewish Christians from the curse of the Mosaic law there was no divine curse from which He redeemed all Christians. On the contrary, in Rom. 2:14f. Paul says that even the Gentiles have the work of the law written in their hearts, their conscience bearing witness. It is entirely in accordance with the teaching of the Apostle, therefore, when the Westminster Shorter Catechism says: "*All mankind by their fall lost communion with God, are under His wrath and curse.*" The curse of God's law rested upon all mankind, both Jew and Gentile, and from that curse both Jew and Gentile were redeemed by Christ.

There is no reason at all to weaken the force of the word "redeem," in the sentence, "Christ redeemed us from the curse of the law." It means "to buy off," "to set free by the payment of a price." Truly Christ did pay a price to set us free, the price of His own precious blood. On this subject the reader is referred to the splendid articles of B. B. Warfield, "The New Testament Terminology of Redemption," and "Redeemer and Redemption," in *Biblical Doctrines*, 1929, pp. 325-398. These articles should forever dispose of the habit of depriving these wonderful Biblical words of their true, rich meaning. We are not saved by the Lord Jesus Christ by some method that cost Him nothing. No, we were bought with a price; in the fullest sense of the word we were "redeemed."

Christ Our Substitute

"Christ redeemed us from the curse of the law by becoming a curse for us." That is only a more forcible way of saying that Christ bore a curse for us, or that He became accursed for us. Perhaps the reason why Paul avoids saying that Christ became "accursed" for us is that the word "accursed" in Greek, like the English word, might mean *"worthy of a curse,"* and in that sense the word would not apply. Christ was not worthy of the curse that He bore upon the cross. We alone were worthy of it; He endured it for us though He was worthy of naught but glory and honor and praise.

But *what* curse was it that Christ bore upon the cross? There ought really to be no doubt about the answer. It was *our* curse, the curse of God's law that rightly rested upon us because of sin.

It is perfectly true, indeed, that the Greek preposition here translated "for" does not necessarily indicate substitution; it does not necessarily mean "instead of."

The preposition that does mean "instead of" is used, for example, in Mk. 10:45, where it is said that "the Son of Man came . . . to give His life a ransom instead of many." There we find the great doctrine of the substitutionary atonement taught in the plainest possible way by our Lord Himself and in that one of the Gospels which is thought by modern skeptical criticism to be the earliest of the four.

But although that preposition, which means most clearly "instead of," is not used in our passage, yet our passage teaches the substitutionary atonement in the clearest possible way. Some scholars think that the preposition which *is* used here shades over in certain passages into the meaning "instead of." There is something to be said for such a view. But the question is here quite unimportant; for even if the preposition means in our passage, as it usually does, "in behalf of," "for the benefit of," and not "instead of," yet the idea of substitution is presented by the entire context in the clearest possible manner. "We were under the curse of the law," says Paul; and "Christ redeemed us by becoming a curse in our behalf." Christ bore a curse when He hung there on the cross. But what curse was it? Paul makes the answer perfectly plain. It was not merely the curse of some human law; but it was the curse of *God's* law. True, Christ died at the hands of wicked men; putting Him to death was a terrible crime. But He died, according to Paul as well as according to Peter, "by the determinate counsel and foreknowledge of God," and the curse which Paul quotes in the very next verse as resting upon Christ is the curse of the law of God.

Here we come to the very heart of Paul's teaching. The curse which Christ bore upon the cross was not a curse that *wrongly* rested upon Him; it was not a curse pronounced upon Him by some wicked human law. No, it was the curse of God's law; it was a curse, therefore,—we tremble as we say it, but the Scripture compels us to say it—it was a curse which *rightly* rested upon Him. But if that be so, there can be no doubt but that the substitutionary atonement is taught in Scripture. The only way in which a curse could *rightly* rest upon a sinless One is that He was the substitute, in bearing that curse, for those upon whom it did rightly rest. That is the heart of Paul's teaching and the heart of the whole Bible.

PART II

ADDITIONAL AIDS TO THE INTERPRETATION OF GALATIANS FROM VARIOUS WRITINGS OF J. GRESHAM MACHEN

I. THE EPISTLE TO THE GALATIANS
Questions on the exegesis of Galatians 1:1—4:4 prepared by Dr. Machen for his students

CHAPTER I

Verses 1-5. The Address.

Verse 1.
 (1) ἀπόστολος. Derivation and meaning of the word. The New Testament usage.
 (2) ἀπ' ... δι'. What progress in the thought?
 (3) ἀνθρώπων ... ἀνθρώπου. Why is the number varied?
 (4) Ἰησοῦ Χριστοῦ contrasted with man.
 (5) Why not καὶ ἀπὸ θεοῦ πατρός? Why is θεοῦ without the article?
 (6) πατρός. Father of whom?
 (7) Why is οὐκ ... νεκρῶν added? Why is τοῦ ἐγείραντος αὐτὸν ἐκ νεκρῶν added?

Verse 2.
 (1) σύν with the dative.
 (2) ἐμοί instead of third person.
 (3) Who are meant by οἱ σὺν ἐμοὶ πάντες ἀδελφοί?
 (4) What part do the persons associated with Paul in the openings of his epistles have in the composition of the epistles? Does Paul ever use the first person plural to refer to himself alone?
 (5) ἐκκλησίαις. Derivation and meaning of the word. The New Testament usage.
 (6) Where was "Galatia"?

Verse 3.
 (1) Text. Position of ημων.
 (2) Meaning of χάρις and εἰρήνη.

Verse 4.
 (1) To what act does δόντος refer?
 (2) Text. υπερ or περι? Meaning of the prepositions.
 (3) Meaning of the word ἐξέληται.
 (4) Meaning of ἐνεστῶτος, and of τοῦ αἰῶνος τοῦ ἐνεστῶτος.

(5) Position of πονηροῦ. Its significance as applied to τοῦ αἰῶνος τοῦ ἐνεστῶτος.

(6) The Jewish doctrine of the two ages. How does it differ from Paul's view?

(7) When does the action denoted by ἐξέληται take place?

(8) Significance of the whole clause, ὅπως etc. Why is it added here?

(9) With what is κατὰ τὸ θέλημα etc. to be construed? Why is it added here?

(10) With what is ἡμῶν (last word) to be construed?

Verse 5.
(1) Meaning of δόξα.
(2) What verb is to be supplied?

Review of Verses 1-5.

Openings of letters, Greek, Jewish, and Pauline. Peculiarites of this opening as over against the openings of other Pauline epistles.

Verses 6-10 (9). The occasion for the Epistle. Absence of the usual thanksgiving.

Verse 6.
(1) μετατίθεσθε. Voice. Significance of the tense.

(2) From what point of time is οὕτως ταχέως to be reckoned? (three possibilities).

(3) How is Χριστοῦ to be construed? Who is the one who called?

(4) Meaning of the word καλέσαντος.

(5) Meaning of ἐν χάριτι Χριστοῦ.

Verse 7.
(1) General sense of the verse.
(2) Antecedent of ὅ.
(3) ἄλλο. Other than what?
(4) What contrast, if any, is there between ἕτερον and ἄλλο?
(5) Meaning of εἰ μή.
(6) οἱ ταράσσοντες. Significance of this form of expression.

(7) μεταστρέψαι. Meaning of the word.
(8) τοῦ Χριστοῦ. What kind of genitive?

Verse 8.
(1) Text. ευαγγελισηται or ευαγγελιζηται? Is the former υμιν to be read?
(2) What is the force of ἀλλά?
(3) Whom does Paul mean by ἡμεῖς?
(4) Meaning of παρά.
(5) ἀνάθεμα. History and meaning of the word.

Verse 9.
(1) When did the action denoted by προειρήκαμεν take place?
(2) Meaning of the word ἄρτι.
(3) εἰ ... εὐαγγελίζεται. Significance of the mood. Cf.v.8.

Verse 10.
(1) What is the force of γάρ?
(2) What is the force of ἄρτι?
(3) Meaning of πείθω. Of ἢ τὸν θεόν.
(4) Meaning of ἤρεσκον.
(5) To what period of time does ἔτι refer?
(6) To whom does ἀνθρώποις refer?
(7) What is the meaning of Χριστοῦ δοῦλος οὐκ ἂν ἤμην? How does it follow from the preceding clause?
(8) ἤμην. The form.
(9) What does this verse tell us about the charges of the Judaizers against Paul?
(10) Does this verse belong to the preceding paragraph or to what follows?

i.11—ii.21. Paul's apostolic authority vindicated.

Verses 11-12. The claim that is to be proved.

Verse 11.
(1) Text. γαρ or δε?
(2) To what does γάρ refer?
(3) ἀδελφοί. Significance of this form of address.
(4) Meaning of κατὰ ἄνθρωπον.

Verse 12.
(1) Text. ουδε or ουτε before εδιδαχθην?
(2) Meaning of οὐδὲ γάρ.
(3) With what is ἐγώ contrasted?
(4) Distinction between παρέλαβον and ἐδιδάχθην.
(5) What kind of genitive is Ἰησοῦ Χριστοῦ?
(6) To what event or events in the life of Paul does ἀποκαλύψεως Ἰησοῦ Χριστοῦ refer? What was the manner and content of this revelation?

i.13—ii.21. Historical review in vindication of Paul's apostolic authority.

Verses 13-14. Before the conversion.

Verse 13.
(1) τὴν ἐμὴν ἀναστροφήν ποτε ἐν τῷ Ἰουδαϊσμῷ. Order of words.
(2) ἀναστροφήν. History and meaning of the word.
(3) Meaning of Ἰουδαϊσμῷ.
(4) Meaning of ἐπόρθουν.

Verse 14.
(1) συνηλικιώτας. What tendency of late Greek is illustrated by this word?
(2) περισσοτέρως. Force of the comparative.
(3) Meaning of the word ὑπάρχων.
(4) What is meant by τῶν πατρικῶν μου παραδόσεων. Importance of verses 13-14 in Paul's argument.

Verses 15-16a. The conversion.

Verse 15.
(1) Text. Is ο θεος to be read?
(2) Is ἐκ κοιλίας μητρός μου to be interpreted temporally or locally? If temporally, what point of time is meant?
(3) Meaning of ἀφορίσας?
(4) To what event does καλέσας refer?

Verse 16.
(1) When did the revealing take place?
(2) What is the force of ἐν ἐμοί? Harmony with other statements of Paul, and with Acts.

(3) ἔθνεσιν. Was this destination made known to Paul at the time of the ἀποκαλύψαι?
(4) With what is εὐθέως to be construed? Harmony with Acts.
(5) What is the meaning of προσανεθέμην?
(6) To whom does σαρκὶ καὶ αἵματι refer?

Verses 16b-24. After the conversion. No dependence on the original apostles.

Verse 17.
  (1) Text. ανηλθον or απηλθον?
  (2) Why is the preposition ἀνά prefixed to the verb?
  (3) Ἱεροσόλυμα. Declension. What other form of the name occurs?
  (4) What region is meant by "Arabia"?
  (5) How long did Paul stay in Arabia? What did he do there?
  (6) What confirmation of Acts is afforded by πάλιν ὑπέστρεψα?

Verse 18.
  (1) Text. ετη τρια or τρια ετη? κηφαν or πετρον?
  (2) The names Κηφᾶς and Πέτρος.
  (3) From what point of time are the three years to be reckoned?
  (4) What other accounts have we of this departure from Damascus?
  (5) Meaning of ἱστορῆσαι.
  (6) Meaning of πρός with the accusative here.
  (7) δεκαπέντε. The form.

Verse 19.
  (1) Does James here appear as an apostle? (Meaning of εἰ μή). If apostle, was he (a) among the twelve, or (b) an apostle in a wider sense?
  (2) In what sense is James called "the brother of the Lord"? History of this James.

Verse 20.
  (1) Construction.
  (2) What does this verse strengthen?

Verse 21.
 (1) Text. Is τῆς to be read before Κιλικίας?
 (2) What region is meant by "Syria"? Harmony with Acts.
 (3) Importance of this departure.

Verse 22.
 (1) Grammar— ἤμην ... ἀγνοούμενος and τῷ προσώπῳ.
 (2) Why does Paul add ταῖς ἐν Χριστῷ?
 (3) What is meant by τῆς Ἰουδαίας?

Verse 23.
 (1) Grammar— ἀκούοντες ἦσαν.
 (2) Tense of διώκων.
 (3) In what sense is τὴν πίστιν used here?

Verse 24.
 Meaning of ἐν ἐμοί.

CHAPTER II

Verses 1-10. The conference with the original apostles. They recognized that Paul had already received his commission from God.

Verse 1.
 (1) Meaning of διά.
 (2) The form Βαρνάβα.
 (3) From what point of time is διὰ δεκατεσσάρων ἐτῶν to be reckoned?
 (4) Was this Paul's second visit to Jerusalem after his conversion? Harmony with Acts.

Verse 2.
 (1) κατὰ ἀποκάλυψιν. Meaning of the phrase and harmony with Acts. Why does Paul add ἀνέβην δὲ κατὰ ἀποκάλυψιν?
 (2) Who are meant by αὐτοῖς?
 (3) Do ἀνεθέμην αὐτοῖς and κατ' ἰδίαν δὲ τοῖς δοκοῦσιν refer to the same meeting?
 (4) Meaning of the phrase τοῖς δοκοῦσιν.

(5) In what two ways may μή πως be interpreted? With what is μή πως etc. to be construed? Mood of τρέχω and of ἔδραμον.

Verse 3.
    (1) Relation to what precedes.
    (2) What is the force of οὐδέ?
    (3) What is the force of Ἕλλην ὤν?
    (4) What is the meaning of ἠναγκάσθη? What are the historical implications?

Verse 4.
    (1) Who are meant by ψευδαδέλφους?
    (2) What is the meaning of παρεισάκτους and παρεισῆλθαν? Into what were they "brought in," and into what did they "come in"?
    (3) What is the force of οἵτινες as distinguished from the simple relative?
    (4) Who are meant by the first person plural in this verse? What is meant by τὴν ἐλευθερίαν ἡμῶν?
    (5) Meaning of ἐν Χριστῷ Ἰησοῦ.
    (6) καταδουλώσουσιν. Mood.

Verse 5.
    (1) Text. Is οἷς οὐδε to be read?
    (2) Was Titus circumcised?
    (3) What is the meaning of τῇ ὑποταγῇ? Explain the case.
    (4) What is the meaning of ἡ ἀλήθεια τοῦ εὐαγγελίου
    (5) Explain the use of the second πρός.
    (6) Who are meant by ὑμᾶς?
    (7) Explain the sentence-structure of verses 4, 5. What is the general sense of these verses?

Verse 6.
    (1) Text. Is ο to be read before θεος?
    (2) Relation of this verse to what precedes.
    (3) What two meanings of ποτέ are possible here? Which is to be preferred?

(4) What is the origin of the phrase πρόσωπον λαμβάνειν?
(5) What is the meaning of οὐδὲν προσανέθεντο? (four possibilities).
(6) Explain the sentence-structure of this verse. What is the force of γάρ? Explain the emphasis on ἐμοί.
(7) What does this verse tell us about Paul's feeling toward the original apostles?

Verse 7.
(1) ἰδόντες. How did they see it?
(2) πεπίστευμαι. Significance of the tense.
(3) Explain the case of τὸ εὐαγγέλιον.
(4) What is meant by τὸ εὐαγγέλιον τῆς ἀκροβυστίας as over against τὸ εὐαγγέλιον τῆς περιτομῆς?

Verse 8.
(1) What is the force of γάρ?
(2) Explain the case of Πέτρῳ and of ἐμοί.
(3) What was the manner of the activity denoted by ἐνεργήσας?
(4) Why did not Paul write εἰς τὴν ἀποστολὴν τῶν ἐθνῶν instead of εἰς τὰ ἔθνη?

Verse 9.
(1) What is meant by τὴν χάριν? How did they recognize it?
(2) Ἰάκωβος καὶ Κηφᾶς καὶ Ἰωάνης. What three persons are meant? Significance of the order.
(3) What is the meaning of the expression δεξιὰς ἔδωκαν?
(4) Position of κοινωνίας in the sentence. Significance of the word.
(5) ἵνα ἡμεῖς etc. What was the meaning of this arrangement between Paul and the original apostles?

Verse 10.
(1) With what is ἵνα μνημονεύωμεν to be construed?
(2) Who are meant by τῶν πτωχῶν?
(3) What is the meaning of ἐσπούδασα?

Verses 11-21 (or 11-14). Paul and Peter. Paul could even oppose one of the original apostles.

Verse 11.
(1) When did the event narrated in verses 11ff. take place?
(2) What is the meaning of κατεγνωσμένος?

Verse 12.
(1) Text. ηλθεν or ηλθον?
(2) What are the implications of ἀπὸ 'Ιακώβου?
(3) What is the force of the tense of ὑπέστελλεν and ἀφώριζεν?
(4) Meaning of the phrase τοὺς ἐκ περιτομῆς.

Verse 13.
(1) Is καὶ to be read before οἱ λοιποί?
(2) Wherein consisted the "hyprocrisy" of Peter's action?
(3) Explain the case of ὑποκρίσει.
(4) Subsequent relations between Paul and Barnabas.

Verse 14.
(1) Meaning of ὀρθοποδοῦσιν.
(2) Meaning of πρός.
(3) Explain the tense of ζῆς.
(4) ἀναγκάζεις. How was the compulsion exerted?

Verse 15.
(1) Where does the speech to Peter end?
(2) Explain the sentence-structure in verses 15, 16.
(3) Meaning of ἁμαρτωλοί.

Verse 16.
(1) Text. χριστον ιησουν or ιησουν χριστον?
(2) What is the meaning of δικαιοῦται?
(3) To what does νόμου refer? Explain the genitive.
(4) Why is there no article with νόμου?
(5) Meaning of ἐὰν μή.
(6) What is the force of ὅτι in the last clause?
(7) οὐ ... πᾶσα. Explain the usage.

Verse 17.
(1) What is the meaning of ἐν Χριστῷ?
(2) What is the meaning of εὑρέθημεν?
(3) In what two ways may ἄρα be accented? What is the difference in meaning?
(4) What is the meaning of μὴ γένοιτο?

Verse 18.
(1) συνιστάνω. Form and meaning.
(2) Wherein consists the "transgression" referred to in παραβάτην?
(3) What is the force of γάρ?
(4) What is the argument of verses 15-18?

Verse 19.
(1) Explain the emphasis on ἐγώ.
(2) What is the force of γάρ?
(3) What is the meaning of νόμῳ ἀπέθανον?
(4) What is the force of διὰ νόμου?
(5) What is the meaning of θεῷ ζήσω?
(6) Explain Χριστῷ συνεσταύρωμαι.

Verse 20.
(1) Text. του υιου του θεου or του θεου και χριστου?
(2) Explain the construction of ὅ.
(3) With what period of time does νῦν imply a contrast?
(4) What is the meaning of ἐν πίστει?
(5) Why does Paul add τοῦ ἀγαπήσαντός με etc.?
(6) What is the significance of με?

Verse 21.
(1) What is the force of γάρ?
(2) What is the meaning of δωρεάν?
(3) Explain the thought of the verse. What is its significance in the Epistle?
(4) What was the result of the meeting with Peter?
(5) What is the place of verses 15-21 in the argument of the Epistle?

Chapter III

iii. I—v. 12. Paul's gospel vindicated.

Verses 1-5. Argument from experience. The Spirit was given through faith, not by works.

Verse 1.
  (1) Text. Is τη αληθεια μη πειθεσθαι to be read after εβασκανεν?   Is εν υμιν to be read after προεγραφη?
  (2) Why does Paul address his readers just at this point as ἀνόητοι?
  (3) What is the importance of ˇΩ ἀνόητοι Γαλάται for the question of the destination of the Epistle?
  (4) Derivation and meaning of ἐβάσκανεν.
  (5) What is the meaning of προεγράφη?   (four possibilities).

Verse 2.
  (1) τὸ πνεῦμα. How manifested? By whom received?
  (2) What is the meaning of ἀκοῆς πίστεως?

Verse 3.
  (1) πνεύματι. Why without the article? Explain the case.
  (2) What is the voice of ἐπιτελεῖσθε?

Verse 4.
  (1) To what does τοσαῦτα refer?
  (2) What is the meaning of εἴ γε καὶ εἰκῇ?

Verse 5.
  (1) To whom does ὁ ... ἐπιχορηγῶν refer?
  (2) ἐπιχορηγῶν. Derivation and meaning of the word.
  (3) Explain the tense of ἐπιχορηγῶν and ἐνεργῶν.
  (4) What is meant by δυνάμεις?

Verses 6-22. Argument from Scripture. Not those who depend upon the works of the law, but those who believe, have the benefits of the covenant made with Abraham.

Verses 6-9. Abraham was justified by faith, and those who are of faith, being his true descendants, share his blessing.

Verse 6.
(1) Does this verse belong to the preceding or to the following paragraph?
(2) Does καθώς introduce a proof or a mere comparison?
(3) What passage does Paul quote? What form of the Old Testament does he use? Where else in the New Testament is the same passage quoted?

Verse 7.
(1) What is the mood of γινώσκετε?
(2) οἱ ἐκ πίστεως. Meaning of the phrase.
(3) οὗτοι. With whom contrasted?

Verse 8.
(1) προϊδοῦσα. How can this verb be used of ἡ γραφή?
(2) What is the meaning of ἡ γραφή?
(3) Explain the tense of δικαιοῖ.
(4) Explain the use of the second ὅτι.
(5) What passage or passages does Paul quote?
(6) What is here the meaning of ἔθνη?
(7) In what does the blessing consist?
(8) What is the meaning of ἐν σοί?

Verse 9.
(1) What is the force of ὥστε?
(2) Compare with verses 6-9 James ii. 20-24.

Verses 10-14. The law, on the contrary, far from bringing a blessing, brought a curse, from which Christ had to free us before the blessing of Abraham might be enjoyed.

Verse 10.
(1) What is the force of γάρ?
(2) Special use of γέγραπται.
(3) What passage or passages does Paul quote?
(4) τοῦ ποιῆσαι. Grammar.
(5) What syllogism is involved in this verse? What part of it is missing? Is that part supplied in what follows?

Verse 11.
(1) What is the meaning of ἐν νόμῳ? Of παρὰ τῷ θεῷ?

(2) Does the first ὅτι mean "that" or "because"? The second ὅτι?
(3) What passage is quoted? Where else in the New Testament is the same passage quoted?
(4) With what is ἐκ πίστεως to be construed? What is the alternative view?
(5) What is the meaning of ζήσεται?
(6) Compare the passage as quoted by Paul with the Hebrew Old Testament and with the Septuagint.

Verse 12.
(1) What is the meaning of ἐκ πίστεως?
(2) What passage is quoted? Where else in the New Testament is the same passage quoted?
(3) What is the significance of the quotation for Paul's argument?
(4) What syllogism is expressed in verses 11, 12?

Verse 13.
(1) Text. οτι γεγραπται or γεγραπται γαρ?
(2) To whom does the first person plural in this verse refer?
(3) Explain the emphasis on Χριστός.
(4) What is the meaning of ἐξηγόρασεν? To whom or to what was the price paid?
(5) Why is the noun κατάρα used instead of an adjective?
(6) What is the meaning of ὑπέρ?
(7) What is the teaching of this verse as to the meaning of the death of Christ?
(8) What passage is quoted? Why does Paul omit ὑπὸ θεοῦ?
(9) What is the meaning and validity of the quotation in Paul's argument?

Verse 14.
(1) Text. ιησου χριστου or χριστου ιησου?
(2) Explain the meaning of this verse in relation to verse 13, giving particular attention to εἰς τὰ ἔθνη.
(3) To what does ἡ εὐλογία refer?
(4) What is the meaning of ἐν Ἰησοῦ Χριστῷ?

(5) Explain the use of ἐπαγγελίαν as the object of λάβωμεν.
(6) λάβωμεν. To whom does the first person plural refer?
(7) τοῦ πνεύματος. Meaning of the genitive. What promise is meant by τὴν ἐπαγγελίαν?
(8) With what is the second ἵνα clause to be construed?

Verses 15-18. The law came after the promise and cannot affect it.

Verse 15.
   (1) Meaning of κατὰ ἄνθρωπον λέγω.
   (2) Meaning and position of ὅμως.
   (3) Meaning of διαθήκη.
   (4) Is οὐδείς to be taken strictly?

Verse 16.
   (1) What is the place of this verse in the argument?
   (2) What is the force of the datives τῷ ... Ἀβραάμ and τῷ σπέρματι?
   (3) αἱ ἐπαγγελίαι. What is the force of the plural?
   (4) What is the subject of λέγει?
   (5) What Old Testament passage is quoted in this verse?
   (6) What is the meaning of οὐ λέγει ... Χριστός? What is the validity of the argument?

Verse 17.
   (1) Text. Is εἰς χριστον to be read after υπο του θεου?
   (2) What is the force of τοῦτο δὲ λέγω?
   (3) μετὰ τετρακόσια καὶ τριάκοντα ἔτη. Compare the number with the parallel passages in the Hebrew and Greek Bibles.
   (4) Does εἰς τό ... express purpose here?

Verse 18.
   (1) What is the force of γάρ?
   (2) What is the force of οὐκέτι?
   (3) How is κεχάρισται to be interpreted?

Verses 19-22. The law was not intended to compete with the promise, but served a subordinate and temporary purpose.

Verse 19.
(1) Text. αχρις αν or αχρις ου?
(2) ἄχρις οὗ ἔλθῃ. Grammar.
(3) What is the meaning of τῶν παραβάσεων χάριν προσετέθη?
(4) What is meant by τὸ σπέρμα?
(5) διαταγεὶς δι' ἀγγέλων. What is the basis for this idea? Where else does it appear in the New Testament?
(6) What is the meaning of ἐν χειρί?
(7) Who is meant by μεσίτου?
(8) Why does Paul add διαταγεὶς ... μεσίτου?

Verse 20.
(1) With what is ἑνός to be contrasted?
(2) What are the most probable interpretations of the verse, and which is to be preferred?

Verse 21.
(1) Text. Is του θεου to be read after επαγγελιων? εκ νομου ην αν or εκ νομου ην or εκ νομου αν ην or εν νομω αν ην or αν εκ νομου ην?
(2) What is the force of οὖν?
(3) What is the force of γάρ?
(4) ὁ δυνάμενος. Significance of this form of expression.
(5) What life is referred to in ζωοποιῆσαι?
(6) How does the apodosis of the second half of this verse follow from the protasis?

Verse 22.
(1) What is the connection with what precedes?
(2) What is meant by ἡ γραφή?
(3) How is συνέκλεισεν ἡ γραφή to be interpreted?
(4) τὰ πάντα. Significance of the neuter.
(5) Does ἵνα etc. here express purpose? If so, whose purpose?
(6) With what is ἐκ πίστεως to be construed?

(7) ἐκ πίστεως, τοῖς πιστεύουσιν, Why are both these phrases used?
(8) What is the argument of verses 21, 22?

iii. 23—iv. 7. The former bondage contrasted with the present freedom.

Verses 23-25. The life under the law was a period of restraint like that of childhood, preliminary to faith in Christ.

Verse 23.
(1) Text. συνκλειόμενοι or συγκεκλεισμένοι?
(2) What is the meaning of τὴν πίστιν?
(3) ὑπὸ νόμον ἐφρουρούμεθα etc. Explain the figure.
(4) To whom does the first person plural refer?
(5) How closely is συνκλειόμενοι to be joined to ἐφρουρούμεθα?
(6) Explain the tenses of ἐφρουρούμεθα and of συνκλειόμενοι.
(7) What idea does εἰς express?
(8) τὴν μέλλουσαν πίστιν ἀποκαλυφθῆναι. Explain the order. What is the significance of ἀποκαλυφθῆναι?

Verse 24.
(1) What was the position and function of a παιδαγωγός?
(2) Explain the application of the figure.

Verse 25.
To whom does the first person plural refer?

Verses 26-29. But now you are all alike sons of God in Christ, and therefore heirs of the promise made to Abraham.

Verse 26.
(1) What is the force of γάρ?
(2) Why is the second person used?
(3) With what is ἐν Χριστῷ Ἰησοῦ to be construed? How is it to be interpreted?

Verse 27.
    (1) What is the meaning of εἰς Χριστὸν ἐβαπτίσθητε?
    (2) What is the meaning of Χριστὸν ἐνεδύσασθε?

Verse 28.
    (1) Text. εις εστε εν χριστω ιησου or εν εστε εν χριστω ιησου or εστε χριστου ιησου?
    (2) What is the derivation and meaning of ἔνι?
    (3) What is the meaning of Ἕλλην?
    (4) What is the meaning of εἷς ἐστὲ ἐν Χριστῷ Ἰησοῦ?

Verse 29.
    ἄρα etc. How does this follow from εἰ δὲ ὑμεῖς Χριστοῦ?

CHAPTER IV

Verses 1-7. Further unfolding and application of the figure of the two stages in the life of a son.

Verse 1.
    (1) Is the father of the κληρονόμος conceived of as living or dead?
    (2) In the application of the figure, to whom does the κληρονόμος νήπιος refer?

Verse 2.
    (1) What were the positions and functions of ἐπίτροποι and οἰκονόμοι?
    (2) What legal difficulty is involved in ἄχρι τῆς προθεσμίας τοῦ πατρός? To what kind of law is Paul referring? What is the solution of the difficulty?

Verse 3.
    (1) Text. Is ημεθα or ημεν to be read before δεδουλωμενοι?
    (2) ἤμεθα. The form. Explain the phrase ἤμεθα δεδουλωμένοι.
    (3) To whom does the first person plural refer?
    (4) What are the leading interpretations of τὰ στοιχεῖα τοῦ κόσμου? Which is correct?

Verse 4.
 (1) What is the meaning of πλήρωμα and of the phrase τὸ πλήρωμα τοῦ χρόνου?
 (2) What is the meaning of ἐξαπέστειλεν? What does this word imply as to Paul's conception of the person of Christ?
 (3) γενόμενον ἐκ γυναικός. What does this phrase imply as to Paul's conception of the birth of Jesus?
 (4) In what two ways may γενόμενον ὑπὸ νόμον be interpreted? Which is correct?

II. SURVEYS OF GALATIANS

Included in this section are (1) Dr. Machen's treatment of Galatians as a whole found in Lesson XVIII, "The Conflict with the Judaizers," in *The Literature and History of New Testament Times* (Philadelphia: The Presbyterian Board of Publication and Sabbath School Work, [1915]), Teacher's Manual, pp. 97-102, and (2) the lesson of the same number and title in the corresponding Student's Text Book, Part II, *The Westminster Departmental Graded Series* (Philadelphia: Publication Department, Board of Christian Education of the Presbyterian Church in the U.S.A., [1914]), pp. 96-101.

(1)

From Teacher's Manual

Excerpt from

LESSON XVIII

The Conflict With The Judaizers

Galatians a Polemic

After studying first the Thessalonian epistles and then Galatians in succession the student should be able to form some conception of the variety among the epistles of Paul. Certainly there could be no sharper contrast. First and Second Thessalonians are simple, affectionate letters written to a youthful church; Galatians is one of the most passionate bits of polemic in the whole Bible. We ought to honor Paul for his anger. A lesser man might have taken a calmer view of the situation. After all, it might have been said, the observance of Jewish fasts and feasts was not a serious matter; even circumcision, though useless, could do no great harm. But Paul penetrated below the surface. He detected the great principles that were at stake. The Judaizers were disannulling the grace of God.

The Address. Gal. 1:1-5

The addresses of the Pauline epistles are never merely formal. Paul does not wait for the beginning of the letter proper in order to say what he has in mind. Even the epistolary forms are suffused with the deepest religious feeling.

The opening of the present letter is anticipatory of what is to follow. Dividing the opening into three parts—the nominative (name and title of the writer), the dative (name of those to whom the letter is addressed), and the greeting—it will be observed that every one of these parts has its peculiarity as compared with the other Pauline epistles.

The peculiarity of the nominative is the remarkable addition beginning with "not from men," which is a summary of the first great division of the epistle, Paul's defense against the personal attack of his opponents. Since the Epistle to the Galatians is polemic from beginning to end, it is not surprising that the very first word after the bare name and title of the author is "not." Paul cannot mention his title "apostle"—in the addresses of First and Second Thessalonians he had not thought it necessary to mention it at all—without thinking of the way in which in Galatia it was misrepresented. "My apostleship," he says, "came not only from Christ, but directly from Christ."

The peculiarity of the dative is its brevity—not "beloved of God, called to be saints," or the like, but just the bare and formal "to the churches of Galatia." The situation was not one which called for pleasant words!

The greeting is the least varied part in the addresses of the Pauline epistles. The long addition to the greeting in Galatians is absolutely unique. It is a summary of the second and central main division of the epistle, Paul's defense of his gospel. "Christ has died to free you. The Judaizers in bringing you into bondage are making of none effect the grace of Christ, manifested on the cross." That is the very core of the letter. In all of the Pauline epistles there is scarcely a passage more characteristic of the man than the first five verses of Galatians. An ordinary writer would have been merely formal in the address. Not so Paul!

The exultant supernaturalism of the address should be noticed. This supernaturalism appears, in the first place, in the sphere of external history—"God the Father, who raised him from the dead." Pauline Christianity is based upon the miracle of the resurrection. Supernaturalism appears also, however, in the sphere of Christian experience—"who gave himself for our sins, that he might deliver us out of this present evil world." Christianity is no mere easy development of the old life, no mere improvement of the life, but a new life in a new world. In both spheres, supernaturalism is being denied in the modern Church. Pauline Christianity is very different from much that is called Christianity to-day.

Finally, this passage will serve to exhibit Paul's lofty view of the person of Christ. "Neither through man," says Paul, "but through Jesus Christ." Jesus Christ is here distinguished sharply from men and placed clearly on the side of God. What is more, even the Judaizers evidently accepted fundamentally the same view. Paul said, "Not by man, but by Jesus Christ"; the Judaizers said, "Not by Jesus Christ, but by man." But if so, then the Judaizers, no less than Paul, distinguished Jesus sharply from ordinary humanity. About other things there was debate, but about the person of Christ Paul appears in harmony even with his opponents. Evidently the original apostles had given the Judaizers on this point no slightest excuse for differing from Paul. The heavenly Christ of Paul was also the Christ of those who had walked and talked with Jesus of Nazareth. They had seen Jesus subject to all the petty limitations of human life. Yet they thought him divine! Could they have been deceived?

The Purpose of the Epistle. Gal. 1:6-10

The thanksgiving for the Christian state of the readers, which appears in practically every other of the Pauline epistles, is here conspicuous by its absence. Here it would have been a mockery. The Galatians were on the point of giving up the gospel. There was just a chance of saving them. The letter was written in a desperate crisis. Pray God it might not be too late! No time here for words of thanks!

In vs. 6-10, Paul simply states the purpose of the letter in a few uncompromising words: "You are falling away from the gospel and I am writing to stop you."

Paul's Defense of his Apostolic Authority. Gal. 1:11 to 2:21

After stating, Gal. 1:11, 12, the thesis that is to be proved in this section, Paul defends his independent apostolic authority by three main arguments.

In the first place, vs. 13-24, he was already launched upon his work as apostle to the Gentiles before he had even come into any effective contact with the original apostles. Before his conversion, he had been an active persecutor. His conversion was wrought, not, like an ordinary conversion, through human agency, but by an immediate act of Christ. After his conversion it was three years before he saw any of the apostles. Then he saw only Peter (and James) and that not long enough to become, as his opponents said, a disciple of these leaders.

In the second place, Gal. 2:1-10, when he finally did hold a conference with the original apostles, they themselves, the very authorities to whom the Judaizers appealed, recognized that his authority was quite independent of theirs, and, like theirs, of directly divine origin.

In the third place, Gal. 2:11-21, so independent was his authority that on one occasion he could even rebuke the chief of the original apostles himself. What Paul said at that time to Peter happened to be exactly what he wanted to say, in the epistle, to the Galatians. This section, therefore, forms a transition to the second main division of the epistle. It has sometimes been thought surprising that Paul does not say how Peter took his rebuke. The conclusion has even been drawn that if Peter had acknowledged his error Paul would have been sure to say so. Such reasoning ignores the character of this section. In reporting the substance of what he said to Peter, Paul has laid bare the very depths of his own life. To return, after such a passage, to the incident at Antioch would have been pedantic and unnecessary. Long before the end of the second chapter Paul has forgotten all about Peter, all about Antioch, and all about the whole of his past history. He is thinking only of the grace of Christ, and how some men are trampling it under foot. O foolish Galatians, to desert so great a salvation!

Paul's Defense of his Gospel. Gal. 3:1 to 5:12

Salvation cannot be earned by human effort, but must be received simply as a free gift. Christ has died to save us from the curse of the law: to submit again to the yoke of bondage is disloyalty to him—that is the great thesis that Paul sets out to prove.

He proves it first by an argument from experience. Gal. 3:1-5. You received the Holy Spirit, in palpable manifestation, before you ever saw the Judaizers, before you ever thought of keeping the Mosaic law. You received the Spirit by faith alone. How then can you now think that the law is necessary? Surely there can be nothing higher than the Spirit.

In the second place, there is an argument from Scripture. Not those who depend upon the works of the law, but those who believe, have the benefit of the covenant made with Abraham. Vs. 6-22.

In the third place, by the use of various figures, Paul contrasts the former bondage with the present freedom. Gal. 3:23 to 4:7. The life under the law was a period of restraint like that of childhood, preliminary to faith in Christ. The law was intended to produce the consciousness of sin, in order that the resultant hopelessness might lead men to accept the Saviour. Vs. 23-25. But now all Christians alike, both Jews and Gentiles, are sons of God in Christ, and therefore heirs of the promise made to Abraham. Vs. 29-36. Being sons of God, with all the glorious freedom of sonship, with the Spirit crying, "Abba, Father," in the heart, how can we think of returning to the miserable bondage of an external and legalistic religion? Gal. 4:1-11.

In the fourth place, Paul turns away from argument to make a personal appeal. Vs. 12-20. What has become of your devotion to me? Surely I have not become your enemy just because I tell you the truth. The Judaizers are estranging you from me. Listen to me, my spiritual children, even though I can speak to you only through the cold medium of a letter!

In the fifth place, Paul, in his perplexity, bethinks himself of one more argument. It is an argument that would appeal especially to those who were impressed by the Judaizers' method of using the Old Testament, but it also has permanent validity. The fundamental principle, says Paul, for which I am arguing, the principle of grace, can be illustrated from the story of Ishmael and Isaac. Ishmael had every prospect of being the heir of Abraham. It seemed impossible for the aged Abraham to have another son. Nature was on Ishmael's side. But nature was overruled. So it is today. As far as nature is concerned, the Jews are the heirs of Abraham—they have all the outward marks of sonship. But God has willed otherwise. He has chosen to give the inheritance to the heirs according to promise. The principle of the divine choice, operative on a small scale in the acceptance of Isaac, is operative now on a large scale in the acceptance of the Gentile church.

Finally, Paul concludes the central section of the epistle by emphasizing the gravity of the crisis. Gal. 5:1-12. Do not be deceived. Circumcision as the Judaizers advocate it is no innocent thing; it means the acceptance of a law religion. You must choose either the law or grace; you cannot have both.

The Results of Paul's Gospel. Gal. 5:13 to 6:10

In this third main division of the epistle Paul exhibits the practical working of faith. Paul's gospel is more powerful than the teaching of the Judaizers. Try to keep the law in your own strength and you will fail, for the flesh is too strong. But the Spirit is stronger than the flesh, and the Spirit is received by faith.

Conclusion. Gal. 6:11-18

This concluding section, if not the whole epistle, was written with Paul's own hand. V. 11. In his other letters Paul dictated everything but a brief closing salutation.

In the closing section, Paul lays the alternative once more before his readers. The Judaizers have worldly aims, they boast of worldly advantages; but the true Christian boasts of nothing but the cross. Christianity, as here portrayed, is not the gentle, easy-going doctrine that is being mistaken for it to-day. It is no light thing to say, "The world hath been crucified unto me, and I unto the world." But the result is a new creature!

In the Library. — Purves, "Christianity in the Apostolic Age," pp. 203-213. Davis, "Dictionary of the Bible": article on "Ephesus"; Purves, articles on "Galatia" and "Galatians, Epistle to the" (supplemented). Hastings, "Dictionary of the Bible": Ramsay, article on "Ephesus"; Dods, article on "Galatians, Epistle to the." Ramsay, "St. Paul the Traveller and the Roman Citizen," pp. 262-282; "Pictures of the Apostolic Church," pp. 247-269, 293-300. Lewin, "The Life and Epistles of St. Paul," chs. xii, xiii. Conybeare and Howson, "The Life and Epistles of St. Paul," chs. xii, xiii, xiv, xv, and xvi. Stalker, "The Life of St. Paul," pp. 82-84, 108-118. Lumby, pp. 239-266. Cook, pp. 476-485. Plumptre, pp. 124-136. Rockham, pp. 331-370. McClymont, "The New Testament and Its Writers," pp. 70-76. Ellicott, "A New Testament Commentary for English Readers," vol. ii, pp. 419-468: Sanday, "The Epistle of Paul the Apostle to the Galatians." "The Cambridge Bible for Schools and Colleges": Perowne, "The Epistle to the Galatians." Zahn, "Introduction to the New Testament," vol. i, pp. 164-202. Lightfoot, "Saint Paul's Epistle to the Galatians." The two last-named works are intended primarily for those who have some knowledge of Greek, but can also be used by others.

(2)

From Student's Text Book

LESSON XVIII

THE CONFLICT WITH THE JUDAIZERS

Lesson Material: Acts 18: 18 to 19:40; The Epistle to the Galatians

DAILY BIBLE READINGS

M. Acts 18:18 to 19:20.
T. Acts 19:21-40.
W. Gal., ch. 1.
Th. Gal., ch. 2.
F. Gal. 3:1 to 4:7.
S. Gal. 4:8 to 5:12.
S. Gal. 5:13 to 6:18.

After having been brought before the judgment seat of Gallio, Paul remained many days in Corinth. His work was not suddenly interrupted as at Thessalonica and at many other places. The proconsul Gallio proved to be less susceptible to Jewish influence than lesser magistrates had been.

Instead of returning by the land route through Macedonia, Paul went direct by sea to Ephesus. At Ephesus, Aquila and Priscilla, who had accompanied Paul so far, were left behind. Paul contented himself, this time, with only a very brief stay, and after a sea voyage landed at Caesarea on the coast of Palestine. After landing, "he went up and saluted the church." What church is meant here—the church at Caesarea or the great church at Jerusalem? The latter view is more probable. Since Caesarea was ordinarily used as the seaport for Jerusalem, the name Jerusalem did not have to be mentioned. Probably, then, we have here Paul's fourth visit to Jerusalem after his conversion.

After spending some time in Antioch, Paul went through the Galatian country and Phrygia, thus beginning the third missionary journey. These were the same regions that had been visited on the second journey, Acts 16:6; but this time they were taken in the reverse order. Probably Galatia proper is meant, rather than some other part of the Roman province Galatia. After passing through the high central portion of Asia Minor, Paul came at last to the coastal plain, to Ephesus. Acts 19:1.

In Ephesus, Paul was able to preach somewhat longer than usual in the synagogue; but finally, after three months, he was driven out, as in so many other cities, and engaged for over two years in a purely Gentile work. A few of the incidents of this Ephesian residence are narrated by Luke, and narrated with characteristic vividness and accuracy. The school of Tyrannus, the Jewish exorcists, the books of magic, Demetrius the silversmith, the craftsmen, the great temple of Diana, the assembly in the theater, the Asiarchs, the town clerk—these are all described in a way that betokens the genuine historian, dependent upon first-hand information. There is scarcely any more absorbing bit of narrative, even in The Acts.

The Date of Galatians and the Location of the Churches

At some time during the three-year stay of Paul at Ephesus, and probably during the earlier rather than the later part of that period, the Epistle to the Galatians seems to have been written. This dating is dependent upon the correctness of the "North Galatian theory," which places "the churches of Galatia" to which the epistle is addressed in the northern part of the Roman province Galatia, and supposes that the churches had been founded on the journey described in Acts 16:6, and revisited at the time of Acts 18:23. Another widely prevalent theory — the "South Galatian theory" — identifies "the churches of Galatia" with the congregations at Pisidian Antioch, Iconium, Lystra and Derbe, in the southern part of the Roman province Galatia. Since these congregations were formed on the first missionary journey, the South Galatian theory admits of an earlier dating of the epistle than is possible on the North Galatian theory. It is very difficult to decide between the North Galatian and the South Galatian theories. Weighty arguments have been adduced on both sides. Provisionally, the North Galatian view has been adopted in the arrangements of this Text Book.

Fortunately, the interpretation of the epistle is very largely independent of "the Galatian question." Wherever the churches addressed in the epistle are to be placed, at any rate the situation that prevailed in those churches—the situation that gave rise to the epistle—can be reconstructed pretty clearly on the basis of the epistle itself, without reference to the narrative in The Acts.

The Situation Presupposed by the Epistle

"The churches of Galatia" to which Paul writes had been founded by Paul himself. Gal. 1:8; 4:12-20. Their membership was composed chiefly of Gentiles; for it was just to prevent the Galatian Christians from becoming Jews that the epistle was written. At Paul's first visit to the churches he had been ill, indeed his illness seems actually to have been the cause of his preaching to them. This illness was a temptation to them to reject his message, for physical weakness was in that day regarded with loathing rather than with sympathy, as a visitation of the divine wrath. Yet the Galatians had overcome the temptation nobly; they had received Paul "as an angel of God, even as Christ Jesus." Gal. 4:14.

Paul's preaching in Galatia no doubt included all the fundamental elements of the gospel. Jesus Christ crucified, he says, was openly set forth before their eyes as on a great placard or picture. The eager faith of the Galatians was followed by the bestowal of the Spirit, who manifested himself not only in a holier life, but also in miraculous powers. Evidently the Spirit became the possession of all who believed. Gal. 3:1-5.

Probably Paul had visited the churches a second time before the epistle was written, Gal. 4:13; and it was probably at this second visit that he took occasion to warn them against false teaching. Gal. 1:9. The danger, however, seems not to have been imminent at that time. The early part of the churches' life was altogether satisfactory. "Ye were running well," says Paul. Gal. 5:7.

A short time before the epistle was written, however, certain Jewish false teachers had entered into the churches from the outside. These men throughout the letter are sharply distinguished from the Galatian Christians themselves, whom despite their faults Paul addresses as "brethren." The false teachers were "Judaizers," and seem to have been very much like the Judaizers who are described in Acts 15:1, 5, 24. They insisted on observance of the Mosiac law, in addition to faith in Christ, as necessary to salvation. The Gentiles, they said, must unite themselves with the chosen people; they must become Jews if they were to become Christians.

In order to gain a hearing for this new teaching, the Judaizers were obliged to undermine the authority of Paul. Paul, they said, had received his apostleship only through the mediatorship of those who had known Jesus on earth and had been commissioned directly by him. If an apostle, therefore, he was at best only an apostle of the second rank. His authority was certainly not equal to that of Peter and the rest. Furthermore he was not even consistent. He adapted his message to the likes and dislikes of men. On occasion he could even advocate what he now opposed. Gal. 1:10; 5:11.

The activity of the Judaizers had been surprisingly successful. The Galatian Christians had already begun to waver in their devotion to Paul, Gal. 4:15, 16; and already they had begun to give heed to the claims of the law. Already they were observing Jewish fasts and feasts. V. 10. The decisive step, it is true, had not yet been taken. They had not yet united themselves definitely with the people of Israel. But they were in grave danger. If they were to be saved for the gospel, there was no time to lose.

Naturally the Epistle to the Galatians is a polemic from beginning to end—and a powerful, sharp polemic, too. It has just one purpose — to prevent the Galatian Christians from yielding to the demands of the Judaizers.

Contents of Galatians

In the first main division of the epistle, Gal. 1:11 to 2:21, which comes after the address, ch. 1:1-5, and a brief statement of the occasion of his writing, vs. 6-10, Paul defends his independent apostolic authority against the personal attack of his opponents. He does so by a review of events of his life. Christ had called him—that and nothing else had made him an apostle.

In the second main division, Gal. 3:1 to 5:12, Paul defends his gospel against the perversion of it attempted by the Judaizers. The Judaizers said: "You are saved by faith and by works. You need Christ's help, but part of your salvation you must earn by keeping the law." "No," said Paul, "you must take your choice. Earn your salvation if you can. Then you must keep the whole of the law; which is impossible. Or else, trust unreservedly in Christ. He will do everything or nothing. By his death he has paid the penalty imposed by the law upon our sins. If, therefore, by faith we are united with him, the law has nothing more to say to us. It is as though we had died. We can start fresh. We can begin a new life, free from the law and free from the wrath of God. Salvation is not something we can earn by keeping the law. It is a free gift."

The third main division, Gal. 5:13 to 6:10, is sometimes called the "practical" part of the epistle. But that term must not be misunderstood. It is not as though Paul had got through the main argument of the letter, and then turned to give some useful hints as to conduct. On the contrary, this last division is an integral part of the argument. The epistle is a polemic from beginning to end. In the "practical" part Paul is refuting a very weighty argument of his opponents. One criticism of salvation by faith has always been that it leads logically to moral laxness. If salvation is a free gift of God, independent of the works of men, then, it is said, it makes no difference what we do; we can go on sinning and yet be saved just the same. This criticism is gloriously refuted in the last division of Galatians. True faith, says Paul, is a faith that works itself out through love. And love is nothing else than the fulfilling of the whole moral law. The law, therefore, is fulfilled by the very man who is free from the law. Only, by him it is fulfilled not by obedience, through his own strength, to a set of external commandments, but by submission to a mighty inward impulse. By faith a new power enters into the life—the power of the Spirit of God. The little world of the soul becomes the scene of a conflict between titanic forces. "The flesh lusteth against the Spirit, and the Spirit against the flesh." Which shall we choose? It is easy to tell, at any rate, what the choice of any man has been. The works of the flesh are manifest, and so is the fruit of the Spirit. The man that does evil is under the power of the flesh, and will never inherit the kingdom of God; the man that does good has by faith submitted himself to the Spirit of God. Salvation brings a new life for the future as well as forgiveness for the past. "Be of sin the double cure, cleanse me from its guilt and power"—these words are a true interpretation of Paul.

Finally, in a few strong concluding words, Gal. 6:11-18, Paul uncovers the motives of his opponents, lays the alternative once more before his readers, and calls upon them to decide aright.

Permanent Value of Galatians

The Judaizers are dead and gone, but not the issue that they raised. Faith or works—that is as much as ever a living issue. "Salvation by character" is just a modern form of Judaizing, and a modern form of bondage to the law. Christ crucified needs still to be held up before our eyes; and still we need to receive by faith the gracious, life-giving power of his Spirit. Paul in Galatians was fighting the age-long battle of the Christian Church. "Just as I am, without one plea but that thy blood was shed for me" —these words would never have been written if the Judaizers had won.

Topics for Study

1. Summarize in your own words (a) Gal., chs. 1 and 2, (b) ch. 3:1 to 5:12, (c) ch. 5:13 to 6:18 (three topics).

2. Where were "the churches of Galatia" to which the Epistle to the Galatians was addressed? Discuss the two possible views.

3. Compare the address of the Epistle to the Galatians, Gal. 1:1-5, with the addresses of the other Pauline epistles, and show how the peculiarities of this address are connected with the peculiarities of the whole epistle.

4. Give a full account of the Judaizers, using both The Acts and Galatians.

5. What does Paul mean in Galatians by "the law"? What is the importance for us of his teaching about the law? Compare Rom. 2:14-16.

III. THE COUNCIL AT JERUSALEM

Dr. Machen has dealt with the Jerusalem Council in a number of his works. However, it may be of service to the reader to include here the succint and illuminating treatment of the Council in the little known and not generally available Teacher's Manual, *The Literature and History of New Testament Times* (see above), pp. 81-85. See also the corresponding Student's Text Book, Part II, pp. 80-84.

LESSON XV

THE COUNCIL AT JERUSALEM

The lesson for today deals with one of the most important events in apostolic history. At the Jerusalem council the principles of the Gentile mission and of the entire life of the Church were brought to clear expression. If the original apostles had agreed with the Judaizers against Paul, the whole history of the Church would have been different. There would even have been room to doubt whether Paul was really a disciple of Jesus; for if he was, how could he come to differ so radically from those whom Jesus had taught? As a matter of fact, however, these dire consequences were avoided. When the issue was made between Paul and the Judaizers, the original apostles decided whole-heartedly for Paul. The unity of the Church was preserved. God was guiding the deliberations of the council.

1. *The Acts and Galatians*

The treatment of to-day's lesson in the Student's Text Book is based upon the assumption that Gal. 2:1-10 is an account of the same visit of Paul to Jerusalem as the visit which is described in Acts 15:1-29. That assumption is not universally accepted. Some scholars identify the event of Gal. 2:1-10, not with the Apostolic Council of Acts 15:1-29, but with the "famine visit" of Acts 11:30; 12:25. Indeed, some maintain that the Epistle to the Galatians not only contains no account of the Apostolic Council, but was actually written before the council was held—say at Antioch, soon after the first missionary journey. Of course this early dating of Galatians can be adopted only in connection with the "South Galatian theory"; for according to the "North Galatian theory" the churches addressed in the epistle were not founded until after the council, namely at the time of Acts 16:6.

Undoubtedly the identification of Gal. 2:1-10 with Acts 11:30; 12:25, avoids some difficulties. If Gal. 2:1-10 be identified with Acts 15:1-29, then Paul in Galatians has passed over the famine visit without mention. Furthermore there are considerable differences between Gal. 2:1-10 and Acts 15:1-29. For example, if Paul is referring to the Apostolic Council, why has he not mentioned the apostolic decree of Acts 15:23-29? These difficulties, however, are not insuperable, and there are counter difficulties against the identification of Gal. 2:1-10 with the famine visit.

One such difficulty is connected with chronology. Paul says that his first visit to Jerusalem took place three years after his conversion, Gal. 1:18, and—according to the most natural interpretation of Gal. 2:1—that the visit of Gal. 2:1-10 took place fourteen years after the first visit. The conversion then occurred seventeen years before the time of Gal. 2:1-10. But if Gal. 2:1-10 describes the famine visit, then the time of Gal. 2:1-10 could not have been after about A. D. 46. Counting back seventeen years from A. D. 46 we should get A. D. 29 as the date of the conversion, which is, of course, too early.

This reasoning, it must be admitted, is not quite conclusive. The ancients had an inclusive method of reckoning time. According to this method three years after 1914 would be 1916. Hence, fourteen plus three might be only what we should call about fifteen years, instead of seventeen. Furthermore, Paul may mean in Gal. 2:1 that his conference with the apostles took place fourteen years after the conversion rather than fourteen years after the visit.

The identification of Gal. 2:1-10 with the famine visit is not impossible. But on the whole the usual view, which identifies the event of Gal. 2:1-10 with the meeting at the time of the Apostolic Council of Acts 15:1-29, must be regarded as more probable. The Apostolic Council probably took place roughly at about A. D. 49. The conversion of Paul then should probably be put at about A. D. 32-34.

2. *The Judaizers*

Conceivably the question about the freedom of the Gentiles from the law might have arisen at an earlier time; for Gentiles had already been received into the Church before the first missionary journey. As a matter of fact, indeed, some objection had been raised to the reception of Cornelius. But that objection had easily been silenced by an appeal to the immediate guidance of God. Perhaps the case of Cornelius could be regarded as exceptional; and a similar reflection might possibly have been applied to the Gentile Christians at Antioch. There seemed to be no danger, at any rate, that the predominantly Jewish character of the Church would be lost. Now, however, after a regular Gentile mission had been carried on with signal success, the situation was materially altered. Evidently the influx of Gentile converts, if allowed to go on unhindered, would change the whole character of the Church. Christianity would appear altogether as a new dispensation: the prerogatives of Israel would be gone. The question of Gentile Christianity had existed before, but after the first missionary journey it became acute.

Perhaps, however, there was also another reason why the battle had not been fought out at an earlier time. It looks very much as though this bitter opposition to the Gentile mission had arisen only through the appearance of a new element in the Jerusalem church. Were these extreme legalists, who objected to the work of Paul and Barnabas— were these men present in the Church from the beginning? The question is more than doubtful. It is more probable that these legalists came into the Church during the period of prosperity which followed upon the persecution of Stephen and was only briefly interrupted by the persecution under Herod Agrippa I.

These Jewish Christian opponents of the Gentile mission —these "Judaizers"—must be examined with some care.

They are described not only by Luke in The Acts but by Paul himself in Galatians. According to The Acts, some of them at least had belonged to the sect of the Pharisees before they had become Christians (Acts 15:5).

The activity of the Judaizers is described by Luke in complete independence of the account given by Paul. As usual, Luke contents himself with a record of external fact, while Paul uncovers the deeper motives of the Judaizers' actions. Yet the facts as reported by Luke fully justify the harsh words which Paul employs. According to Paul, these Judaizers were "false brethren privily brought in, who came in privily to spy out our liberty which we have in Christ Jesus, that they might bring us into bondage." Gal. 2:4. By calling them "false brethren" Paul means simply that they had not really grasped the fundamental principle of the gospel—the principle of justification by faith. They were still trying to earn their salvation by their works instead of receiving it as a gift of God. At heart they were still Jews rather than Christians. They came in privily into places where they did not belong — perhaps Paul means especially into the church at Antioch—in order to spy out Christian liberty (Gal. 2:4). Compare Acts 15:1.

The rise of this Judaizing party is easy to understand. In some respects the Judaizers were simply following the line of least resistance. By upholding the Mosaic law they would escape persecution and even obtain honor. We have seen that it was the Jews who instigated the early persecutions of the Church. Such persecutions would be avoided by the Judaizers, for they could say to their non-Christian countrymen: "We are engaged simply in one form of the world-wide Jewish mission. We are requiring our converts to keep the Mosaic law and unite themselves definitely with the people of Israel. Every convert that we gain is a convert to Judaism. The cross of Christ that we proclaim is supplementary to the law, not subversive of it. We deserve therefore from the Jews not persecution but honor." Compare what Paul says about the Judaizers in Galatia. Gal. 6:12, 13.

3. *The Apostolic Decree*

At first sight it seems rather strange that Paul in Galatians does not mention the apostolic decree. Some have supposed that his words even exclude any decree of that sort. In Gal. 2:6 Paul says that the pillars of the Jerusalem church "imparted nothing" to him. Yet according to The Acts they imparted to him this decree. The decree, moreover, seems to have a direct bearing upon the question that Paul was discussing in Galatians; for it involved the imposition of a part of the ceremonial law upon Gentile Christians. How then, if the decree really was passed as Luke says it was, could it have been left unmentioned by Paul?

There are various ways of overcoming the difficulty. In the first place it is not perfectly certain that any of the prohibitions contained in the decree are ceremonial in character. Three of them are probably ceremonial if the text of most manuscripts of The Acts is correct. Most manuscripts read, at Acts 15:29: "That ye abstain from things sacrificed to idols, and from blood, and from things strangled, and from fornication; from which if ye keep yourselves, it shall be well with you." Here "things offered to idols" apparently describes not idolatrous worship, but food which had been dedicated to idols; and "blood" describes meat used for food without previous removal of the blood. This meaning of "blood" is apparently fixed by the addition of "things strangled." Since "things strangled" evidently refers to food, probably the two preceding expressions refer to food also. According to the great mass of our witnesses to the text, therefore, the apostolic decree contains a food law. A few witnesses, however, omit all reference to things strangled, not only at Acts 15:29 but also at v. 20 and at ch. 21:25. If this text be original, then it is possible to interpret the prohibitions as simply moral and not at all ceremonial in character. "Things offered to idols" may be interpreted simply of idolatry, and "blood" of murder. But if the prohibitions are prohibitions of immorality, then they cannot be said to have "imparted" anything to Paul; for of course he was as much opposed to immorality as anyone.

However, the more familiar form of the text is probably correct. The witnesses that omit the word "strangled" are those that attest the so-called "Western Text" of The Acts. This Western Text differs rather strikingly from the more familiar text in many places. The question as to how far the Western Text of The Acts is correct is a hotly debated question. On the whole, however, the Western readings are usually at any rate to be discredited.

In the second place, the difficulty about the decree may be overcome by regarding Gal. 2:1-10 as parallel not with Acts 15:1-29 but with Acts 11:30; 12:25. This solution has already been discussed.

In the third place, the difficulty may be overcome by that interpretation of the decree which is proposed in the Student's Text Book. The decree was not an addition to Paul's gospel. It was not imposed upon the Gentile Christians as though a part of the law were necessary to salvation. On the contrary it was simply an attempt to solve the practical problems of certain mixed churches—not the Pauline churches in general, but churches which stood in an especially close relation to Jerusalem. This interpretation of the decree is favored by the difficult verse, Acts 15:21. What James there means is probably that the Gentile Christians should avoid those things which would give the most serious offense to hearers of the law.

In the Library.—Purves, "Christianity in the Apostolic Age," pp. 125-166. Lightfoot, "Saint Paul's Epistle to the Galatians," pp. 123-128 ("The later visit of St. Paul to Jerusalem"), 292-374 ("St. Paul and the Three"). Ramsay, "St. Paul the Traveller and the Roman Citizen," pp. 48-60, 152-175. Lewin, "The Life and Epistles of St. Paul," ch. ix. Conybeare and Howson, "The Life and Epistles of St. Paul," ch. vii. Stalker, "The Life of St. Paul," pp. 108-118. Lumby, pp. 185-200. Cook, pp. 451-458. Plumptre, pp. 93-101. Rackham, pp. 238-259, 263-270.

IV. FAITH AND WORKS

The following passage concerning Faith and Works and the reconciliation between the teaching of James and of Paul on this subject is taken from the Student's Text Book mentioned above, Part III (Philadelphia: The Presbyterian Board of Publication and Sabbath School Work, [1915], pp. 181-82).

(1) *Apparent Contradiction of Paul.*—In James 2:14-26 the writer is apparently in direct conflict with Paul. According to Paul, justification is by faith alone and not by the works of the law — see for example, Gal. 2:14-21; according to James, a man is justified by works and not only by faith (James 2:24). Upon closer examination, however, the contradiction is seen to be one of form and not of substance; and like other apparent contradictions in the Bible it serves only to reveal the Scripture combination of rich variety with perfect unity.

(2) *What Is Meant by Faith?*—According to James faith without works is dead; according to Paul faith is all-sufficient for salvation. But what does James mean by faith? The answer is perfectly plain. The faith which James is condemning is a mere intellectual assent which has no effect upon conduct. The demons also, he says, have that sort of faith, and yet evidently they are not saved (James 2:19). What Paul means by faith is something entirely different; it is not a mere intellectual assent to certain propositions, but an attitude of the entire man by which the whole life is intrusted to Christ. In other words, the faith that James is condemning is not the faith that Paul is commending.

The solution of the whole problem is provided by Paul himself in a single phrase. In Gal. 5:6, he says, "For in Christ Jesus neither circumcision availeth anything, nor uncircumcision; but faith working through love." "Faith working through love" is the key to an understanding both of Paul and of James. The faith about which Paul has been speaking is not the idle faith which James condemns, but a faith that works. It works itself out through love. And what love is Paul explains in the whole last division of Galatians. It is no mere emotion, but the actual fulfilling of the whole moral law. "For the whole law is fulfilled in one word, even in this: Thou shalt love thy neighbor as thyself" (Gal. 5:14). Paul is fully as severe as James against a faith that permits men to continue in sin. The faith about which he is speaking is a faith that receives the Spirit who gives men power to lead a holy life.

(3) *What Is Meant by Works?*—Moreover, as the faith which James condemns is different from the faith which Paul commends, so also the works which James commends are different from the works which Paul condemns. Paul is speaking about "works of the law"—that is, works which are intended to earn salvation by fulfilling the law through human effort. James says nothing in chapter 2:14-26 about works of the law. The works of which he is speaking are works that spring from faith and are the expression of faith. Abraham offered Isaac as a sacrifice only because he believed God. His works were merely an evidence that his faith was real. Such works as that are insisted upon by Paul in every epistle. Without them no man can inherit the kingdom of God (Gal. 5:21). Only — and here again James would have been perfectly agreed—such works as that can spring only from faith. They can be accomplished not by human effort, but only by the reception of the power of God.

(4) *The Value of James.*—If James had had the epistles of Paul before him he would no doubt have expressed himself differently. He might have said not that faith without works is dead, but that faith without works is not true faith at all. This is what he clearly means. But the expression of his thought is all the more poignant because it is independent. His stern, terse insistence upon moral reality in religion, of which the passage just considered is only a typical example, provides a valuable supplement to the rest of the New Testament. Of itself it would be insufficient; but taken in connection with the Gospels and with Paul it contributes a necessary fiber to the woven cord of Christian character.

V. REVIEW OF BURTON ON GALATIANS*

A Critical and Exegetical Commentary on the Epistle to the Galatians. In *The International Critical Commentary.* By Ernest De Witt Burton, Professor of New Testament Interpretation in the University of Chicago. New York: Charles Scribner's Sons, 1920. Pp. lxxxix, 541.

Professor Burton's long-awaited commentary on Galatians is perhaps the most elaborate New Testament exegetical work that has appeared within the past thirty or forty years. The author declares in his preface that he began work on Galatians in 1896, and the finished product bears abundant testimony to the diligence with which the twenty-four intervening years up to the appearance of the book were spent. Attainments in various fields, moreover, served to equip the author for his task; Professor Burton is a notable grammarian and lexicographer who had already—even before the appearance of this his most important work—placed students of the New Testament very deeply in his debt.

The method of the commentary allows free play for the exercise of the author's gift for analysis and classification. In addition to Professor Burton's own view, rival exegetical opinion with regard to all questions of any importance whatever is carefully noted, and minute differences of opinion are distinguished and classified. The result may at times make difficult reading, but only superficiality can ignore the value of such work. The Epistle to the Galatians is such a supremely important piece of writing that no amount of labor is too great if the exact meaning can finally be attained. And it may sometimes appear that the elaborate classification, the minute grammatical distinctions, may be an aid to common sense. The painful process of determining what a passage does not mean is often the very best way to determine clearly what it does mean, although after the result has been attained the process of its attainment may sometimes be forgotten.

In the elaborate "detached notes on important terms of

---

*This Review originally appeared in *The Princeton Theological Review*, XX (1922), pp. 142ff.

Paul's vocabulary" which follow the commentary proper, the author has exercised his notable gifts as a lexicographer. The results are at times destructive of conclusions which in the modern school of comparative religion have attained almost to the position of dogma. Particularly refreshing are the notes on Πνεῦμα and Σάρξ and on Τὰ Στοιχεῖα τοῦ κόσμου. . In the former note, which is an abridgment of part of the author's admirable monograph (*Spirit, Soul and Flesh*, 1918), Professor Burton exhibits the basis in the Old Testament for the Pauline use of the term "Spirit," and the lack of basis in Greek writers. By a careful exhibition and classification of the actual usage, which is in marked contrast to the unmethodical roamings of certain recent writers, the conclusions of Reitzenstein and others are tacitly but convincingly refuted. In the latter note, Professor Burton is bold enough to reject the current interpretation, almost hallowed with the sanctity of a modern exegetical tradition, which finds personal beings in the στοιχεῖα τοῦ κόσμου and attributes to Paul all kinds of strange opinions about the identity of the heathen gods with the angels of the Old Testament dispensation. For very good and cogently presented reasons, our commentator returns to the sensible view which makes of the στοιχεῖα τοῦ κόσμου simply "the rudimentary religious teachings possessed by the race." Somewhat related to this conclusion is the author's insistence that the implied contrast with ἑνός in Gal. 3:20 is duality, not plurality, and his rejection of any interpretation which makes Paul's argument turn on the view that the angels, and not God directly, were the givers of the Law. On the positive side, Professor Burton's treatment of this passage is less satisfactory. He is inclined to treat Gal. 3:20 as rabbinical, and to question whether either this verse or Gal. 3:16b belongs really to Paul

It is impossible, here, to follow any further the lexicographical investigations of Professor Burton. Enough has perhaps been said to show that the commentary, with its detached notes, is valuable not merely as an aid to the understanding of Galatians, but also as a mine of information about the entire history, both profane and Biblical, of New Testament words.

Nevertheless, despite the many virtues of Professor Burton's great work, despite the gratitude which all students of the New Testament must feel toward the learned author, it must be confessed with sorrow that this most recent and most elaborate commentary marks distinctly a backward step in the history of New Testament exegesis. For the plain fact is that the method of grammatico-historical exegesis is here actually though not consciously abandoned. The author does not present to his readers the real Paul as he actually lived in the first century, but a strangely modernized Paul, who will subserve the interests of the current liberalism.

This modernizing of the apostle runs all through the commentary. It appears in many directions.

In the first place, the Paul of Professor Burton presents a totally un-Pauline view of the seat of authority in religion and of the validity of the gospel message. In the year 1921, after all the boasted development of modern historical method, it is nothing short of amazing to find Professor Burton writing as follows (p. lxi): "Thus Paul neigher approves nor disapproves all that the Jewish church had conanised, but assumes towards it a discriminative attitude, finding much in it that is true and most valuable, but denying that being in the Old Testament of itself makes a teaching or command authoritative. This discriminative attitude towards the Old Testament, coupled with the apostle's clear recognition of its value as a whole and his insistence, despite his dissent from many of its precepts, upon connecting the Christian religion historically with that of the Old Testament, is most significant. Though he has left us no definite statement to this effect, possibly never formulated the matter in this way in his own mind, he in effect accepted the principle that while each generation is the heir of all the ages, it is also the critic of all, and the arbiter of its own religion." No doubt these sentences correctly represent the views of Professor Burton. But to think of them as representing the views of Paul is to fall into an error so preposterous as to make all refutation needless. It is surely difficult to recognize a "discriminative attitude towards the Old Testament" in the way in which Paul—as did Jesus before him—appeals again and again to Scripture as the absolutely final instance. No doubt Paul did not inculcate the continued observance of the ceremonial Law. But that does not mean that he regarded the ceremonial Law as of lesser authority than any other part of the Old Testament. Indeed it is just in the Epistle to the Galatians that Paul makes his attitude perfectly clear. The Mosaic Law, he says in effect, was given by God, and was of absolute authority. It could never be set aside, even in its minutest particulars, by any merely practical considerations. It could only be set aside by an act of God. But such an act had actually been accomplished in the redemptive work of Christ. The Law served a divine purpose. But the divine purpose was a temporary purpose. The Law was a schoolmaster to bring Israel to Christ, and when Christ appeared the work of the schoolmaster was done.

The "discriminative attitude towards the Old Testament" which Professor Burton attributes to Paul is of a piece with the principle—also supposed to have been accepted, at least in effect, by Paul—"that while each generation is the heir of all the ages, it is also the critic of all, and the arbiter of its own religion." Such a Paul would have been perfectly at home in modern committees on Church union, with their indifference toward truth and their politely veiled skepticism. But it is a little difficult to recognize here the Paul who pronounced anathemas upon the very angels in heaven if they proclaimed a different gospel, and who withstood Peter to his face. Professor Burton believes that what Paul "claimed for himself, viz., a divine commission and a corresponding responsibility, he freely admitted might be possessed by other men who did not wholly agree with him. Sitting in council with them he neither consented to conform his own course of action or message to their practice nor demanded that they should conform theirs to his. The gospel of the circumcision and the gospel of the uncircumcision had certain elements in common, but they were by no means identical. Yet he claimed for himself the right and duty to preach his gospel, and admitted the right and duty of the other apostles to preach theirs" (p. lxiii). Such words have a familiar sound. They are heard everywhere at the present day. They are an expression of that "undogmatic Christianity," which is really a veiled agnosticism. But certainly they are not Pauline. Paul defended his right to preach his gospel not because every man has the right to formulate a gospel on the basis of his experience, but because by a unique interposition of God he had had revealed to him the gospel which was true. Professor Burton says on page 380: "Limiting his own efforts to Gentile lands (Gal. 1:16; 2:8, 9) and within these lands to fields not already occupied by others (II Cor. 10:13; Rom. 15:20), and equally denied the right of others to attempt to win his converts to their views (Gal. 1:8, 9; 5:12)." Such exegesis as this ought not to need refutation in detail. Paul is here reduced to the level of a modern "practical" Christian—putting life above principle and practice above truth. The real Paul was vastly different.

Of course Professor Burton fails to recognize the historical character of the Pauline gospel. He seems to regard the Epistle to the Galatians merely as a plea for "spiritual religion." There could be no greater error. The gospel of Paul did not consist in the enunciation of eternal truths—the truths of an underlying, ideal religion—but in the proclamation of something that had happened, namely the death and resurrection of the Lord Jesus Christ. Without that happening, according to Paul, the truth about "religion" would have brought nothing but blank despair. The gospel, according to Paul, as indeed the very word for "gospel" implies, was not the discovery of what had always been true, but the proclamation—with explanation of the meaning—of something new. It is no wonder that Professor Burton is very much puzzled by Paul's emphasis upon the physical evidence of the resurrection. "On the one side," he says (p. 374), "the general type of his thought, his emphasis on the purely spiritual as against the physical in religion, would favour the view that he did not attach vital importance to his having seen Jesus." But as a matter of fact, our commentator is obliged to admit that Paul apparently did attach importance to his having seen Jesus. The Paul of Professor Burton never ought to have done so. But the real Paul believed that the resurrection was a plain fact of history.

But the most fundamental error of all has not yet been mentioned. That error consists in a total misunderstanding of the purpose of the Epistle. In the last sentence of the commentary proper (p. 362), Professor Burton characterizes the Epistle to the Galatians as "one of the noblest pleas ever written for Christian liberty and spiritual religion." These words might be interpreted in a way consonant with the truth. But unfortunately, the entire book renders it only too plain that "spiritual religion" is here regarded as an explanation of "Christian liberty." Professor Burton regards the Epistle to the Galatians as directed against ceremonialism and externality and a piecemeal morality which divides the Law of God into separate rules. There is of course a certain measure of truth in this opinion. In one passage, somewhat obscure it is true, Paul does apparently characterize the Jewish forms which the Galatians were adopting as belonging to the period of childhood from which the Christian man has emerged, but in the Epistle as a whole the thought of externalism, as against spiritual religion, is entirely subordinate. The real point of the Epistle is quite different. What Paul is really attacking in Galatians is not ceremonialism in religion, or a divisive morality, but the principle of merit. The real controversy in Galatia was not between outward works and inward works, but upon human merit however attained and the divine grace.

The question between these two conceptions of the purpose of the Epistle is highly important to Professor Burton. For if the Epistle is directed against externalism in religion, then Professor Burton belongs, in the controversy in Galatia, with Paul, whereas if the Epistle is directed against a religion of merit, Professor Burton belongs with the Judaizers. And as a matter of fact the latter alternative is correct. Modern liberalism is clearly a religion of merit, which brings satisfaction to its adherents only because they hold a lax view of sin and of the law.

It is true, Professor Burton repudiates the "law in the legalistic sense," and believes that Paul repudiated it. But he believes that there is a higher sense of the word "law," in accordance with which it designates a complete expression of the will of God including mercy, and that Paul maintained the law when it is so considered. The meaning seems to be that Paul supposed God to look with complacency upon the transgressions to which all men are subject if only there be a true effort on man's part to obey God's will. In other words, God is content with a relative goodness, and the mistake of the Judaizers was to suppose that he dealt with men on the basis of strict justice. There could be no greater error. As a matter of fact, the whole of Paulinism is founded not upon a lax interpretation of the law of God, but upon a strict interpretation. The demands of the Law could not be set aside in the interests of practical religion. And all were under the curse. But Christ took the curse upon Himself, and paid the Law's penalty for us. Such is the teaching of Paul. The Pauline doctrine of justification is absolutely unintelligible except upon the basis of a strict view of law; it is absolutely unintelligible upon the basis of "liberalism." It is because Paul was not a liberal Jew that he could be the apostle of Christian liberty.

Starting from a radically different view of sin and of the law of God from that of Paul, Professor Burton seeks to force the apostle into the modern mould. It might seem as though he would have been discouraged by the hopelessness of the task. It is rather difficult to make out of the writer of Galatians 2 and 3 a complacent believer in the religion of modern naturalism, who uses the term "justification" to designate the mere acceptance by God of a lower goodness than that which His law requires, and who regards faith itself as a meritorious work. With regard to the religion of modern liberalism as with regard to the teaching of the Judaizers in Galatia, the real Paul would have said: "I do not make void the grace of God: for if righteousness is through the law, then Christ died for nought" (Gal. 2:21). But it is useless to quote individual verses to Professor Burton, no matter how plain they may seem. The ingenuity of our commentator is equal to any task. Thus the verse just quoted, the key verse of the Epistle, coming though it does after a glorious passage where even one who is unprepared to accept the gospel of Paul might be expected to understand something of what it meant to him, our commentator actually makes "the grace of God" refer to the giving of the law to Israel. Paul, he says, is answering an attack of the opponents to the effect that he was making of no account "the special grace of God to Israel in giving them the law." In the presence of such exegesis the reader may well stand aghast. Paul has poured out his soul before us. But all to no purpose.

Professor Burton, in other words, with modern liberalism in general, occupies in all essentials the position of the Judaizers. He believes that the grace of God is necessary in order to salvation. But human goodness, he believes, is also necessary; man keeps the law the best he can, and then God meets him half way. That was exactly the view of the Judaizers. They believed that in addition to the law it was necessary to have the grace of Christ, but that human merit, though not sufficient, was necessary. And it was against such a position that the Epistle to the Galatians was written. There are two possible ways, says Paul, of attaining salvation—in the first place perfect obedience, and in the second place acceptance of the sacrifice of Christ. But the whole Epistle is directed against any mingling of the two.

What will Professor Burton do with Galatians 6:14—"Far be it from me to glory save in the cross of our Lord Jesus Christ"? Will he recognize at least in the Pauline doctrine of the new creation the tremendous supernaturalism of the Pauline gospel? Not at all. "To this world [the world of earthly relationships]," he says, Paul "became dead by the cross of Christ, because in Christ's death on the cross he saw a demonstration that God's way of accepting men was not on the basis of works of law, but on that of faith in Christ." Our commentator then proceeds to speak of the evidence "that the significance of the cross is in what it proves respecting God's real attitude towards men." It would hardly be possible to get further away from any true historical method of exegesis. Modern naturalism may be true or it may be false—that is another question—but certainly Paul was not an adherent of it. And the death of the believer to the world, according to Paul, was certainly not an act of man, but an act of God.

In order to learn something of the true nature of Paulinism, Professor Burton would not have had to turn to "conservative" scholars who accept Paulinism as their own religion; he could have learned also from those who see Paulinism somewhat as it is and then reject it. He could have learned from Baur. He could have learned from Wrede, who with all his exaggerations at least faced the problem of Paulinism as a redemptive religion. He could have learned from Bousset. But Bousset's "Kyrios Christos," which appeared in 1914, is not even mentioned by our commentator. Professor Burton, in short, has hardly come to grips at all with the really great problems of the apostolic age.

The Epistle to the Galatians, "the Magna Charta of Christian liberty," has fallen again upon evil days. It had fallen upon evil days at the close of the middle ages. It was buried then under the Roman Catholic system of merits, and under the trivialities of mediaeval exegesis. And now again, in the pages of Professor Burton's commentary, it is buried under the neo-legalistic slavery of the modern "liberal" Church. But the message of the Epistle is essentially plain, and cannot permanently be obscured. It was discovered by Luther at the beginning of the sixteenth century. Will some man of God discover it again, and set humanity free?

VI. INDEX OF REFERENCES TO GALATIANS IN VARIOUS OTHER WORKS OF MACHEN

The volumes referred to in this Index, the brief designations given to them, and the dates of the editions or printings consulted are as follows:

1. CL   *Christianity and Liberalism* (New York: The Macmillan Company, 1930)
2. OPR   *The Origin of Paul's Religion* (New York: The Macmillan Company, 1928)
3. VB   *The Virgin Birth of Christ* (New York and London: Harper & Brothers, 1930)
4. WF   *What Is Faith?* (New York: The Macmillan Company, 1925)
5. CFMW   *The Christian Faith in the Modern World.* (New York: The Macmillan Company, 1936)
6. CVM   *The Christian View of Man* (New York: The Macmillan Company, 1937)
7. GT   *God Transcendent* (Grand Rapids: Wm. B. Eerdmans Publishing Company, 1949)
8. WC   *What Is Christianity?* (Grand Rapids: Wm. B. Eerdmans Publishing Company, 1951)
9. LHNTT   *The Literature and History of New Testament Times.* (Philadelphia: The Presbyterian Board of Publication and Sabbath School Work, [1915]), Teacher's Manual
    STB   The corresponding Student's Text Book [1914]
10. BBH   James Oscar Boyd and John Gresham Machen: *A Brief Bible History* (Philadelphia: The Westminster Press, 1931)
11. BTS   "Jesus and Paul" in *Biblical and Theological Studies* by the Members of the Faculty of Princeton Theological Seminary (New York: Charles Scribner's Sons, 1912), pp. 545-78

INDEX

A. TOPICAL (Selected References)
Galatia   LHNTT 78ff.; BBH 110, 114
Galatians, The Epistle to the, BBH 116ff.
    The Acts and, OPR 40
    Baur, F. C., and, OPR 107; BTS 554
    date of, OPR 81ff.
    I Corinthians 15:1-11 and, OPR 144f.
    genuineness of, OPR 31; BTS 550
    James, Epistle of, and, (Faith and Works;
       James 2 and Gal. 2)   WF 183-218
    Romans, Epistle to the, and, LHNTT 118
Grammatico-Historical Exegesis   WF 23ff., 183f., 186ff.;
    WC 226ff.

B. TEXTUAL

GALATIANS

Chapter I

Chapters I, II OPR 21, 37ff., 144ff.
Chapter I BTS 560f., 563ff.
1:1   CL 96; OPR 22, 129, 145ff., 199; CFMW 221;
    WC 42, 173f.; BTS 557f., 560
1:2   OPR 81
1:4   LHNTT 103
1:8   CL 22
1:12 OPR 145ff.
1:14 OPR 47
1:16-17 OPR 74
1:16 OPR 71ff.
1:17 OPR 49f; BBH 105
1:18-24 BBH 107f.
1:18-19 OPR 74-77, 84, 300; CFMW 220
1:18 OPR 79, 80; CFMW 210
1:19 OPR 75, 299f.; CFMW 219f.
1:22 OPR 50-52, 75, 76
1:23 OPR 52

Chapter II

Chapter II OPR 166f.: WF 201; BTS 549
2:1-10   OPR 78-100, 104, 121f., 139; CFMW 220; BBH 111
2:1-2   STB 82
2:1   OPR 79, 80, 84, 85, 137
2:2   OPR 83f., 95, 120ff.
2:6   OPR 87, 95f., 120ff.
2:9   CL 83; OPR 100, 104, 120ff.; BTS 554
2:10   OPR 99f.
2:11-21 OPR 87, 93, 100ff., 122ff.; STB 83f.; BBH 112f.; BTS 554f.
2:11-13 OPR 97
2:12   OPR 101
2:14-21 OPR 123f.
2:14   OPR 123f.
2:16   WF 199
2:19   OPR 103
2:20   CL 44, 46, 139, 145f.; OPR 150; WF 151, 154, 169; BTS 560
2:21   OPR 279

Chapter III

Chapter III WF 201
3:1   OPR 103, 149f.; BTS 562f.
3:2   OPR 287
3:5   OPR 271f.
3:23   WF 44f.
3:24   OPR 18; WF 119-42; CVM 232
3:26-28 GT 57-63
3:27   OPR 287
3:28   LHNTT 103

Chapter IV

4:4-5   VB 259f.
4:14   OPR 58ff.
4:25   CL 144

Chapter V

5:6   CL 146f.; WF 209-18; BBH 110
5:13—6:18   CL 146f.
5:14   CL 146; WF 213
5:19-21 OPR 160; CVM 217, 223

Chapter VI

6:3   OPR 121

Other Related Titles

In addition to *Notes on Galatians* by Machen we are happy to offer the following related titles:

Biblical and Theological Studies by the professors of Princeton Seminary in 1912, at the centenary celebration of the Seminary. Articles are by men like Allis, Vos, Warfield, Machen, Wilson and others.

Theology on Fire: Vols. 1 & 2 by Joseph A. Alexander is the two volumes of sermons by this brilliant scholar from Princeton Seminary.

A Shepherd's Heart by James W. Alexander is a volume of outstanding expository sermons from the pastoral ministry of one of the leading preachers on the 19th century.

Evangelical Truth by Archibald Alexander is a volume of practical sermons intended to be used for Family Worship.

The Lord of Glory by Benjamin B. Warfield is one of the best treatments of the doctrine of the Deity of Christ ever written. Warfield is simply masterful.

The Power of God unto Salvation by Benjamin B. Warfield is the first book of sermons ever published of the sermons of this master-theologian.

The Scripture Guide by James W. Alexander is a helpful guide to lead young people and new converts into a deeper appreciation of the Word of God.

My Brother's Keeper by James W. Alexander is a book of letters Alexander wrote to his 10 year old brother. It is full of sound advice on a wide variety of subjects.

Mourning a Beloved Shepherd by Charles Hodge and John Hall is a little volume containing the funeral addresses for James W. Alexander. Very informative and challenging.

John Eadie Titles

Solid Ground is delighted to announce that we have republished several volumes by John Eadie, gifted Scottish minister. The following are in print:

Commentary on the Greek Text of Paul's Letter to the Galatians
Part of the classic five-volume set that brought world-wide renown to this humble man, Eadie expounds this letter with passion and precision. In the words of Spurgeon, "This is a most careful attempt to ascertain the meaning of the Apostle by painstaking analysis of his words."

Commentary on the Greek Text of Paul's Letter to the Ephesians
Spurgeon said, "This book is one of prodigious learning and research. The author seems to have read all, in every language, that has been written on the Epistle. It is also a work of independent criticism, and casts much new light upon many passages."

Commentary on the Greek Text of Paul's Letter to the Philippians
Robert Paul Martin wrote, "Everything that John Eadie wrote is pure gold. He was simply the best exegete of his generation. His commentaries on Paul's epistles are valued highly by careful expositors. Solid Ground Christian Books has done a great service by bringing Eadie's works back into print."

Commentary on the Greek Text of Paul's Letter to the Colossians
According to the New Schaff-Herzog Encyclopedia of Religious Knowledge, "These commentaries of John Eadie are marked by candor and clearness as well as by an evangelical unction not common in works of the kind." Spurgeon said, "Very full and reliable. A work of utmost value."

Commentary on the Greek Text of Paul's Letters to the Thessalonians
Published posthumously, this volume completes the series that has been highly acclaimed for more than a century. Invaluable.

Paul the Preacher: A Popular and Practical Exposition of His Discourses and Speeches as Recorded in the Acts of the Apostles
Very rare volume intended for a more popular audience, this volume begins with Saul's conversion and ends with Paul preaching the Gospel of the Kingdom in Rome. It perfectly fills in the gaps in the commentaries. Outstanding work!

DIVINE LOVE: A Series of Doctrinal, Practical and Experimental Discourses
Buried over a hundred years, this volume consists of a dozen complete sermons from Eadie's the pastoral ministry. "John Eadie, the respected nineteenth-century Scottish Secession minister-theologian, takes the reader on an edifying journey through this vital biblical theme." - Ligon Duncan

Lectures on the Bible to the Young for Their Instruction and Excitement
"Though written for the rising generation, these plain addresses are not meant for mere children. Simplicity has, indeed, been aimed at in their style and arrangement, in order to adapt them to a class of young readers whose minds have already enjoyed some previous training and discipline." – Author's Preface

Call us Toll Free at 1-877-666-9469
Send us an e-mail at sgcb@charter.net
Visit us on line at solid-ground-books.com

www.ingramcontent.com/pod-product-compliance
Lightning Source LLC
Chambersburg PA
CBHW031140160426
43193CB00008B/198